A MODEL OF THE BRAIN

A MODEL OF THE BRAIN

BY

J. Z. YOUNG
M.A., D.Sc., F.R.S.

Professor of Anatomy in the
University of London at University College

BEING

THE WILLIAM WITHERING LECTURES
DELIVERED TO THE FACULTY OF MEDICINE
OF THE UNIVERSITY OF BIRMINGHAM

1960

WITH THE TITLE

MECHANISMS OF LEARNING AND FORM DISCRIMINATION

OXFORD
AT THE CLARENDON PRESS

Oxford University Press, Amen House, London E.C.4

GLASGOW NEW YORK TORONTO MELBOURNE WELLINGTON
BOMBAY CALCUTTA MADRAS KARACHI LAHORE DACCA
CAPE TOWN SALISBURY NAIROBI IBADAN ACCRA
KUALA LUMPUR HONG KONG

FIRST PUBLISHED 1964
REPRINTED 1964

PRINTED IN GREAT BRITAIN
AT THE UNIVERSITY PRESS, OXFORD
BY VIVIAN RIDLER
PRINTER TO THE UNIVERSITY

PREFACE

THIS book is based upon the William Withering Lectures given to the Faculty of Medicine of the University of Birmingham in the spring of 1960. I must apologize to the Faculty for the long delay in publication and also for the fact that little remains of the lectures as originally given. There are good reasons for both facts. The publication of lectures, even with much modification, remains an ambiguous form of communication. Material collected for a lecture should be different from that used for a book. A more important cause for the delay and alterations has been that I was dissatisfied with the general picture or 'model' of the brain that I tried to present in 1960. Yet I am most grateful to the Faculty for the stimulus that made me attempt to produce one. Though it was certainly very inadequate at the time I venture to think it is somewhat more satisfactory now. Of course many fresh data have accumulated in the last few years about the brain of the octopus, on which the model is mainly based, and many more data on other brains. As a result of the sustained attempt to think how to fit these data together it might now be said that we begin to 'understand' the octopus brain. The scheme is no doubt wrong in many ways, but in some respects it is reasonably complete. Some kind of statement can be offered about the function of each region of the brain in the behaviour and learning system of these animals. It is indeed most exciting to be able to produce and use even such a manifestly imperfect model. Yet its main function remains the rather pedestrian one of providing a framework that carries the facts. For this reason the reader may feel at times that he is learning too much about cephalopods and too little about brains. Yet perhaps the very multiplicity of themes that are introduced may suggest the various aspects from which the nervous system may be approached.

The present model is mainly built on data from anatomy and behavioural experiments but this may not be altogether a disadvantage. Perhaps two of the most pertinent questions that may be asked about the nervous system are 'What can it do?' and 'How are its units connected to enable it to carry out its functions?' The light microscope and electron microscope are probably the most powerful tools for investigating the second question. The microelectrode certainly follows closely in the study of connectivity and provides much further information about the activities of the units of the system. That information is, of course, fundamentally important, but curiously enough the very importance of the study of the physiology of the *units* often seems to distract attention from the *system* of which they are a part.

Yet there is really no excuse for a book about the brain that contains so little reference to its electrical properties. Inevitably this leaves the model that is presented as a mere lifeless doll. Anyone even vaguely familiar with the rich sources of information about activity within the nervous system may well close this book quickly in disdain. I can only suggest that one cannot read about all relevant aspects of a subject at once, or even in one book, least of all when the subject is the most complicated device that is known to us. If this book gives anyone the opportunity to play with ideas about the brain it will have served the function of a good toy. Writing it has had this effect for me and I am deeply grateful to the Birmingham Faculty, to Professor A. L. d'Abreu, the Dean at the time, and to the Professor of Anatomy, Sir Solly Zuckerman, for giving me this stimulus.

It is also a pleasure to thank all those who have contributed to the production of the book. Mrs. J. Astafiev has prepared the drawings. Many colleagues have criticized the text, B. B. Boycott, M. J. Wells, N. S. Sutherland, and W. R. A. Muntz from their special knowledge of the nervous system of *Octopus* and of its behaviour. J. T. Aitken has criticized the anatomical, W. K. Taylor the engineering, and G. Sommerhoff the logical concepts. They have all made many improvements and the errors that remain are due to my refusal to accept their advice. Mrs. Bruce Young made constant revision possible by repeated re-typing and Mrs. M. Nixon followed and corrected all the stages of the drafts. P. N. Dilly helped with the early drafts and V. C. Barber with the later stages.

The extensive programme of work with octopuses has been carried out at Naples and it is difficult to express adequately the debt we owe to all those who have made it possible, from Dr. P. Dohrn, the director, to his laboratory assistants and fishermen. Similarly, the facts and ideas here could never have been accumulated without the financial help that we have received for work in Naples and London from the Nuffield Foundation and the Office of Aerospace Research of the United States Air Force. Neither organization has ever shown dismay at financing work that must often have seemed of remote importance. We shall be well pleased if they can feel that the result is a tribute to their vision.

Finally, it is a special pleasure to thank my many colleagues in the Department of Anatomy at University College and particularly those who have been responsible for making the immense number of microscopic preparations upon which much of this work depends. The collection of more than 100,000 slides has been largely produced under the direction of J. Armstrong and Miss P. Stephens. It is due to their skill that so much detail of the organization of the brain has been revealed, and the collection remains for others to study.

J.Z.Y.

February 1964

CONTENTS

Contents

1

MODELS OF THE BRAIN

1. *In what sense can we expect to know how brains work?*

THE question 'How do brains work?' may seem at first sight to be reasonably clearly formulated, though we should, of course, expect the answer to be complicated. Our first task is to examine the question, so that we may know what sort of answer we expect to give it. It will be found that the question is not really simple in form at all, and moreover, that the problem of how to express it is of great importance. It is not too much to say that the whole structure of our logic and language is influenced by the words we use to discuss this problem. It is, I suppose, no accident that Descartes, who has affected the ways of thought of the world more than most people, was an anatomist and physiologist, and was deeply concerned with how to speak about the brain.

2. *Similarities in the procedure of biologists and engineers*

What answer do we expect when we ask 'How does the brain work?'? How should we know whether we had found the right answer? There is clearly some relation between this form of words and that of an engineer, who would say 'I know how it works' of a machine with the structure and connexions of whose parts he was so familiar that he could take it to pieces and put it together again. Do we mean to imply that we should hope to be able to do this with a brain? I believe that in the last analysis this is the most useful criterion by which we should consider ourselves satisfied that we understand a living system. However, we are obviously such a long way from achieving this end that it may be found to be expedient to compromise on this definition.

Of course there are senses in which we can be said to understand a system without taking it to pieces. For example, an engineer who has found the relationship between voltages and amperes in various parts of a network will say that he understands it, without having to study the individual parts. It may be even more important for a radio engineer to appreciate the principles with which a system handles information than to be able himself to analyse and synthesize the equipment available. If he does make a synthesis, it may be only a simulation of the significant features of the flow of signals, in the form of equations, a diagram, or a model.

It is often claimed that a similar approach to the nervous system can provide us with adequate understanding, even if there is little or no detailed information about nerve cells, and certainly without trying to synthesize a brain. There is something in this as a pragmatic approach, though in the last analysis I believe it to be unsatisfactory. The equations and diagrams of the engineer are 'understood' if they refer to situations that have been realized in practice, or could conceivably be so. The abstractions refer, that is to say, to known equipment and experimental situations. When we have similar relevant information about nerve cells, then indeed equations and diagrams become really useful.

It may be valuable even at this early stage of discussion to pursue further the various senses in which an engineer represents the functions of the various parts of a complicated device. As Gregory (1961) explains, we may use any of the three types of diagram shown in Fig. 1. The first shows the actual characteristics and anatomy, the second its idealized components, and the third their functional value. Biologists, like engineers, are concerned with the performance of the whole system (though they usually call it 'behaviour'). As Gregory points out, knowledge such as is represented by Fig. 1a and 1b is of little use unless we can also draw diagram 1c. In a radio set a faulty condenser or valve at almost any point in the circuit may cause a 'howl', but it does not follow that the part concerned is a 'centre' for howling. The point for the present is that there are subtleties we may not suspect in the discussion of the 'functioning' of machines and its 'explanation'.

We may obtain some help from considering why there are similarities and interrelations between the procedures of the

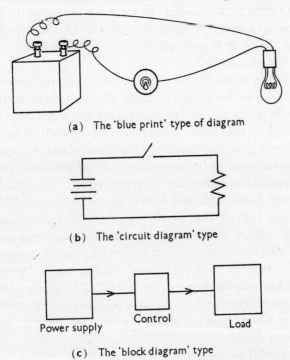

(a) The 'blue print' type of diagram

(b) The 'circuit diagram' type

Power supply   Control   Load

(c) The 'block diagram' type

FIG. I. To illustrate possible methods of describing the same system. (From Gregory.)

biologist and the engineer. Both are concerned with the study of the ways by which living things meet their needs. When we say that living things have 'needs' we emphasize that they are self-maintaining systems; 'homeostats' in modern terminology. These are systems so organized that they are able to interchange with their surroundings without merging with them. One of the features of a homeostat is the presence of detectors that indicate tendencies of imbalance within it and set in motion actions that tend to correct them. These are the systems of 'need' and 'motivation' which, more than any other features, seem to set living things apart from the rest of the universe. By taking the 'right' actions, in good time, living organisms avoid the otherwise inexorable tendency to dissipate into their surroundings. To trace the history of the growth of this power of self-maintenance and to find adequate ways to speak about it is perhaps the major task for biology, and indeed for philosophy.

The biologist studies all the aspects of the processes of self-maintenance or homeostasis: understanding them he may be able to help in the better control of the organisms, as in agriculture or medicine. The engineer is concerned to supply means to help in the meeting of human needs, for example, by transportation or by transmission of information. Both the doctor and the engineer are therefore equally concerned with the human homeostat, and how it meets its 'needs'. Historically it has proved that as the engineer develops means for assisting with a living function, the language and methods that he uses have been applied to describe and investigate that function itself as it is performed by the body. In order to operate his machines man has created a language that goes with them and increasingly he uses this language in preference to others when speaking about the parts of his own body, in health and disease.

It is useful to remember how greatly we already depend upon the analogies of physics and engineering for the descriptions that we have of the nervous system, imperfect though they are. The anatomist, when studying the connexions of its parts, is unravelling its 'wiring diagram'. In his description and discussion he makes use of whatever similar systems he knows, whether it is the hydraulic devices used as parallels by Descartes or the components of modern electronic equipment. There is no doubt that making such analysis and comparison is one of the meanings that people give to 'understanding' a brain.

A physiologist tests the actions of the parts precisely as does an engineer, with voltmeter and ammeter. Indeed, the history of knowledge of the physiology of the nervous system has largely been the history of the development of methods for measuring electric currents and potentials. At the same time physical theory has provided a language in which the physiologist can describe the characteristics of a nerve fibre and its membranes in terms of resistances, capacities, currents and potentials, when it is at rest or in action. By the use of a computer it has been possible to test rigorously the implications of models of nerve-fibre functioning that have been suggested as a result of experimental observation (Hodgkin and Huxley, 1952).

The point is so obvious that it may not seem to be worth labouring. Yet if we are to find a language in which to speak of 'how the brain works' it is important to recognize fully that the use of the language of the physical sciences is already commonplace in biology. Indeed, it plays the central part in much that is considered most exciting in the subject. It has produced results that we all make use of every day in applied biology and medicine.

3. *Are there fundamental differences between the methods of biology and physical science?*

We all hope that the physician or surgeon will 'understand' the workings of our bodies and as we say 'put them right'. In doing this he may not use exclusively the language of physical science, but his power to help us increases when he can do so. This does not, of course, necessarily mean that by using any technique known at present we can 'explain' a living system, still less produce one. The language of physics and the other sciences that are basic to the production of our machines is not yet ready for that, but it is itself continually growing. It is stimulated from many sources not least by investigations of the actions of living matter. There is evidently a complicated relationship between (1) the words used originally to talk about man and other living things (e.g. energy, information, memory); (2) development of new techniques in the physical sciences and engineering, in the course of which some of these words are taken over and used to describe the actions of machines; (3) the development of exact meanings for these words in the physical sciences; (4) the undertaking of investigations, by means of the new physical methods, of ourselves and our relations with the world around us.

We are becoming accustomed to expect that the 'workings' of the body will be at least partly 'understood' by the use of terms similar to those used by physical science. We find it less easy to believe that this may be possible when considering those actions of the brain system that take place in what we ordinarily call our 'minds'. It seems at first that there is a distinction here between biology and engineering, a gap that cannot be bridged. The engineer may be able to build apparatus to help us to fulfil our needs but can we call him in to make that which is itself the subject of need? It will be a thesis of this book that in spite of appearances and prejudices to the contrary there is nothing absurd in supposing that this is possible. As machines that assist our brains develop we shall learn from them a language much more useful than the present one for speaking about brains and their 'products', such as 'mind'. Many of the difficulties we now experience about such problems come from the fact that only for a short time have we possessed machines that perform actions in any way similar to those of brains. We have become thoroughly familiar with the implications of the statement that 'steam engines and muscles both do work', but we are uneasy with 'calculating machines and brains both think'.

There will, of course, be many who are prepared to argue that all such usages are confusing and moreover degrading and derogatory to some central entity, the soul of man (perhaps also to God or some general principle of the universe). Sincerely though such resistence is held, my belief is that it is the product of a verbal tradition appropriate to an earlier state of knowledge. With the growth of information and of new usages it will be found to fade away, leaving us better able to face these great problems about ourselves and the universe.

There are undoubtedly many respects in which living systems differ so greatly from non-living ones that the current techniques of the physical sciences cannot be fully applied to them. Living organisms are heterogeneous systems continually interchanging with their surroundings but maintaining their integrity. The procedures of physical science, such as isolation, purification, and the restriction of experimentation to change of single variables are therefore difficult or impossible to apply to living things. The continued existence of such systems depends (as we shall see) on what we shall call the 'instructions' that they receive from their past history. Prediction about individual organisms therefore has in a sense a different status from prediction in physical science.

It is true that a physicist has in theory to consider the whole past history of the elements he is studying. In practice he is able to postulate an initial state in which the relevant properties are known. In biology this is not so, the homeostatic properties of any type of creature depend on the information that has been stored within that line since life began. Until we can read off this information (notably from the DNA) we cannot know the initial state of the individual organisms that we investigate. Such difficulties are serious but do not alter the fact that great areas of discovery have been opened by applying the concepts of the physical sciences in biology and this development will certainly continue.

Although biology increasingly uses the equipment and language that are made available by physical science and engineering, yet there remain many differences between the methods of physical and biological science. For example, we often try to investigate the function of the nervous system by removing some part of it and looking for the absence of particular actions as a result. This is a crude procedure, which would rarely be used by an engineer, even though in man-made systems individual components with single 'functions' are perhaps more common than in the body. As knowledge grows it becomes apparent that the brain is a machine of a type very different from those made hitherto by man. Its success is largely due to the richness of its parallel circuits and redundancies.

This makes it very difficult to assign particular functions, especially by the technique of removal (see Gregory, 1962).

A further difficulty is that it has been felt in the past that the exact language of the scientist is appropriate only for use in dealing with certain 'material matters'. The supposition that 'things of the spirit' are necessarily dealt with in another language has persisted only because we have not yet been able to extend our scientific treatment to the brain. Nor is there any reason to suppose that, as we learn to control brains better, the results will be deleterious to human dignity. Many people are worried that the application of such knowledge will somehow reduce the powers of each individual. Is there any reason to fear the intrusions that may be made possible by increased understanding of cerebral processes? It is noticeable that such apprehensions about 'brain washing' are usually expressed in relation to new methods adopted by enemies, whereas other names are used for the even more powerful and restrictive conventional procedures by which each of us is taught to conform in his own society. It is difficult until one thinks about it to realize how utterly our brains are *already* conditioned by the traditional methods applied in our upbringing. No doubt these are 'good' methods; if they were otherwise we should not be here. But does anyone really believe that they could not be improved, especially if we could understand more of the delicate instrument that learns from those methods?

In particular, the place of the individual and the contribution he can make personally to the group should become more apparent rather than less as we come to understand the relative importance of information acquired by the individual and by the population (Chapter 18). 'Traditional' methods of instruction often in practice make very great demands on the individual to conform. It could even be argued that a chief danger of increased understanding of the brain may be that it will give too much emphasis to the individual. It will certainly help him to assert the value of his own contribution, and will provide him with better methods for ensuring free communication with his fellows, which we all so greatly need.

The fear that knowledge of the brain will be harmful fails, then, to pay attention to the degree to which *all* our actions are already ruled by the conventions that we learn. If we did not speak and behave approximately in the 'correct' way we should be helpless, uncommunicating idiots. Further exploration of the working of the brain may well give us new powers that are at least as great as those already given by language. There is every reason to expect that what we call our emotional and imaginative life will be enlarged rather than restricted as we come to understand the cerebral processes that are involved. It can hardly be doubted that the evolution of *Homo sapiens*, with his languages, has produced a species in which the individuals are more free to exercise creative ability than were their non-human ancestors. It may well be that in future a language and symbolism will emerge at least as much richer than those of today, as ours are than the simple communication systems of apes.

Part of the difficulty of this problem arises from the fact that for the first time new techniques are beginning seriously to probe the very nature of the communication system that must itself be used among us. For thousands of years philosophers and linguists have speculated upon these matters without changing greatly our fundamental concepts such as those of 'body' and 'mind'. As yet, study of the brain has not indeed produced very powerful alternatives either, and we cannot say more than that there are signs that it is about to do so.

I shall discuss later the suggestion that in a certain sense we can describe the brains of higher animals as embodying models of the world. This is not a mere figure of speech and I shall try to describe some characteristics of the model in the simple example of the octopus.[1] There is some evidence that we are on the right lines in the analysis in that case, but we know so little of the more interesting situations, for example in our own brains, that speculation and further claims may seem ridiculous. Perhaps they are. At least by considering how these

[1] The use of octopus refers throughout to *Octopus vulgaris* Lamarck.

models are constructed and how they operate we may find a
means of organizing our knowledge of how the brain works.

It is important to approach the subject of how brains work
gradually and with humility. Clearly we cannot expect immediately to have full understanding of the more complicated
brains such as our own. Investigation of somewhat simpler
animals, such as the octopus, is probably the best way of finding the principles that are at work. This comparative method
has proved to be a most powerful tool for investigating digestion, respiration, excretion, and other bodily functions. Similarly there is every reason to think that we shall learn much by
studying the various experiments that have been made by the
action of natural selection in the design of nervous systems.
The actions of the human brain are so complicated that it may
be difficult to see the similarity with simpler animals. It will
indeed be a long time before we can really say that we understand our brains.

4. *Making and remaking nervous systems*

Let us return to the conception that if we understand the
nervous system we should be able to take it to pieces, repair it,
and even make others like it. Steps have indeed already been
taken in this direction. A nervous system is made every time
that an embryo develops. From the studies of embryologists
much is known about the influences that guide the nerve fibres
as they grow out from the nerve cells and form their elaborate
patterns. By operations on young embryos, especially of frogs,
newts, and chickens, it has been possible to regulate growth
and to produce much information about the controlling factors
that are at work. For example, if some organ is removed, say
the rudiment of a leg or an ear, then the nerve cells that should
innervate it will develop normally for quite a long time. The
'instructions' to do so come from the hereditary make-up.
Sooner or later, however, the nerve cells whose nerve fibres
have been unable to make connexion with the appropriate end
organ will begin to shrink and may finally disappear completely. In normal development, therefore, there must be some

influence that proceeds from the end organ up the nerve fibres
to the cell body. Evidence has been produced that such influences may be quite specific, so that each nerve cell becomes
'typed' to correspond to some particular muscle or receptor
organ. This 'typing' would then presumably influence the connexions that are made with it by other fibres of the central
nervous system. The problem of the nature of these influences,
reminding one of immunological effects, remains to be solved.
We are certainly a long way from being able to make nervous
systems to order, but we begin to see, in outline, the principles of how to do so. Although we cannot yet make a fully
functioning nervous system it is possible to produce, for
example, an embryo newt with ten eyes (Nieuwkoop, personal
communication). The result may not be a very good newt, but
at least it is in a sense a living creature partly constructed by
man.

Somewhat similar experiments can be made with adult
animals. In mammals functional regeneration in the nervous
system is limited to peripheral nerves. But in other animal
groups brain tissue is capable of very effective growth. The
fibres of the optic nerve of the frog and the toad grow back into
the mid-brain roof in two or three months after they have
been severed and normal vision is restored (Sperry, 1951;
Maturana *et al.*, 1960; Lettvin *et al.*, 1959; Parriss, 1963*a*).
The experimental evidence shows that each fibre returns to
make connexions similar to its original ones (Sperry, 1951;
Gaze, 1960). This at once directs attention to the fascinating
problem of specificity of connexions in the nervous system—
how far it exists, how it is built up, and how maintained. What
is the blue-print of instructions for the design of even a relatively simple nervous system such as the frog's? Is all the
information specified in the genes?

Other experiments have shown that whole pieces of amphi-
bian brain can be transplanted, for example the fore-brain of
one newt to the mid-brain of another (Wiemer, 1955). Optic
nerve fibres apparently grew into this strange organ and it was
said to function well for the recognition of simple patterns of

movement and for the taking of food. The internal organization of such composites is very different from any normal
brain and this seems to show the opposite of Sperry's experiment, namely that almost any nervous pattern will do for
a particular task. This is a thesis that I find difficult to believe
and certainly more experiments of this sort are needed and
much will be learned from them.

The making of nervous systems to order can be done in
other ways, for example in tissue culture or by the technique
of 'deplantation' in which, say, a piece of nerve cord and
a piece of muscle are placed together among the connective
tissues of a tadpole's tail (Weiss, 1950; Szentágothai, 1961).
Small autonomous nervous systems can be formed in this way,
producing sporadic muscular movements, or reflex action if
afferents are added. Once again we see glimpses of powerful
techniques to come. It is not beyond possibility that cells
grown in tissue culture might make more suitable elements
than transistors for the computers with numerous parts that
we shall discuss later. Man has learned how to tame cattle
that contain bacteria that turn grass into beef to keep him
alive. Why should he not make chick's neurons grow in patterns that will make a thinking machine to help him to decide
how to ensure that a maximum population lives to enjoy the
beef?

I cannot pretend to say how this can be done, or that it will
be done. The point is that if we believe that our analysis of
living systems is on the right lines, there is surely no reason
why we should not proceed with the logical next step of constructing similar systems. This, incidentally, applies also to
the study of the origin and production of living matter itself.

The whole discussion takes a new turn, however, when we
consider that in such attempts at synthesis there is no need
simply to follow nature's way exactly, or to use the same
materials, which take millions of years to fashion by natural
selection. Man's way is to find other materials and by short
cuts produce what he calls 'machines' that do the work more
easily for him.

And so, if you notice, the argument has gone round the circle and we are answering the question whether we should use machine language in asking how the brain works by saying that our brain works by making machines. To say this may seem to be an oversimplification; many people live without making machines and are concerned with other things. But all normal humans make models, or at least use words. By speech we produce, as it were, models of the world. Words influence other people because they fit with the models that those others have in their heads. In his writing and art, his speech and his machines man manages to transfer outside his head at least some features of the information that is within it. The formation of such artefacts, available for the use of many, is our unique feature. The modern electronic apparatus that assists with communication of information and with computation is only the latest stage of a development that has been going on throughout the history of man. Indeed, it goes much farther back than this. In Chapter 7 we shall see that in a certain sense the brains of all higher animals embody models of the animal's world. Because of this correspondence they are able to issue instructions that appropriately regulate the homeostat.

2

THE BRAIN AS THE
COMPUTER OF A HOMEOSTAT

1. *The need for a more general terminology*

IT may be that there is less difference than at first appears between making calculating machines and the development of brains. A calculating machine is something assembled by a human being outside his body to help him to make useful predictions about the future. We shall show later that in his brain there exists a not wholly dissimilar 'model', made by him, of different components, but serving the same purpose. We can add either in our heads, or with an abacus, or with an electronic computer. It is, I suppose, possible that each of these pieces of 'apparatus' operates so differently that there is nothing to be gained by comparing them, but since all serve the same function of (among other things) addition, it is unlikely that there are not sufficient similarities to make the comparisons worth while. We are certainly in serious need of ways of speaking about the higher nervous centres, not only for research but so that we may teach the medical student and he may help his patients. It is worth while to consider this point further because it is sometimes complained that 'all this comparison of men and machines does not really help research'. Is this perhaps because much of our research, however revealing in some ways, still fails to provide solutions to the questions we want answered?

Biology has made so many advances recently that there is a temptation to sit down and exploit the new techniques, say, of biochemistry, electron microscopy, or microelectrodes, without spending much time to think whether with them we are finding out the right things for any particular purpose. In neuroanatomy, for example, we discover details of many tracts

and centres, and make the student learn their names, some of
which he may occasionally hear again in clinical practice. But
do we provide him with any general 'picture' of how the brain
is constructed and how it works? Can he say that he 'understands' the behaviour of his more abnormal patients, let alone
the minor aberrations of nervous functioning that he meets in
himself and others every day? This is not to say that our
neuroanatomical studies are wrong or wasted. On the contrary,
they are fundamental; without them we cannot begin to describe the instrument we have to deal with. But in themselves
they only tell us about 'pathways' and 'connexions'.

Physiological investigations give us further concepts, such
as 'reflexes' and 'conditioned reflexes'. We can speak of 'inte-
gration' or 'association centres', but unfortunately these are
still not sufficiently powerful concepts to describe what goes
on in an animal as it devises a complicated course of action,
say for hunting or flight, in the light of what has happened in
the past. Still less do such terms serve to describe what goes
on while a human being 'thinks'. We cannot honestly claim to
produce an effective science of neurology only by using the
system of language that we already know. We literally *must*
try to find stimulation from other studies, so that we may
recognize significant features that we have not 'seen' before,
although we may have 'looked' at them many times.

Whenever we examine a normal or pathological section of
nervous tissue under the microscope, we are studying the plan
of a computer or control system, able to regulate some part of
life. Surely we should try to speak of it in terms that indicate
the operations it performs, rather than by simply giving it
names indicating the similarity of its shape to a nut, a rind, an
olive, or a pear.[1] Every neuroanatomist should be ashamed if

[1] The amygdaloid (nutlike) nucleus among the basal ganglia of the forebrain
is concerned with smell and the control of a complex of higher visceral activities
and hence enters into 'emotion'. There is a cortex (rind) both in the cerebral
hemispheres (our main computers) and in the cerebellum (which is perhaps
a timing device, Braitenberg and Onesto, 1962). There are two 'olives'; a superior one in the pons (bridge) is concerned with hearing, while the inferior olive
in the medulla plays an unknown part in the cortico-fronto-cerebellar-motor
system. The pyriform (pear-like) lobe receives fibres from the olfactory bulb and

he lives through his life without providing facts that show how to improve on at least one such term.

The difficulty of fitting 'functional' names to these centres, chosen at random, shows the extent of our ignorance. It may be that our laziness in not finding better names has contributed to the obscurity. It is hard to share the complacency that accepts terminology as traditional, as picturesque, or 'good enough'. Perhaps the risks of mistaken functional names are worth accepting.

I have no illusions that this will be a popular thesis among the learned, who will rightly say that the task is difficult and that we do not yet know enough. It is true that even with all the information from anatomy, surgery, pathology, electrical recording, biochemistry, and other sources, we are still only beginning to be able to consider the functioning of the nervous system as a whole.

Indeed, discussion of this problem of nomenclature may prompt us to realize some of the complexities of the whole process of description and the growth of language. When someone discovers an object hitherto unknown, he must describe it in the terms that will be understood. He can only do this by comparing the new object with some familiar one—as was done with the names just discussed. The problem is to find the most suitable field from which to draw in making comparisons. In talking about the nervous system it is not the shapes of the centres that are interesting but the parts that they play in the life of the homeostat. Description by comparison with the known parts of artificial machines, may, therefore, be more 'meaningful' than earlier terminology. However, it undoubtedly also has great dangers. The new comparisons may prove to be inept or at least incomplete, indeed in our present ignorance they are almost bound to be so. Rejecting the old and almost arbitrary names may lead us to worse trouble with the new, and is certainly rather unfair to our predecessors, who did their best. In spite of all these

is probably concerned with the coding system for smells or with the early stages of computation of appropriate responses.

difficulties I still find that the more meaningful terminology is the better, and especially that it is more likely to be understood and to lead to further diffusion of knowledge about the brain.

2. *The analysis of a homeostat*

We may therefore begin with the aim of describing the nervous system as an engineer would describe the control system of a homeostat. That this is likely to be a good plan of attack is witnessed by all the evidence of scientific biology— our success in understanding the heart depends upon treating it as a pump, and so on for other organs. The fact that artificial homeostats are produced by men to assist human survival need not trouble us here. Heat engines also have this character but we find it useful to measure human needs in calories. Whatever may be the philosophical problems that this raises, the scientific issue is that in the attempt to give an *exact* description of biological processes it is useful to compare them with the *exact* specifications of the physicist or engineer. To put it in another way, the job of the engineer is to describe human needs so exactly that artefacts can be made to assist them. His language is, therefore, of the greatest value in describing any living process.

It would be very useful here to have an extended and detailed discussion of the terms that are used in specifying the control system of a homeostat. This indeed would be really necessary for a full treatment. My purpose, however, is rather to suggest a general line of orientation of study and to discuss some problems that arise in attempting to pursue it.

The conception of a homeostat involves the existence of a system with a given organization, distinct from its surroundings (environment). The system maintains certain features of its organization constant in spite of changes in the environment that would tend to vary them. Thus a thermostat is a device for controlling the addition or subtraction of heat to reverse the effects of environmental temperature change. The essential features for such action may be discussed as (1) detectors of environmental change; (2) a communication

C

system that carries afferent signals recording such changes to (3) a computing device (controller), which issues further signals in efferent communication channels that reach to (4) effectors, which take appropriate action. Finally, and most interesting of all, the system must have (5) instructions, both in general as to what sort of thing it is to do and in particular at what

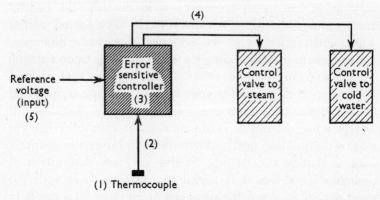

FIG. 2. Diagram of a thermostatic control system. A thermocouple (1) responds to changes in temperature and the consequent changes in current flow in the channel (2) leading to the controller (3) constitute 'signals' in a 'code' because the system has been so designed that particular changes in current produce particular effects in the controller. Similarly the reference voltage (5) constitutes a further signal in a code 'recognized' by the controller and telling it what to do on receipt of signals from (1). The result of the computations in the controller is to produce 'decisions' as a result of which further signals pass in the efferent channels (4), having the effect of turning on either cold water or steam as required.

level it is to operate (for example, for a thermostat, at what temperature). In the diagram of Fig. 2 there is a simple example of such a system designed to regulate the temperature, say, of a bath of liquid used for silver plating.

None of these concepts is simple; all would bear extended discussion. Indeed, the subsequent chapters constitute an attempt to discuss and illustrate some of them. We notice first of all that a homeostat is evidently a system that can exist in several states. A major problem for biology is to find ways of describing the process of 'adaptation' by which each individual organism reaches a particular state and survives for a time in its environment. The thesis we shall suggest is that a useful means of doing this is to compare the process of adaptation with the transmission of information by selection of written or spoken words from a language.

This way of speaking is valuable partly because it is reasonably easily understood at the present time and in such an obscure field we need aids to understanding. Further than this, however, the analogy makes definite predictions, which we can proceed to verify. It tells us that the 'adaptation' of the homeostat is achieved by selection among sets of possible actions, sets that must have been provided previously by some antecedent processes. We are all familiar with the fact that evolutionary adaptation proceeds by selection of genes from a pool provided in the population by mutation. In the shorter term process by which bacteria become 'adapted' to their medium we look for the array of enzymes from which selection is made (p. 52). Similarly the 'adaptations' by which muscles become enlarged or the blood comes to contain more haemoglobin at high altitudes depend upon selection among possible states of the system. Finally, if the same mechanism occurs in the nervous system we may expect to find that 'learning', which is a form of adaptation, depends upon selection of certain elements among a set. We shall try to show later that this set is indeed provided by the various shapes of the dendritic trees of the cells.

The description of the process of adaptation in the terms of the communication engineer is certainly powerful if it can accurately encompass all these things. One may even suspect that its power derives from the fact that communication is a fundamental feature of living things and that our language is only a special case. Perhaps, however, we should be careful to avoid letting enthusiasm run away with us at this point. There are plenty of other ways of describing adaptation. A good case may be made for regarding the 'goal-directed' properties of living systems as 'objective system-properties that require an independent abstract analysis within the framework of a general and exact system research' (Sommerhoff, personal communication). Those who think like this, point to the fact that the techniques of communication theory were devised for one particular type of engineering problem alone. More seriously still, our knowledge of the brain is so scant and the dissimilarity of the brain from computers is so great that we may easily be badly misled by speaking of the one in the language of the other.

Nevertheless, I believe that it is wise to try to do so. Indeed it is inevitable because these terms are those that people increasingly use in other spheres and they will apply them to the brain even if we dislike it. Others may devise more abstract systems that avoid these dangers and if they are truly more powerful they will supplant our, perhaps crude, attempts to speak usefully about the brain partly at least in the terms of communication and computer engineering.

The conceptions of 'signals' carrying 'information' in a 'code' are among the most fruitful and yet misused of these ideas. They will be further discussed in the next chapter. 'Information' may be defined as the feature of certain physical events in the communication channels of a homeostatic system that allows selection among a number of possible responses. The physical events in the channels are called 'signals', and they transmit information in a 'code'. A code is thus essentially a set of physical events among which the appropriate members are selected to represent any given change in the surroundings. Encoding is the process of selecting the appropriate signals to represent any given change. Decoding is the action of an effector producing some operation on the environment that appropriately relates to the change encoded by the given signals. The fact that the signal adequately represents the situation is shown only by the fact that the homeostat responds by an appropriate action to the environment. The appropriateness, in turn, is attested by the fact that the homeostat continues its self-maintenance. In this sense we shall say that the organism is (or contains) a representation of its environment.

Many different sorts of physical change can serve as signals to represent any given change, the relationship of signal to that which it represents being (in general) arbitrary and decided separately for each homeostat by its history. The conversion from one sort of physical signal to another is called re-coding (e.g. speech into writing). Information is thus that feature of the system that remains invariant under re-coding.

The conception of 'computing' involved in the third operation listed on p. 18 is clear in general, but endlessly complicated in particulars. It involves setting up the appropriate interactions between the incoming afferent signals and whatever represents the instructions of the machine. A comparison is thus achieved and the appropriate outgoing signals are sent off. This may be quite simply achieved, but in more elaborate computers it is a most complicated process and is divided up into many parts. This involves what the engineer calls a 'memory', namely a store of the results of previous parts of the calculation, which can be consulted later. We shall discuss the analogy with living memory later. For the moment we may notice its relation to the 'instructions'. The instructions are, of course, in general embodied in the design of the machine— a homeostat is made to do one sort of job. However, in more sophisticated machines the details of the instructions are included in the memory system, in such a way as to play a part in the computing when required. The memory system is a store of signals, that is, representations in code of past events (or at any rate of their general effects). Instructions, in the same code, can obviously be made to intervene in the calculations in such a way as to produce an effective result.

It may be objected that since the instructions of all artificial homeostats are given by men, the analogy with a brain must remain imperfect. One of our most interesting tasks will be to show that this is not so and that it is very profitable to extend this terminology to describe a self-instructing computer. Here we approach the limits of exact knowledge because no such computers have been made (at least none that approach living performance). But here the interaction of engineer and biologist becomes two-directional. The existing engineering terminology has been helpful in devising ways of speaking about the general performance of the body and in particular of the nervous system. This enables us to begin to devise experiments that reveal how it is arranged so as to learn its own instructions. It may well be that the hints as to how it does this will help to devise computers with greater capabilities than any yet in use.

3. *The basic equipment of the nervous system*

It is quite clear that the body operates in something like the same way as the homeostatic system that we have described. We now have to ask whether and how this helps us to describe the actions of the nervous system and the means it uses to regulate behaviour. Sherrington, in his *Integrative action of the nervous system*, as long ago as 1906, provided a model of how this could be done with the concepts then available, including those he had himself invented. Even fifty years later it is hard to do better, but he would have been the last to suppose that his methods were final and the first to hope that with new methods there would grow new ways of thinking. It is not a question of leaving existing pathways of research and adopting entirely new techniques. Perhaps what we need is to go about the investigations that we already know we can undertake with the determination to think constantly where they are leading and how we may improve them. Many people will suppose that all research workers do this all the time, but in fact few do so. Most of us continue with what we have begun. We sometimes think about what to do next, but seldom of the wider scheme into which our studies fit and only very seldom are we brave enough to think that we ourselves might attempt a new synthesis.

The brain can be studied in so many ways, indeed, that one is tempted to be satisfied with a multitude of investigations of particulars. The very conception that the brain has 'a method of working' will seem to have something absurd for anyone who knows anything about it. Nevertheless, if we look upon it as the mediator of the control by which, with the signals from the receptors, homeostasis is maintained, we shall have some sort of plan with which to begin.

By means of Sherrington's elegant scheme we may understand much of the reflex activity of the spinal cord. This was no abstract idea but was supported by a mass of evidence, and it has proved fruitful in allowing supplementation ever since. Indeed, it is only by the gradual accumulation of such detailed knowledge that a reliable understanding of a complicated system can be achieved. We should beware of short cuts.

Already, in Sherrington's thesis it was clearly established that we can recognize two distinct agents in the equipment of the nervous system, nerve fibres, which transmit 'information', and synaptic junctions at which 'decisions' are taken (as we might now say). Everything that has been discovered since has confirmed the brilliant simplicity and depth of this distinction. It was made possible by a combination of physiological analysis with microscopical study of the elements of the nervous system, made largely by Cajal and by Sherrington himself.

Some people may deny that it is useful to 'translate' these physiological discoveries into the newly evolved language of the communication engineer. Many biologists find the new language unpleasing and unnecessary. It is true that it has been slow to prove itself as a stimulant to research, perhaps because it prompts the asking of some questions that the physiological techniques cannot yet answer. To show how this language is relevant and helpful to understanding of the system, we shall first survey briefly some characteristics of the nervous system. Then we can consider the terms in which an engineer might analyse a homeostat of this sort. The result should be to give us a new insight as to the variables that we need to study if we are to understand the system.

We now know that nerve fibres are able to propagate all-or-nothing signals with a high safety factor and without decrement. They are the transmission system of the brain, and one of our main tasks is to study the code by which they carry information. Receptor nerve fibres are in contact with sensitive transducer systems such as the eye and ear, which respond to small changes in the world around. We have to study how these changes are 'encoded' to produce sequences of signals in the nerves.

At their transmitting ends nerve fibres are in contact either by synapses with other nerve-cells or by motor end plates with muscles, glands, or other effector organs. At these stations, as Sherrington also long ago realized, transmission depends upon the arrival of certain patterns of signals. The synapses and cell bodies and branches of the nerve cells are thus the places at which the effective calculations are performed. We may say that the muscles and other effectors finally decode the signals sent out from the brain and the organism takes the actions that are appropriate.

The task is, then, to examine these features of the nervous system and discuss whether they can usefully be analysed in the engineer's manner.

3

INSTRUCTIONS FOR THE COMPUTER AND BRAIN

1. *Codes and computers in animals and machines*

IF we are to understand how a brain works we must first answer the rather obvious question 'What does it do?' One could not expect to understand a motor-car until one found that it was for movement, or a television set for visual communication. Many people might give as an answer that the brain is used for thinking, but we shall pursue the machine analogy and say that the brain is the central controller of a self-maintaining homeostat. This feature of self-maintenance raises subtle difficulties of logic and language, but we shall not be distracted by these. We now have many machines with some homeostatic properties, from automatic factories to refrigerators, but they are, of course, all made by us for our ends. Whether or not this introduces fundamental weaknesses into the comparison, there is no doubt that those who work with these engines provide us with a powerful language for talking about the nervous system. In particular, in making calculating machines a language has been evolved that helps in so many ways in describing the brain that today it is indispensable for the neurologist. These machines are ways devised by brains for doing the work of brains. It is not surprising that the words that brains use to talk about the machines can also be used of brains. It does not follow, of course, that they are the *only* relevant words. Indeed, how could they be, for we have not made a calculating machine that will do all that we ourselves can. If we had made one we should, as we say, fully understand the brain.

2. *Definition of a 'code of instructions'*

Computing machines are said to operate by systems of

logical instructions or codes.[1] In this context a code is defined as any set of physical events that causes a system (specifically an automaton) to perform some organized task. I take this definition (amended) from v. Neumann (1958). You will see that a code of instructions is something that produces an 'organized task'. The attempt at further definition of an 'organized task' should bring us closer to understanding the nature of the problem involved in asking 'How does the brain work?' 'Organized tasks' we might say are the sort of activities that homeostats engage in. The tasks may be said to be 'organized' because they keep the system in its steady state. To say this, however, does not bring out any novel features. Clearly, we need to know something more about the relationship between these coded instructions and the environment within which the system is to operate. Obviously the homeostat must be so planned as to be able to take the right sorts of action. A thermostat must respond to changes of temperature by heating or cooling, not by, shall we say, moving away. A usual way of describing this relationship is to say that the homeostat is 'adapted' to a particular environment (Sommerhoff, 1950). For present purposes we shall prefer to say that it 'represents' the environment.

That the whole organized activity of each type of creature is so arranged that it re-presents appropriate actions to the environment is clear enough. Our problem is to discover how the organization of events within the control system is able to produce these adequate patterns of behaviour. It is hardly an exaggeration to say that physiology can, as yet, give us almost no ideas about this. We have so little information about the type of organization that is involved that we cannot even say whether our brains function in any particular way (say like a digital computer) or not. It is very important to bring out and discuss this problem of the basic nature of the neural control system, so that we can be sure that we are setting about our searches by looking in directions that may give us the answers to our questions.

---

[1] Unfortunately usage varies. We here follow v. Neumann. Others would use 'set of signs', 'alphabet', or 'language system'.

In a digital computer that has to function as the controller of a homeostat, say an automatic factory, the correspondence between the operations within and the events in the world around is ensured by an elaborate programme of instructions. The physical events in the communication channels, operating organs, and memory cause the system to perform its 'organized' task for the very simple reason that they have been designed by the engineer to do so. The plan of this design will include very long series of instructions. Some are of the type that enables the machine, say, to multiply or divide (matters that are logically quite complicated). Other instructions tell the system what 'address' in the memory to consult at each particular stage, or what to do when a value at some point in the calculation is exceeded. The essence of the functioning of the computer is in fact as much in the instruction book as in its physical organs. By varying the instructions the type of task the computer can perform can be varied—it is a general-purpose computer.

The question is where, if anywhere, shall we find a similar set of 'instructions' in the brain? But this is a question to which, unfortunately, neurology as yet provides no answer. As we shall see shortly it does not seem likely that the brain operates with a detailed programme of logical instructions. We can only grope our way, therefore, in the attempt to specify how it does operate. One of the means for doing this is to study a brain very different from our own, as we shall try to do with the octopus.

Our present purpose is to examine the status of the concept of a code. The computing engineers' definition, given above, seems now to be less useful for us than we had hoped, since we have to admit that we do not know what feature of the brain it is that enables it to produce its 'organized tasks'.

We can, however, build up a provisional system with which to operate in the attempt to find out more. The concept that the organism functions by making 'decisions' between alternative courses of action provides a starting-point. 'Signals' are the physical events in the communication channels that operate the decision-taking mechanism. The signals thus carry 'information', but it does not necessarily follow that each channel of the nervous system can carry a whole series of different messages, using an elaborate 'code'. One of the outstanding features of the nervous system is that it contains a very large number of channels, many operating in parallel. One of the principles that it uses for 'encoding' may well be the use of different channels to indicate particular events, each channel functioning only at a small number of significantly different levels of activity.

A 'code' that involves a very large number of channels in this way may seem to be a very different thing from the 'code' in which information is conveyed in a single channel, say the Morse code. Whether the difference is fundamental or not it is certainly true that the idea of using the concept of a code in speaking about the operations of the nervous system begins to reveal unexpected complications and perhaps to seem less attractive.

One feature of a code as usually conceived is that there is a one-to-one correspondence between each signal (or set of signals) and that which they represent. The code should be 'reversible'. Probably everyone will agree that in an animal that has learned there must be in the brain some feature that could be called a 'record' of the situations that have been experienced. But is this record likely to be precise enough to be comparable in respect of reversibility with the record that is stored in code form in the memory of a computer? When an animal learns, it gradually comes to take actions that are appropriate to certain aspects of the situations it has experienced. Only in this sense can it be said to 'represent' those situations. It may be argued that it would therefore be better to speak of the animal as 'becoming adapted to' the situations that have been experienced. There is no need, it may be said, to bring in any questions of 'encoding'.

There is certainly some force in this argument, but I consider that it is not decisive. The record that is set up in the brain certainly often falls far short of being a full representation of the details of each occasion of the experience in the past. But then no record that we know of in any code system can really be considered *by itself* to provide all such details. We use the word 'code' to indicate a set of physical events that accurately corresponds to another set, *given certain conditions*, namely the presence of a particular type of communication channel. There are great differences in the degree of exactness of the codes that we use. A digital computation uses a code that approaches more nearly to 'one to one reversible correspondence' than is found in an after-dinner conversation. The representations that we can detect in animals after training may give us little sign of corresponding to the individual occasions of the past. However, under suitable conditions the brain *can* store very accurate records of individual past occasions. We know this for certain in man, and there is no reason to think that we are unique in this respect. It may be that the reason we do not usually consider animals as giving an accurate record of individual occasions of the past is that we are not used to providing experimental situations where they can do so. That we cannot detect the efficiency of the coding may be our fault and not evidence that it does not exist. Instead of agreeing that the imperfection of the record is a reason for not speaking about 'encoding', because it emphasizes that there is a unique change at each learning occasion, we should reverse the procedure and find new means of study that will show whether the record is exact.

The future will tell which point of view is right. It may be that the use of the concept of 'coding' is actually of positive value in the search for the nature of the changes that occur during learning. In spite of all the difficulties that have been experienced in locating the nature of the memory trace, I believe that it will be possible to find some changes in certain specific places after each learning occasion. I think it is our business to try to identify those changes as they occur and not merely as they accumulate in the apparently slow process of learning. For this reason I welcome the difficulties we have been discussing, which are associated with the use of the terms 'coding' and 'representation'. I prefer to speak in this way, rather than of the organism becoming 'adapted', for the very reason that the latter suggests a slow process of moulding rather than a series of specific choices. But in any case it is important not to be too concerned about terminology. What matters is to find out as much as possible about the changes in the brain during learning.

3. *The alphabet of the nervous system*

Our immediate task is to find how the nervous system takes, from all the varied things that go on around it, some record of those events that provide clues as to how it should act in the future to ensure survival. We are accustomed to look for this power in a principle of 'adaptation' by which organisms, from bacteria upwards, adjust their metabolism to suit the requirements. Adaptation is indeed a fundamental capacity and it may be that all systems of learning are based upon it. Any given organism has only a certain range of powers of adaptation, conferred on it presumably by the hereditary mechanism. We know a good deal about the mechanism of adaptation, e.g. of enzyme systems, and it is reasonable to suppose that there is a set of possible molecular configurations available, out of which the appropriate ones are somehow selected.

The thesis I wish to propound is that learning in the nervous system is similarly a selection among a previously available set of possible alternatives. The Pavlovian formula of conditioning may make it appear that, in learning, any 'stimulus' can become associated with any response. The conditioned reflex is very often considered to be 'the simplest example of learning' and therefore the best model to choose when thinking about the physiological processes involved (see, e.g. Eccles, 1953). It has often been pointed out that the apparent simplicity of the conditioned reflex conceals many implicit assumptions (e.g. Konorski, 1948). Perhaps its main defect is that it omits the most significant feature in any system for transmitting and storing information. This is that there shall be a code set of possible signals and actions, among which selection is made.

In the classical example of a conditioned reflex, the ringing of a bell might initially produce either more saliva or less. If food is given, the tendency to produce *less* saliva is suppressed. We shall find much evidence that learning involves preventing access to one of two pathways (p. 155).

Animals learn to respond adequately to relevant features of the world around them. For this they have a code of pre-set detectors, and the signals provided by these must be made to produce certain actions. The means by which the signals from the receptors are combined and linked to effectors are among the most complicated activities of the nervous system. This is especially true in ourselves, since we react to extremely numerous and complicated sets of stimuli. In simpler animals fewer combinations are possible and it may be better to begin by studying the process of 'encoding' in them. Then eventually we may be able to see how the signals set up in our own receptor channels are combined to give our complicated pattern of behaviour.

The obvious principle upon which an efficient code operates is that it puts the events to be signalled into the elements of a limited set of classes, for each of which there is a previously determined signal or symbol. This signal is then able, when transmitted, to produce some effect or reaction corresponding to the event that it represents. Clearly, there must be some relationship between the number of classes in the code and the number of things that the homeostat can do. However, we shall find that octopuses have quite elaborate coding systems for visual and tactile events, although the decisions that are made are essentially simple, whether to attack or retreat.

4. *The colour alphabet*

A good example for the discussion of coding is colour vision, where the continuous spectrum of wavelengths is analysed into a limited number of named colours. According to classical theory this is done by using combinations of three main categories, red, green, and blue. I make the excuse of reverence for my ancestor Thomas Young for not examining the complexities of this system, but shall assume that colour vision is possible because we are provided by heredity with a small number of types of primary receptors, with which we encode the visual information into a small number of primary categories, associated with such fundamental features of the environment as blood and meat, leaves and fruit, and the open sky and sea. We can then make a moderately subtle system of recombinations with this alphabet of symbols, without 'measuring' the wavelengths in units as a physicist would do.

The point is that our code of symbols for wavelength differences is limited by the provision of quite a small set of receptors, tuned to wavelengths that occur frequently as features of the environment that are important for our lives. Then, appropriate means of combining these categories are provided by the retinal nervous layers and the brain. I shall try to show that at least in the octopus even such complicated matters as discriminations between shapes are performed by similar pre-set systems for detecting certain features of the surroundings.

5. *The frog's visual alphabet*

Studies of the visual system of the frog have shown recently how the information provided by the rods and cones about the retinal image is simplified into a form that can be used by the animal (Lettvin *et al.*, 1959; Maturana *et al.*, 1960). Action potentials recorded by microelectrodes in the optic nerve show that the fibres may be classified into six types. (1) 'Contrast detectors', giving a sustained response when any object moves into the visual field and stops there. (2) 'Convexity detectors', responding to a small object moving into the field, with a frequency proportional to the convexity, i.e. increasing as the object gets smaller. These two types correspond to the 'on' fibres of earlier workers (Hartline, 1938; Barlow, 1953). (3) 'Moving edge detectors' respond with a frequency increasing with the speed of an edge moving over the field ('on–off' fibres). (4) 'Dimming detectors' discharge when the light intensity is reduced; these are the fastest conducting fibres in the nerve (10 m/sec). (5) The fibres of the fifth class are 'Darkness detectors', measuring the intensity of illumination, firing continuously with a frequency inversely proportional to the light intensity and increasing to a maximum in darkness.

These sets of fibres project to sheets of endings in the mid-brain tectum, at increasing depths, in the order given (except that the fifth end with the third). Together they provide the information that leads to the tracking of flying insects (presumably type 2), sudden approach of a large attacker (the fast conducting type 4) and presumably other situations, for it is known that toads, if not frogs, can distinguish visual shapes (Parriss, 1963b). A sixth type of fibre responds when there is an increase of light intensity in the blue waveband (Muntz, 1962a). It has also been shown that frogs jump towards blue in preference to other colours; that is, they may jump to open water rather than to, say, vegetation. This type of fibre is connected not with the optic tectum but with the thalamus. It is not clear what may be the significance of the fact that this thalamic pathway, which becomes so highly developed in mammals, serves for escape in the frog.

The response of each of the six types of fibre in the optic nerve must be determined by the form of its connexions in the retina with bipolar cells, themselves connected in turn with rods and cones. As Maturana and Lettvin and their colleagues express it 'they extract differently weighted samples of simple operations done by the bipolars'. The changes that occur at the dendritic trees of the nerve cells of the retina (presumably summative and subtractive actions) are thus the active agents involved in coding the input, separating it into one of six suitable types (more detailed analysis suggests that there are further subdivisions). The important point is that the information passed to the brain is already simplified and, as we may say, 'coded'. The authors express this picturesquely by saying that 'the eye speaks to the brain in a language already highly organised and interpreted, instead of transmitting some more or less accurate copy of the distribution of light on the receptors'. 'Speaking in a language' means selecting suitable items from a pre-selected code. We shall suggest that this is exactly the way that in octopuses the information about the shape of objects seen is reported by selection among sets of cells with different dendritic patterns. Moreover, there is evidence that in mammals, also, visual shape discrimination depends upon the patterns of the dendritic trees (p. 162).

6. *The representation of information in a machine*

In any encoding system the problem is to set up a representation of external changes in a form that is suitable for the operations required. Thus for transmission of information to a distance by telegraphy we may code into a system of dots, dashes, and pauses. Hereditary transmission is by a code of combinations of nucleotides, controlled by natural selection. Again, to multiply or divide we may encode numbers into lengths measured logarithmically on a slide rule and then manœuvre the lengths. Alternatively we may represent numbers in whatever physical form is used by a particular digital calculating machine. Whatever method is used the encoding operation consists in choosing the appropriate members among a set of physical conditions that by some previous operation has been selected to constitute the code. The principles of efficient coding have been much explored (see, e.g. Ashby, 1960; Barlow, 1959). In order to transmit the maximal amount of information per signal there are certain principles that produce 'optimal coding'. An obvious one is that the most frequently occurring items should be indicated by the shortest signs (Morse). So little is known of the details of the coding system employed in the brain that we cannot yet apply these principles in detail. We are, however, beginning to be able to say something about the physical operations involved in encoding. Sometimes this is performed by a set of specifically selective responders (transducers) as in the cochlea of the ear, which operates partly like the tuned reeds or resonance circuits of certain radio control devices. I shall suggest the hypothesis that in the visual system of an octopus and perhaps of other animals the set in question is to be found among the various dendritic trees of the cells, differing in lengths and directions of orientation.

It is clear that the subject of coding must be of some relevance to the study of the brain. It does not necessarily follow that coding systems that have proved efficient for particular machines for assisting communication will be found to apply in the workings of the body. There is, however, a certain likelihood that similarities will appear. A telephone must transmit 'speech' and a television picture must be not only 'seen', but 'understood'. It would be surprising if the language used by the engineer to describe the systems he creates to ensure the part of the transmission outside the body was found to have no relevance to the events that follow within the ear, eye, and brain. This question has become of special importance in recent years since the development of very rapid calculating machines raises the question whether the brain operates with similar methods. We shall find that there are both similarities and differences. Undoubtedly the language and mathematics developed for the study of computers helps to provide us with ways of talking about the brain and hence of finding out more about it.

Since the language is still not generally familiar to biologists I shall try to give a very simple version of it, following the method used by the mathematician v. Neumann in his very clear account (1958). His comparison of the properties of computers and brains is most stimulating to the neurologist and suggests many further ideas. It is a melancholy reflection on the effects of specialization that some of these ideas had not occurred to v. Neumann himself, in spite of years of interest in the problem and excellent opportunities for discussion. The need for mathematicians and biologists to learn each other's languages and facts is sufficient justification for discussion even at an elementary level.

7. *Analogue and digital representation*

Calculating machines proceed by three steps. First, numbers are encoded, that is to say represented by some physical state in the machine. Then some organs operate upon these representations in a manner that is equivalent to (i.e. represents), say, addition or multiplication. Finally, in a decoding operation the result is read off as a number. Transmission of the representations of numbers from one place to another within the machine may be an important part of the operations. Numbers may be put aside and stored in an organ known as the memory of the machine and then recalled again to be used at a later stage in the calculation.

Two different types of machine may be recognized and understanding of the difference between them is important in finding a language for talking about the nervous system. The difference depends upon the type of code that is used to represent the numbers, which determines the type of operation by which the calculation is performed.

In *analogue machines* each number is represented by allowing some physical quantity to vary to the requisite extent. Thus on a slide rule each number is represented by a length. Calculation is then done by manipulating two lengths. In the calculating machines suggested in the last century to solve differential equations, which were among the earliest modern computers, numbers were to be represented by the amount which a disc rotated on a system of shafts, which were so geared together that their movements represented the required calculations. In more modern versions the numbers may be represented by the strength of currents or related voltages, which can be added or subtracted and, by various means, multiplied or divided. Many parts in an analogue machine may have to interact in performing a desired calculation. Obviously there is a sense in which we may say that these parts and their operations show at least some degree of physical correspondence to the calculations they perform. In that sense we can say that they are 'models' of these calculations. We shall see the importance of this as we come to consider in what sense the organism is an 'analogue' of its environment and in particular whether we can usefully consider that the brain contains a 'model'.

In an analogue representation the physical quantity usually varies continuously, but in *digital representation* it can assume only certain arbitrary states, such as the conventional digits 0–9, after which the system is named. In nearly all modern computing machines the binary system is used, there are only two states, presence or absence of a particular condition, e.g. an electrical pulse. This simplification obviously makes it a great deal easier to perform operations with the numbers, but equally clearly it demands a form of coding that is somewhat more elaborate than the analogue system, since the latter allows a distinct physical value for each number. In particular, digital coding requires that the value to be assigned to each mark depends upon its position in a series. Thus, in binary digital coding, instead of the ten digits of the decimal system, there are only 0's and 1's. The number 1 is represented by 01, 2 by 10, 3 by 11, 4 by 100, and so on. Provided the rules imposed by the logic of the system are observed arithmetic is easy. For addition of two numbers:

$$
\begin{array}{ccc}
01 & 10 & 11 \\
01 & 01 & 01 \\
\hline
10 & 11 & 100 \\
\end{array}
$$

The rule is that the sum is 1 if the added digits differ and 0 if they are the same, 1 being then carried.

Such processes are easily carried out by physical means and they can be performed very rapidly. This is the secret of the success of digital computers and we have to ask whether the brain operates by similar methods of binary coding or whether it sets up analogues. Perhaps it does both, for they can be combined. In the system known as pulse-density coding each number is represented by the frequency of pulses averaged over a suitable time. Thus 1 1 11 1 11 1 1 11 might represent 'three' and 11 1 111 1 111 11 1111 1111 'six'. (Larger sequences than this would be needed for adequate averaging.) Arithmetical operations can be performed with such pulse sequences, for example they can be added and, by suitable devices, multiplied. Moreover, they can be stored, by making them operate suitable analogue accumulating devices. It is possible that the nervous system operates as a mixed digital/analogue system of this sort, with pulse-frequency modulation.

8. *Impulse frequencies in the nervous system*

There is usually a relationship between the frequency of response in an afferent nerve fibre and the intensity of stimulation of the receptor that is connected with it. Presumably the effects of such trains of impulses at the next cells of the chain vary with these frequencies and durations. In this sense we are dealing with a frequency code. However, it is improbable that individual nerve fibres usually carry a wide variety of specific impulse-frequency patterns. Each nerve fibre usually transmits the information that a particular type of transducer at the periphery is being activated. The frequency serves to signal the intensity of the peripheral change. Information about the various types of change that occur in the world around is provided for by the presence of numerous channels, each connected with a different transducer.

This picture of a multi-channel system obviously requires modification when we come to consider the interaction between signals in different primary afferent channels. Neurons of higher order may receive impulses from many afferent sources. The impulse-frequency pattern that the second-order neuron emits may then be dependent upon the distribution pattern of the first inputs (Melzack and Wall, 1962). The third neurons must then be able to recognize the different frequency patterns. Only in rare cases has it been possible to follow the frequency patterns through chains of neurons. In the auditory system the rate of firing becomes less as the impulses proceed through various synapses from the ear to the cortex (Whitfield, 1957). The frequency also becomes less closely related to intensity of stimulus.

Impulse frequency is obviously a most important variable in the nervous system but it is not very likely that we shall find that single nerve fibres carry large amounts of information by an elaborate system of pulse-frequency modulation.

In the higher centres there are some signs that the storage of records of particular frequencies are accompanied by discharge patterns at those frequencies (Morrell, 1963). 'The temporal pattern of events at a place in the brain can serve as information' (John, 1963). This is, however, a special type of situation and there is no evidence that storage of data about, say, visual or tactile shapes involves the maintenance of particular discharge frequency patterns in higher neurons. But so little is known that it would be difficult to deny that this is a possibility.

We shall assume, however, that in the visual system the coding does not depend upon selecting one among a large number of possible frequency patterns that each fibre can carry. Instead we shall suggest that the coding depends upon initiating action in some among a number of possible anatomically distinct pathways. The intensity of the activity in each of these is represented by the frequency of its impulse discharges. The elements of the code are thus provided by the restrictions placed upon connectivity by the anatomical and physiological properties at each stage. For example, a central neuron with an elongated oval dendritic field will act as an encoding agent recording the presence of a visual event of that shape (p. 162). If this is a correct approach we shall obviously have to devote much study to the restrictions on connectivity, which may provide us with the secrets of the code.

9. *Some differences between brains and digital computers*

So far we have been talking only about the principles of coding and performing the simple operations of arithmetic. In order to solve any particular problem, other than the simplest, a machine must be so constructed or controlled as to operate upon a series of numbers in the manner suited to find a solution. We shall be much more likely to find out how any particular part of the brain works if we ask carefully 'What problems does it solve?' This may seem obvious, but curiously enough the neglect to make this formulation might be said to be one of the great weaknesses of classical physiology of the brain, which is apt to separate the study of receptors from that of 'higher centres' and both of these from study of the motor pathways and behaviour. The whole subject becomes fragmented, isolating psychologists, who study what problems are solved, from the rest of us who are supposed to study the mechanisms by which it is done. Let us try to formulate a scheme of work that avoids this fragmentation and enables us to speak more exactly about the action of each part of the brain.

The brain is the part of the homeostat that chooses from the various possible actions those most likely to ensure survival under the conditions obtaining. It operates in part by the transmission of nerve impulses, which have an all-or-nothing character and therefore seem obviously to be part of a digital system. Notice that the nerve impulses as such are involved in the transmission system within the machine. It does not follow that the active organs that make the calculations also operate on digital principles. The body uses the simplest possible method of transmission, namely signalling by presence or absence, but how does it encode before transmission and how does it operate upon the signals?

If we think about what is involved in making digital calculations, it seems less likely that the method used in digital computers is the only one that is used in the brain. The digital method uses pulses, each in its correct place in a sequence, and representing, as v. Neumann puts it, 'patterns of alternative actions, organized in highly repetitive sequences and governed by strict and logical rules, . . . [which] have a quite complex logical character' (p. 10). The machines are able to do this because they pass the pulses very fast, each lasting as little as 10^{-6} or 10^{-7} seconds in modern machines. The impulses in a nerve fibre cannot follow each other at intervals of less than 10^{-3} seconds, usually the frequency is even lower.

The machine achieves its speed and accuracy by doing all the calculations in one or few computing organs, which are expensive pieces of apparatus with an elaborate structure, ensuring that they operate with great precision. Numbers are fed in in the right order, each is then added, perhaps, to the previous one and the result is transferred to the memory register if it is not to be involved in the next operation. The memory, therefore, consists of a physical record of numerous presences or absences, each at a particular place in the sequence, this position being known as its 'address'. When needed later in the calculation a number is recalled to the computing organs. Are we to consider that the memory in the nervous system is also a record of numerous presences or absences, each neatly addressed and recalled to the active organs exactly as and when needed?

We do not know precisely where or how the record is kept in the brain, but as we shall see later we can localize it approximately, and it seems unlikely that it is stored entirely on these principles or in such an individualized form. The nerve impulses, with their rather low frequency (up to 1,000/sec) and slow conduction velocity (up to about 120 m/sec) do not seem to be reliable enough components to be the indicators of presence or absence at exactly the right place in rigidly determined patterns of sequences. Notice that the need for the reliability of a digital computer comes from the fact that every element in the calculation must be performed at exactly the right place and any error will lead to wildly wrong results. As v. Neumann puts it, the calculation is performed in great arithmetical and logical depth, and the result is either exactly right or so wrong that the error is easily made apparent by repeating the calculation (or doing it in parallel). Living organisms do not seem to operate like this; their components may have a low reliability individually but the whole system produces answers that ensure an astonishing continuity of existence of these very complicated systems. We may meditate that the mammals are much older than the Alps, and yet they are relatively newcomers among living creatures. Very efficient predictors must be at work to ensure such long survival.

10. *Some similarities between brains and analogue computers*

The need for great accuracy and depth in the digital computations comes from the fact that there is only one calculating organ (or few of them). The actions that it is to perform must be controlled by a programme of instructions, which are also coded in digital form in the memory. If the instructions are correct the machine, given sufficient time, can answer any problem that can be set to it in its code. Its great value is that it is a general-purpose computer. Its chief limitation is that much time and ingenuity are needed to take the data from real life, to put them into code, and to programme the machine. Analogue computers have different advantages and limitations. Here there are typically as many active organs as there are operations to be performed. Some of these can be put into direct connexion with the environment and made to represent numbers. The sequence in which the calculation is done in a differential analyser is determined by the way the organs are geared together, or connected by plugging if the numbers are represented by voltages. Thus the pattern of connexions that determines what computation is made is part of the structure or pattern of the machine. These features at once suggest to the biologist, and especially to the anatomist, that the nervous system is likely to work at least partly on analogue principles. What we commonly call the 'structure' of the nervous system determines what it does. It is not a general-purpose computer at all, but consists of a number of analogues set up to perform a few particular tasks.

One of the great advantages of an analogue machine is that it can receive information direct from particular environments. That is to say, the machine may be itself a representation of the environment and its parts are pre-selected to perform certain calculations in relation to the latter. It is possible to find many senses in which animals thus represent, in their structure and behaviour, the conditions under which they live. Some of these will be discussed in later chapters. The many examples of parallel evolution show how species that begin with different basic structures become alike if they live under similar conditions.

An obvious complication that we have to consider is how the setting up of the living analogue is done. It may be partly or largely by heredity, but it may also be influenced by learning. Indeed, we shall see that the perfecting of self-modifying analogue systems may be the feature in which higher nervous systems excel. If this is so, it should be well worth while to try to make artefacts to imitate them, as some engineers are doing. As an example, Dr. W. K. Taylor's machine will be described later (Chapter 19).

The first step is to find the basic principles on which the nervous system computes, and for this it may be best to use an animal whose brain makes relatively few decisions and, being less flexible than our own, is less likely to give the impression of being a general-purpose computer. For this and other reasons we have found it convenient to work with octopus brains, in which we think that we may be beginning to see how the analogue is physically constructed.

One of the great limitations of man-made analogue machines is imposed by the need to have one organ for each component operation involved in the calculation. The fact that the nervous system has available a vast number of very small organs again suggests that it uses analogue principles. Even the most expensive man-made analogues contain only a few hundred units (though Dr. Taylor plans to have 4,000). The 10^8 cells of an octopus, or more than 10^{10} in a man, present an immense advantage. In any case it may be that we should consider the individual synaptic junctions. Counts based on measurements of dendrites by Drs. Aitken and Bridger (1961) would give up to 30,000 of these synaptic knobs for a large cell of the spinal cord of a cat, so the total number in man might be 10^{15}. However, there are good reasons for thinking that the cells are the units involved in the computations and we must be content with some factor of 10^{10}.

The way that the nerve-cells are arranged does not suggest that they are involved in long chains of actions, such as those that represent computations in a digital computer. In general, they are spread out in layers, and impulses are passed in parallel from layer to layer by complex interweaving patterns of fibres, which represent the plugging system of the analogue.

We find this sort of arrangement over and over again, in different animal groups (arthropods, cephalopods, vertebrates). Analysis of such layered systems presents a most stimulating challenge to the anatomist and physiologist and it might be fair to say that it has only just begun. One of the chief aims of the present discussion is to try to devise ways of investigating the computing operations that are conducted by these layered analogues.

But, of course, we must be cautious about guessing in advance at the extent to which digital and analogue procedures are used in the nervous system. There are many self-re-exciting systems in the brain. Particular sets of signals might pass through these many times and they might be part of systems performing computations in depth and even for calling for numbers from addresses in a memory register. However, it is more likely that the memory is somehow embedded in the connexions of the machine, a question to which we shall return later.

Even the way that we perform calculations does not seem to follow a logical pattern, as digital machines do. We do not consult the full logic of multiplication every time that we solve 4 times 4; we simply say 16. It may be argued that we can do it like that because we once learned the logic as children, but is this true, or did we just learn that $4 \times 4 = 16$? In any case, digital machines do not necessarily carry every detailed instruction in digital form in the memory. Some routines can be embodied in analogues. However, this discussion of theory and of the machines of engineers has perhaps already gone on long enough. Its aim is to provide us with an insight into the types of problem that are involved, and the means available for solving them. Our task now is evidently not simply to speculate how the nervous system *might* work, but to find evidence of *how* it does.

4

SOME VARIABLES OF THE
NERVOUS SYSTEM

1. *The numbers of cells in various nervous systems*

IT is clear that there are interesting ways in which we can speak about the nervous system with the language used for computers. We may now consider some of the variables that are likely to be relevant. The numbers of units involved is surely one of these, and of this much could indeed be written, though accurate counts are surprisingly few. The number of nerve cells is small in animals that produce a limited range of behaviour. In the nematode worm *Ascaris* there are exactly 162, mostly arranged in the anterior neural ring (Hanström, 1928). This does not, however, include the receptor cells, which are more numerous. The life of a nematode as an internal parasite requires only a few wriggling movements to keep the material around it stirred. Complicated migrations are performed during the life cycle, to ensure reaching a new host. Many of the movements are passive and produced by the host. Thus, the 'instructions' that ensure that the needs of the worm are met are mainly included in the genetic mechanism. This ensures that large numbers of suitably endowed eggs and larvae are passively carried from host to host. Perhaps the only decision the nervous system makes is whether to wriggle or not, but it may be that a few other actions are possible.

The lowest limit of this condition is found in the worm *Myxicola*. The longitudinal muscles that draw it into its tube are all controlled by a single nerve fibre. Ordinary earthworms have a system of three giant fibres, two conducting forwards, one backwards. In squids the sack-like mantle contracts as one entity to produce the jet that drives the animal through the water. This is operated by a system beginning with only two nerve cells, and these are joined by a bridge so that signals set up in one always pass in both nerves (Fig. 3, see p. 56).

We can learn the elements of the coding system from these simple nervous systems. A single impulse in the giant fibre of *Myxicola* or a squid produces a single twitch of the muscles (Roberts, 1962*a*). In an earthworm, on the other hand, the response produced by a single giant fibre impulse is small. Stimulation of the body surface usually produces bursts of impulses in the giant fibre. The strength of the contraction depends on the number of impulses and this in turn upon the intensity and duration of the stimulus (Roberts, 1962*b*). The escape reaction of these worms can thus be graded whereas *Myxicola* gives an all-or-nothing retreat into its tube. In a squid the number of twitches and hence the speed and distance travelled by the animal presumably follows the number of nerve impulses, though it may not always be one twitch per impulse (Prosser and Young, 1937; Wilson, 1960).

The setting up of the impulses is a more complicated matter. The dendrites of each first-order giant cell in the squid (Fig. 3) are covered by numerous end-feet, the terminals of fibres that bring signals from many parts of the brain. It is not known in detail how the co-operation of these signals determines how many impulses shall be fired. This is in any case only the last stage of the computing process that determines whether the squid moves following the appearance of some object, say a fish, in its visual field.

Much is known about the organization of the motor pathways that control the muscles in other animal groups. Relatively few neurons are involved and each controls a certain number of muscle fibres, the so-called motor unit, which is thus large if the muscle is a powerful one, smaller if its actions have to be finely graded. Thus the soleus muscle of the cat was calculated by Eccles and Sherrington (1930) to be controlled by 233 neurons, each innervating 143 muscle-fibres. A single twitch produces 580 g of tension. In the eye muscles, on the other hand, there is one neuron to every two or three muscle-fibres and this can elicit only a very few grammes tension.

The pattern of what the animal can do is thus determined by the number of units into which its muscular system is divided. No very precise list of the repertoire of possible actions by any animal has yet been produced. It would be difficult to prepare, but worth attempting. In a mammal it would be complicated by the arrangement of the bones as levers, often with many muscles pulling across each joint. But these muscles work as simple antagonists or in limited combinations, and the specification of the order of magnitude of the number of states should be possible. Although it might not seem that this would be of great practical value, it would be a help in giving some firm basis for discussion of the mechanisms that are operating. We have the impression that our actions and those of animals are of unending complexity. The first task is to try to find measures for them.

A very important feature is that the muscle-fibres are nearly always arranged in pairs, or antagonists (e.g. the flexors and extensors of the fingers, wrist, elbow, &c.). The nervous system sends to each muscle fibre the instruction 'contract'. This may vary from 'contract once' (twitch) to 'contract several times in rapid succession' (tetanus). There is no instruction to relax. All movements are therefore controlled by the issuing of a properly programmed sequence of instructions to contraction by members of opposing muscle pairs.

The number of nerve cells in the motor centres gives some measure of the complexity of the control. Thus in a squid, while there is one pair of giant cells to control the mantle, there are thousands of smaller ones to control the chromatophores. In an octopus, which can produce more elaborate colour patterns than a squid, there are about a million cells in the centres that control the chromatophores, and most of them are small. However, a mere fraction of these cells send axons to the periphery. Only 32,000 nerve fibres have been counted in the bundles that contain motor nerve fibres running to the skin. Even if this is a serious underestimate it seems that many of the cells of the chromatophore centres send no axon to the periphery.

The ventral horn of the spinal cord of the cat contains about 120,000 cells, giving rise to the motor fibres, which are in the ventral roots (Holmes and Davenport, 1940). The fibres are relatively more numerous in the regions that control delicate movements, namely the eye and limb muscles. There are, of course, many other (smaller) cells in the spinal cord, concerned in various ways in establishing patterns of movement.

Animals with simpler movement patterns certainly have fewer motor neurons. An amphioxus has at most a few hundreds. Arthropods operate their movement patterns with few motor neurons. There are said to be 350 in the bee and 80 cells in each abdominal and 150 in a thoracic ganglion of a dragon-fly larva (see Wiersma, 1952).

In an octopus the action pattern is perhaps more varied. It can do many different things with its arms, show a variety of colour patterns, swim, eject ink, to mention only a few. Correspondingly, there are about 700,000 cells in the suboesophageal motor centres, excluding those for control of the chromatophores and blood vessels (Young, 1963a). However, as in the spinal cord, not all of these cells send axons to the periphery. Counts of fibres that are presumed to lead away from the brain show only about 110,000 (excluding those for chromatophores, blood vessels, and viscera). This gives us some idea of the number of channels available for producing the major action patterns of octopus behaviour and is comparable to the number in the cat. The total number of cells involved is actually much greater in an octopus because there are elaborate ganglia in the arms, containing altogether no less than 300 million cells. An isolated arm is capable of quite complicated, independent, and well-directed actions. For instance, it can transfer food towards the place where the mouth should be.

Over a million nerve-cells are contained in the centres that control the flow of blood to different parts of the body, which is obviously a factor of great importance for the octopus homeostat. An interesting feature is that all the vasomotor and viscero-motor fibres are small ($< 3\mu$). In the regulation of internal activities there is no need of great speed and this presumably explains the small size of the fibres concerned, in octopuses as in vertebrates. It is less clear why in both groups these small fibres are very numerous.

These figures give us some rough idea of the sizes of the repertoires of actions that are possible for animals. Of course, we should need to know also something of the codes that these neurons use and the extent to which they are able to produce gradations of response in the muscles they control. The situation described for the giant fibres in which each impulse produces a twitch is rare. More usually the effects of impulses at short intervals summate to produce a tetanic contraction of the muscle-fibres, whose tension is proportional to the frequency. The decoding is produced by the effect of each impulse in releasing a certain quantum of the stimulating transmitter acetylcholine. This produces a depolarization of the muscle-fibre surface, which, if sufficient, will be propagated over the fibre to make it twitch, with summation at suitable frequencies.

2. *Number and size of cells in various parts of a nervous system*

There are enormous differences between the sizes of neurons in parts of the nervous system that perform different functions. These differences should provide us with valuable clues about the functions of the parts, but it must be admitted that neurology has so far made little use of such data. In a squid there are about 20 giant nerve fibres, up to 1 mm in diameter, controlling the whole mass of the mantle. The two largest of them are 10 cm or more long in a large squid, and the volume of each approaches $80 \times 10^6 \mu^3$. Perhaps the smallest cells in the animal are the tufted 'amacrines' of the optic lobes (p. 144). There are over 50 million of these, with a maximum diameter of $5\ \mu$ and a bush of minute twigs each of $1\ \mu$ diameter and $10\ \mu$ length. The whole cell can hardly have a volume greater than $80\ \mu^3$ (but the surface area is proportionately very great).

E

The clue to the significance of these immense differences may be in the fact that the conduction velocity of nerve fibres is a function of diameter (among other variables). The giant motor neurons must excite large masses of muscle without excessive delays (see Pumphrey and Young, 1938). The tiny neurons need to conduct whatever signals they carry for such short distances that speed is unimportant. By having them of small size the animal can have many of them, and the question is to discover *what is gained by the presence of such large numbers of channels, most of which carry nearly the same information and would therefore seem to be redundant.*

Further investigation of cell sizes shows that a large range is present both in cephalopods and vertebrates. The cells of the 'higher motor centres' are smaller than the final motor neurons, but much larger than those concerned with the analysis of the information that comes from the receptors. This gradation in octopuses is considered further in Chapter 6 and summarized in Table 1. In a mammal the largest motoneurons of the spinal cord may have a dendrite spread of 1 mm, and axon of 20 μ in diameter and of length 1 m. The volume of the whole cell may be 0·001 mm³ ($10^6 \mu^3$) (Hydén, 1961). There are perhaps 100,000 of them in the human spinal cord. By contrast the amacrines of the retina and smaller 'stellate' cells of the cortex have dimensions comparable to those of the small cells we have considered in squids and octopuses. No one really knows how many of them there are but there may well be 10^8 amacrines in each eye and 10^9 stellate cells in the cerebral cortex. Between these extremes there are in vertebrates as in cephalopods many cells of intermediate size.

3. *Determination of cell size*

Part of our aim is to gain a picture not only of how the nervous system works, but how it is made. Indeed, we aspire to make one (p. 1). It is interesting, therefore, that something is known about the influences that control the diameters of nerve-cells and fibres. Of course in the young animal they are all small. Then, as the nervous system grows and is used, some of them become bigger, partly through the operation of hereditary instructions and partly by the stimuli derived from the very fact of their use.

TABLE 1

Numbers (10^3) of cells with nuclei of various diameters found in suboesophageal and supraoesophageal centres, optic lobes, and arm ganglia of Octopus (Young, 1963a).

Lobes	Total nuclei 10^3	< 5 μ	5–10 μ	10–15 μ	15–20 μ	20–25 μ
Lower motor centres:						
Total	692	183 / 26·4%	302 / 43·6%	164 / 23·7%	37 / 5·3%	6 / 0·9%
Intermediate motor centres:						
Vasomotor centres	1,307	233 / 17·8%	968 / 74·0%	106 / 8·1%	..	..
Chromatophore centres	526	98 / 18·6%	272 / 51·7%	140 / 26·6%	16 / 3·0%	..
Higher motor centres:						
Total	1,540	548 / 35·6%	910 / 59·1%	77 / 5·0%	5 / 0·3%	..
Highest supraoesophageal centres:						
Inferior frontal	1,085	999 / 91·1%	68 / 7·1%	17 / 1·7%	1 / 0·1%	..
Subfrontal	5,308	5,307 / 99·9%	1 / < 0·1%	..	..	..
Superior frontal median	1,772	1,772 / 100%	..	..	..	..
Superior frontal lateral	82	42 / 51·5%	40 / 48·5%	..	..	..
Vertical	25,066	25,000 / 99·7%	66 / 0·3%	..	..	..
Subvertical	810	459 / 56·6%	344 / 42·5%	7 / 0·86%	..	..
Optic lobes:						
(total both)	92,660	85,890 / 92·7%	6,640 / 7·2%	130 / 0·1%	..	..
Arm ganglia:						
Total for eight arms	347,040	107,680 / 31%	237,520 / 68·4%	1,600 / 0·5%	240 / 0·1%	..

This can conveniently be studied in the adult animal when nerve fibres regenerate after they have been severed. Once again all the new nerve fibres are very small. They grow out towards their old destinations—whether they are guided back to these is uncertain—but they only grow in diameter to a limited extent unless they have made an appropriate re-connexion (Aitken, Sharman, and Young, 1947). There must, therefore, be some means by which information is transmitted up the nerve fibre from the muscle or receptor with which it has become connected, instructing the cell to build more material. A neat way of showing this is to overload a neuron. When a lizard regenerates its tail it does not grow a new spinal cord. The whole new tail is, therefore, innervated by the hinder remaining roots and the cells and fibres of these become excessively large (Terni, 1920). Conversely, any nerve cell that has no means of receiving from the periphery or sending an output fades away (atrophies) and may die altogether.

Unfortunately, we do not understand how these increases or decreases in growth activity are initiated or controlled. They are presumably similar in a general way to other processes of hypertrophy and atrophy, but these are mysterious enough. The basic property is perhaps that cells starved of normal substrate direct themselves to make enzymes for the substrate available, a process that has been much investigated in bacteria. How such 'adaptative' actions of enzyme systems come about is not well known. It may be that small quantities of all the enzymes that the species is capable of producing are present in every cell. Most will be in an inhibited state. The effect of a particular demand would thus be to disinhibit the relevant enzyme system (Jacob and Monod, 1961).

Such inquiries are not as far as they may seem to be from the problem that is under investigation, namely the significance of number and size of nerve-cells. The presence of very numerous small cells seems to be characteristic of parts of the nervous system that store much information and these small cells seem also to have some connexion with inhibition or suppression of the spread of nervous excitation. These clues will be followed later. Very small cells can presumably change their effects by very small growth movements. This may be important, especially if learning involves the making of a 'choice' by suppression of some channels. Perhaps we can learn much because we have many channels among which selection can be made.

4. Numbers of receptor channels

In a human being there are estimated to be about 3×10^6 afferent nerve fibres of all types. The figure may be low by a factor of two or more since electron-microscopy has shown the abundance of fibres below the limit of resolution with the light microscope. Thus, Maturana (1959) estimates a total of 485,300 fibres in each optic nerve of a frog, of which 470,000 are less than 2 μ in diameter and only 15,300 are medullated. In man it is estimated that there are 1 million fibres in the optic nerve all with myelin sheaths (but this is not strictly a peripheral nerve since there are nerve cells and elaborate synaptic arrangements in the retina). In man there are about 1 million cones in the fovea and 100 million rods in the peripheral part of the eye. Each cone is connected to one or few nerve fibres in the optic nerve. It follows that many rods, used mainly to detect faint light, are connected to one optic nerve fibre.

The nose contains many million receptor cells even in man with his reduced sense of smell. In other animals there are even greater numbers (100 million in the rabbit, Allison and Warwick, 1949). The auditory system on the other hand works with relatively few units. There are 25,000 receptor cells in the organ of Corti of man and 30,000 fibres in the cochlear nerve. The importance of absolute differences of frequency and time for the proper identification of sounds has probably determined in the auditory system characteristics not found elsewhere.

The number of afferent channels in an octopus brain is less easy to calculate because there are nerve cells just beneath the skin. The situation is thus somewhat as in the vertebrate eye and optic nerve. Rather curiously the octopus eye does *not* contain any nerve cells. There are about 20 million retinal receptor cells in each eye, each cell with a nerve fibre proceeding to the optic lobe.

The number of primary receptor cells in the rims of the suckers has been calculated at 6 million by Graziadei. The fibres from these make contact with only some 300,000 large nerve-cells lying in the skin. There is some further reduction on the way to the brain, within the ganglia at the centres of the arms. Only some 130,000 fibres enter the brain itself via the brachial nerves.

For receptors from other parts of the skin of *Octopus* we have few data. From the various cutaneous nerves about 70,000 fibres enter the brain, and we might assume 1 million primary sense cells in the skin, outside the arms.

To complete our survey of afferent channels there are 200,000 fibres in the labial nerves, carrying the important signals for taste, arising in perhaps five times that number of primary receptors. The olfactory nerves, however, are very small and contain only about 2,000 fibres. All the afferent fibres mentioned so far have been *small* (3 μ or less). We have finally to consider the important static nerves, 1,300 of whose fibres are as much as 20 μ in diameter, presumably to give greater conduction velocity (p. 50). There are also 10,000 fibres of less than 4 μ in the static nerves.

For our total count of afferent pathways we then have:

	Peripheral receptors 10^6	Fibres entering C.N.S. 10^4
Eyes	20	2000
Skin of suckers	6	13
Other skin	1	7
Lips	1	20
Olfactory	?	0·2
Static	0·1(?)	1
	8	41

Thus, if we exclude the eyes, we find that some 8 million peripheral receptors, mainly in the arms, send their information into the brain along only some 400,000 channels. There are many possible errors in these calculations and they must only be used to tell us the order of magnitude, which seems to be similar for the octopus and human systems.

5. Numbers of cells in the central nervous system

It is, of course, in the systems that lie between the input and output that our chief interest lies. These are the working parts of the brain containing the memory stores and performing the computations. Figures of total numbers are only of rather general interest here because an important characteristic of brains is that they are divided up into numerous subdivisions, lobes, or 'boxes', as the engineer would put it. We understand so little of brains that we cannot begin to express the operations that are performed even by such prominent 'boxes' as the cerebellum or thalamus.

The human brain has between 1 and 2×10^{10} cells, arranged in several hundred distinct and named groups. However, by far the greatest part of these are in the cerebral cortex (more than 95 per cent). The brain of an octopus, with which we shall be much concerned, has a hundred times fewer, $1-2 \times 10^8$, in about fifty named groups. Again, the great majority of the cells are in the 'highest' centres, concerned with the discrimination of shapes and with memory. The octopus's nervous system differs from our own, however, in that the arms contain even more nerve cells than the brain (3×10^8). The brain decides main courses of action, the arms execute these.

6. Number of synaptic junctions per cell

This varies greatly and provides us with an important measure of the computing powers of the unit. Thus, in an earthworm there are one-to-one junctions at which every impulse passes and the computing powers are zero. (The significance of the presence of the interruption is obscure; it may be a vestige of an earlier condition.) In the initiation of impulses in the final units of the giant fibre system of the squid (Fig. 3) there are two pre-synaptic units to each post-synaptic one. An impulse in either pre-synaptic fibre is said to fire one impulse post-synaptically, so even in this simple case we are

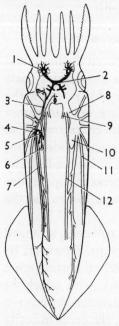

unable to see clearly what computations are involved (Hagiwara and Tasaki, 1958). A further complication is that each pre-synaptic fibre divides up many times and its points of contact with the post-synaptic unit are numerous and spread over a large area. If we did not know that all these knobs were branches of a single fibre we might well suppose this to be a system playing some elaborate part in computation or re-coding. Can it be simply a means of ensuring transmission with a high safety factor? Again we do not know.

When we come to more elaborate synaptic arrangements our ignorance is profound. Aitken and Bridger have recently made new estimates of the dimensions of cells of the ventral horn of the spinal cord of the cat (Fig. 4). The dendrites are much longer than had been supposed. The number of endings that the cell receives is calculated from the area of the dendrites. Wyckoff and Young (1956) calculated that there are 20 synaptic terminals (*boutons*) per $100\,\mu^2$ on the dendrites of ventral horn cells. Aitken and Bridger (1961) increase the estimate of the cell surface area of a large cell from 10,000 μ^2 to 80,000 μ^2 and the total of endings from 2,000 to about 30,000. This figure is still probably too low.

FIG. 3. Diagram of giant fibre system of *Loligo*, as seen from above, the ganglia shown disproportionately large. The nerves are shown in outline on the right and the giant fibres filled in on the left.

1, giant cell, with end-feet attached to its dendrites; 2, interaxonic bridge; 3, second-order giant axon; 4, distal synapse between second- and third-order axons; 5, proximal synapse between fibres arising independently in the C.N.S. and third-order axon; 6, cell bodies of third-order axons. These are unusual in fusing to form a syncytium; 7, third-order axon; 8, mantle connective (joining C.N.S. to stellate ganglion); 9, nerve to retractor muscle of head; 10, giant fibre lobe of stellate ganglion; 11, stellar nerve; 12, fin nerve.

The synaptic endings in the cerebral cortex are much smaller than those in the cord. They can just be seen with the light microscope by the use of special methods (Armstrong,

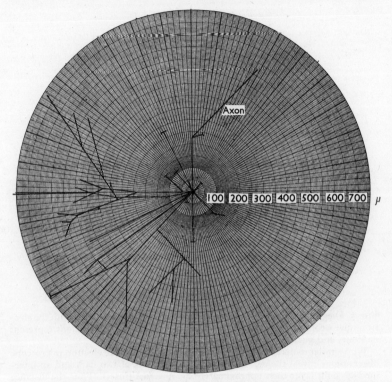

Axon

100 200 300 400 500 600 700 μ

FIG. 4. Polar graph of the dendritic pattern of a cell from the lumbrosacral region of the cat's spinal cord. The central point represents the surface of the perikaryon whose area was estimated to be about 25,000 μ^2. Some of the dendrites (marked with a cross-bar) were cut off by the plane of section. The measured surface of the dendrites was about 81,000 μ^2 but this could possibly be increased to about 220,000 μ^2 on estimates of the truncated branches. The ratio of dendritic surface to perikaryon surface is estimated as 8·5 to 1. (After Aitken and Bridger, 1961.)

Richardson, and Young, 1956). Gray (1959, 1961) has shown many details of them with the electron microscope (Fig. 5). No reliable counts are available but the total for a large pyramidal cell may well be 20,000 or more.

The mass of detail revealed by the electron microscope brings us to face another problem. Are we justified in regarding these synaptic terminals as units in any important sense? In some situations the electron microscope shows that the dendrites are indeed covered by *boutons* of classical form (Fig. 6).

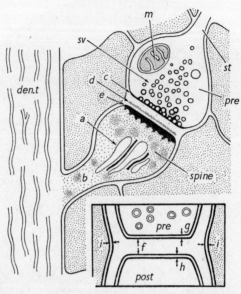

Fig. 5. Diagram of a synaptic contact on a dendrite spine, observed with the electron microscope after osmium tetroxide fixation. The stippled regions represent neuronal and glial processes of the neuropil. (Gray, 1959.)

With similar material fixed with potassium permanganate electron microscope observations reveal the cell membrane as a complex of two dark and an intermediate light layer each approximately 25 Å across (inset). Thus the distance between the arrows at g, h, and i is 75 Å whereas the gap between the pre- and post-synaptic membranes f is some 350 Å.

a, membrane system of unknown function, 'the spine apparatus'; b, dendrite branch; c, presynaptic membrane; d, dense layer lying between the pre- and postsynaptic membranes; *den.t.*, dendrite tubules; e, postsynaptic membrane; m, mitochondrion; *pre*, presynaptic process; *st*, commencement of enlargement of the presynaptic process; *sv*, synaptic vesicles. There is some evidence that these membrane-bound spheres contain the transmitter substance of the synapse.

Even here we have to ask what is the effective surface of contact. Parts of the area where the two cells meet show increased 'density' of their surface membranes. On the presynaptic side of these thickenings there are usually aggregations of 'synaptic vesicles'. These have often been considered to be the carriers

of the excitant chemical synaptic transmitter though there is
no real proof of this. They occur abundantly at motor end-
plates, where the transmitter is known to be released in quantal
'packets' (Fatt and Katz, 1952).

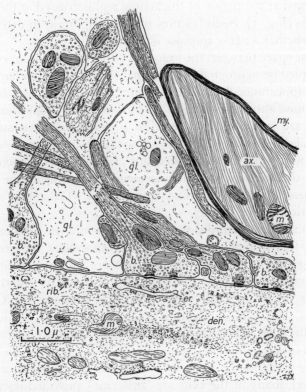

FIG. 6. Synaptic end-feet on surface of a dendrite of the hippocampus of the rat
(Ammon's horn). Drawn from an electronmicrograph provided by the late Dr. L.
Hamlyn.

    ax., medullated axon; *b.*, terminal *boutons*, filled with vesicles; *den.*, dendrite;
er., endoplasmic reticulum; *f.*, fibres leading to the boutons, filled with filaments
(?tubules), which break up distally into vesicles; *gl.*, protoplasm of glia cells;
m., mitochondria; *my.*, myelin sheath; *rib.*, ribosomes.

Is 'the synapse' then to be considered only as these specialized areas of contact? What are the variables that control its
functioning? Assuming that a chemical transmitter initiates
a process of depolarization or hyperpolarization in the post-

synaptic cell, what are the factors that allow summation between the actions at different synapses? Is such interaction the basis of the computing function? The synaptic space between the surface membranes of the two cells is often enlarged at the region of thickening and narrowed at the sides of this (Fig. 5). Such features may be important in determining whether a nerve impulse is initiated.

The space between the branches of the neurons is, of course, occupied by neuroglial protoplasm. This has its own characteristic appearance under the electron microscope (Fig. 6), but we know almost nothing of its physiological properties. Glia cells are said to show electrical phenomena when suitably stimulated (Tasaki and Chang, 1958). It has been held that they may function as 'antineurons', taking up ions discharged from the neurons and thus increasing or decreasing the effectiveness of changes going on near by (Galambos, 1961; Svaetichin et al., 1961).

To all these complications we have to add the further difficulty that in many parts of the nervous system the pre- and post-synaptic branches and the glia are interwoven to form a sponge-like mass of quite baffling complexity. Apart from the technical difficulty of distinguishing between axons, dendrites, and glia in electron micrographs, there is the probability that many of the neurons do not have any single differentiated efferent axon at all. In many of the most interesting parts of the nervous system (retina, perhaps cerebral cortex), many of the cells are 'amacrine', provided only with a bush of branches, all alike, embedded among the branches of other larger neurons (see p. 144). No one has any clear idea as to how these cells act. Some would classify them with the glia, but to the histologist they look like neurons. Yet it hardly seems likely that their function is to conduct discrete signals from any one of the branches to any other one. A further complication is that electron micrographs of the retina show fibres that are post-synaptic on one side, pre-synaptic on the other, judging by such criteria as are available (Kidd, 1962). These may be images of parts of amacrine cells and they suggest processes of transmission of which we can at present form no very exact picture. They warn us against the assumption that the nervous system can be understood by thinking only of a finite number of discrete channels, connected at definite switching points.

Yet we must also beware of abandoning the sure pieces of information that we have, simply because of the complications introduced by recent research. Through many years of study of the nervous system I find that my attitude to this problem has oscillated. The difficulties of building a realistic model that will include all the complexities of the connexions drives one at times to despair and to think of the brain as a 'soup' of chemical processes or electrical fields. But then one's courage returns, one continues with the microscope and microelectrode, and is drawn back to the ideal of Cajal and Sherrington, namely to understand the system in terms of the pathways and units that can be exactly studied in it.

The value of estimates of the number of possible switching points in the nervous system is unfortunately lessened because of our ignorance at present of other features. Usually we do not know how many end-feet there are attached to any one fibre that approaches the cell. Nor, conversely, how many fibres there are that influence each cell, nor whether all their terminals are collected together, or scattered over the dendrites.

Investigations with microelectrodes have done much to explore the sources from which individual cells are stimulated (Eccles, 1961). An electrode can be placed in the cell body, but not, usually, in the dendrites. The interpretation of the potential changes that are seen then, of course, depends upon assumptions about the relative dimensions of dendrites and cell body and their influences upon each other. Thus Eccles has concluded that sources of potential more than $300\,\mu$ from the cell body can hardly contribute to the record given by a microelectrode, yet Aitken's measurements show that, if this is so, half of the surface of the dendrites fails to contribute. Since all dendrites are covered with end-feet they must surely have some significance.

Bodian has made an interesting comparison between the extent of the dendritic fields of various types of cell (Fig. 7). He suggests that the abundance of dendritic branching is approximately proportional to the 'magnitude of sources of

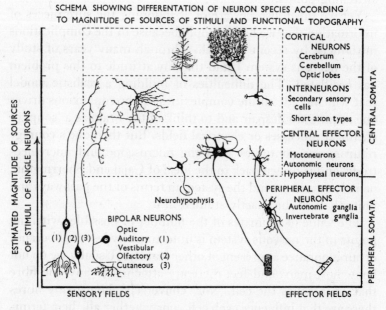

SCHEMA SHOWING DIFFERENTIATION OF NEURON SPECIES ACCORDING TO MAGNITUDE OF SOURCES OF STIMULI AND FUNCTIONAL TOPOGRAPHY

FIG. 7. Neuron types in the mammalian nervous system arranged according to their functions and according to the magnitude of sources of synaptic stimulation (measured on an arbitrary scale). The dendritic fields become more elaborate with increasing stimuli but there are exceptions such as the cerebellar granule cell shown top right. These, however, make up by very large numbers for their paucity of dendrites. (From Bodian, 1952.)

stimuli'. The relationship is clearly not a very simple one (as Bodian himself points out), but the dendritic fields of some of the neurons of higher centres are strikingly complex. The fields are not all spherical, nor are they wholly irregular. In some parts of the nervous system they show specific geometric forms. These may be significant, as we shall see, for the functioning of the system. It is thus reasonable to regard the dendrites and synapses as essentially the 'computing' regions of the nervous system.

The fact that so many of these fundamental data about neurons are continually undergoing revision, involving alteration of important constants by factors of two or more, shows how far we have to go in improving measurements with microscope and microelectrodes. A major difficulty is appropriate sampling among the vast numbers of cells. This will become especially important if it should prove, as will be suggested, that the dendritic trees constitute a set of different sizes and shapes, among which there is selection during learning (p. 162).

In order to deal with these varied populations of cells it seems certain that we shall need to develop mechanical counting methods. It is still an anomaly that the microscope, which is one of the most precise scientific instruments invented, yet yields relatively few results that are quantitative. This has long been realized by pioneers such as Bok (1928), but development of new methods is still slow. We attempted an attack on this problem with the flying-spot microscope (Roberts, Young, and Causley, 1953). Unfortunately, as built, this proved to be an effective device only with materials giving a high level of contrast. This, together with other difficulties of sampling and recognition, has inhibited further progress. Only the human eye has yet proved competent to make the judgements that are needed to provide measurements of the branches of a nerve-cell in a Golgi preparation. Yet this difficulty must somehow be overcome if we are to have useful estimates from all the various areas and centres of the brain.

7. *Extent of connectivity in the cerebral cortex*

One of the greatest gaps in our knowledge is of the extent to which there is overlap between the endings of fibres at each stage passing through the nervous system. Clearly this feature must be fundamental in determining operations of the system. The late Donald Sholl (1956) made some interesting estimates in the cortex of the cat. Each large pyramidal cell may share its dendritic field with up to 4,000 others. Any incoming afferent fibre has the possibility of connecting with some among a group of 5,000 cortical cells, spread through a volume of

0·1 mm³. This may prove to be a particularly important figure since it limits the possibility of making all combinations of a group of input fibres. The problem of such combinations becomes central when considering possible modes of functioning of the brains of higher animals. In the model developed by Taylor combinations of 10^4 input channels to make selection among 10^4, outputs are considered (Chapter 19). These figures are of the order of those shown by Sholl in the cat. These are among the many facts that we need to know if we are to discuss how the cortex stores information and uses it to decide between possible courses of actions. Clearly, as Sholl showed, we must approach these problems statistically, because the operations of the cortex are themselves statistical.

8. *Estimates of the capacity of the nervous system as an information channel*

Another way in which we could attempt to study the working of the nervous system is to estimate, as the communication engineer would do, the rate at which it processes information. Unfortunately we are handicapped for lack of a measure of 'information' such as is available to the engineer, who assumes the use of a language whose statistics are known. An information flow can only be measured for defined units. However, it is possible to make various estimates of the number of 'bits' or decisions between alternative possibilities in the system (Barlow, 1959).[1]

Thus, the maximum capacity of a mammalian nerve fibre is about 1,000 impulses/sec. We might make the large assumption that the interval between pulses is used to convey information and that it can be estimated to an accuracy of 0·05 msec. Then since about 3×10^6 receptor nerve fibres enter the brain, the total capacity would be 3×10^9 bits/sec. The actual capacity is certainly much less, for many reasons, among them that the frequency is rarely as much as 1,000/sec and the coding probably involves pulse-frequency modulation, that is,

[1] In engineering language, if a choice is made between n mutually exclusive possibilities then the information content of the choice is counted as $\log_2 n$ 'bits'.

trains of impulses of similar frequency, rather than pulse-interval modulation.

Definite estimates of actual operating capacity have been made for the eye and ear (Jacobson, 1950, 1951; Barlow, 1959). The human ear can discriminate about 1,450 pitches at about 230 intensities, allowing $\frac{1}{4}$ sec for each discrimination. This seems to give 50,000 bits/sec. However, one tone greatly interferes with another and this masking is calculated to reduce the capacity to 8,000 bits/sec, which is 0·3 bits/sec for each of the 30,000 nerve fibres in each cochlear nerve. Of course the ear can also make other sorts of discrimination, which must be ignored for the moment.

The eye is calculated to be able to resolve 240,000 distinct points, at two intensity levels, and at a rate of one per $\frac{1}{18}$ sec. This omits colour discrimination and much else, but gives a figure of $4·3 \times 10^6$ bits/sec or 5 bits/sec for each of the million nerve fibres in one optic nerve. That an optic nerve fibre carries more information than an auditory one agrees with the fact that in the retina a large amount of coding has already taken place. That is to say, the nervous system has selected features of the input that are relevant for the decisions to be taken and rejected others as redundant. The pulses that pass in the optic nerve are, of course, then well suited to produce the decisions that are made, that is to say, they carry a large amount of information. An important part of our task in understanding how the nervous system works is to discover how such coding is done.

These estimates by Jacobson for the ear and the eye suggest that the 3×10^6 receptor nerve fibres of the body together carry at most 10×10^6 bits/sec, that is to say, much less than $3,000 \times 10^6$ suggested by the maximum frequency of nerve fibre conduction. [Many of the bits of information are concerned with activities such as walking and speaking, which are largely reflex and unconscious in their working.] Ten million bits/sec is still a very large flow of information and is even more surprising when it is found that a human being can only make conscious decisions at a maximum of 25 bits/sec, usually much less (Quastler, 1956; Hick, 1952; Barlow, 1959).

Probably the actual inflow is much less than 10 million bits. Many of the channels operate in parallel and in any case are brought into action only from time to time, just as the individual items of response are mostly brought into play only occasionally.

The problems of how to measure the number of things that an animal or man can do and how often each is done are only beginning to be understood. Human language has provided us with the most useful, if somewhat atypical, example. The techniques of information theory estimate the amount of information conveyed as a function of the frequency of the words in the language. A similar technique might be applicable to animal behaviour generally, if we could isolate the individual actions involved. One of the difficulties is that the measures of information content used assume that the statistics of a language are constant. This is, at best, an approximation and for the study of behaviour in general would often be untrue—always untrue for an animal that is learning or forgetting.

Finally, we must consider that part of the input that is stored for use in making decisions in the future. With fifty years of waking life the total inflow may approach perhaps 10^{15} bits. There is no way of knowing how much of this is stored, certainly by no means all of it is. We shall try to show that the method of storage is not to record the occurrence or absence of each item separately. As each event occurs the receptors and associated centres signal only certain features that have been found significant during past evolutionary history (colour, shape, direction of sound, &c., &c.). The signals reporting these features are then combined with others recording the reward value of the situation (e.g. food, pain), to build a system that will produce a higher probability of biologically correct response in the future. This is necessarily a very vague account of the memory system at this stage and the rest of the book contains an attempt to make it more precise.

We may perhaps approach this end by studying as much as

possible of the behaviour of one single animal type and correlating this with its structure and the method of operation of the units of the nervous system. Boycott and I, with many other colleagues, have endeavoured for some years to make such a study of cephalopod molluscs and the following chapters are a summary of some of the data as I interpret them.

5

CEPHALOPODS AND THEIR
ENVIRONMENTS

1. *Some requirements for homeostasis*

EVERY animal is a homeostat whose inherited instructions so build it that it maintains itself in a particular environment. We shall, therefore, best understand its control systems, in particular the nervous system, if we consider that in a sense it 'represents' the environment, in other words, living organisms remain alive because there is a certain correspondence between the actions that they take and the changes that go on in the environment. The animal continues to live because it does the 'right' things. It is able to do this because it is a system provided by its past history with a number of alternative possibilities of action relevant to the situations that it is likely to meet. The status of this 'adaptive' quality of living actions is, of course, one of the greatest problems of biology. Many different techniques have been devised for discussing it (Sommerhoff, 1950). The feature that we wish to emphasize is that survival depends on a particular type of correspondence between organism and environment. It seems appropriate to express this by saying that the organism 'represents' the environment. The test whether a particular species does or does not represent a stated environment is whether it re-presents appropriate reactions to that environment. If it does so, it survives in that place. The value of this particular formulation is that it emphasizes that the organization of the behaviour of each creature is arrived at by a series of detectors responsive to changes that are likely to be relevant, and that it has at its command effectors that are able to take the necessary actions. In between these there is a computing system able to make whatever decisions are required as to the responses that will be most appropriate to the combinations of messages that are likely to arrive. Its actions are thus forecasts, based on information stored from the past.

In particular we are interested in a self-teaching homeostat, that is to say, one whose information and instructions are not entirely built in by heredity. Such a learning device alters its performance as a result of experience so as to produce results that are satisfactory for its self-maintenance. In order to do this it must record certain features of the input in a code, recording also whether they were accompanied by conditions that were 'good' or 'bad' for the homeostat. We shall try to study the principles by which such a system uses 'rewards' and 'punishments' to control its performance and how it finds the optimal rate of change of behaviour as it learns in any given environment.

Our task is thus to try to produce a scheme that presents the features of the nervous system in a way that shows their relevance to the continuing life of the animal, and indeed of the species. It is not at all easy to find the best words for doing this, especially for the more complicated parts of the nervous system. It is perhaps made easier by starting with unfamiliar animals such as the cephalopods. With them we are less liable to be confused by the overtones of our pre-scientific terminology. Fortunately it is possible to give at least some relevant facts about the searching, coding, and memory systems of these animals. With these facts we may be able better to approach the study of other nervous systems such as those of insects and vertebrates. Some of the principles that control even the most complicated activities of motivation, searching, and learning may well be similar in all animals and in man.

We shall begin, therefore, with a short description of some aspects of the behaviour and biology of the octopus and then compare these with the habits of related cephalopods. In this way we can begin to see the sense in which each species represents its environment.

2. *The basic food-collecting system of an octopus*

In the search for food an octopus uses mainly its eyes and the receptors in the arms for touch and for chemical conditions. Having no shell or powerful defensive apparatus the animal lives protected in a cranny of the rocks that is its home. From this it puts out an arm to seize crabs or other likely food objects that pass within reach. If something appears farther away the octopus may emerge from its home, swim forward by means of the jet from its funnel, and seize the moving object with its arms. The prey is then carried back to the home, paralysed by a secretion of the salivary glands, and held by the jaws of the parrot-like beak and broken up by a rasping file, the radula. In this method of life it is clearly important that the animal should attack only those objects that are likely to yield food, and retreat from any that may sting or bite. There are certainly many enemies lying in wait, for it is common to find that one or more of the arms of an octopus is in process of regeneration, having been bitten off at the tip.

The octopus's brain therefore makes repeated decisions whether or not to put out an arm, or to swim out, when objects move in its visual field or are touched by the arms. Recognition of what is suitable to be attacked depends not on an inherited or built-in system, but on learning by 'experience' whether attack at a given object is likely to produce food or a painful stimulus.

It has not been possible to study the first 'inborn' reactions of *Octopus vulgaris*. Directly after hatching from the egg the larvae swim to the sea surface and live there in the plankton. Later they settle and begin life on the bottom, but they are rarely caught in these early stages. The smallest animals readily available for experiment have already lived for some time on the sea bottom. However, on the west coast of North America there lives a species, *O. briareus*, in which the young are hatched essentially similar to the adult (Messenger, 1963). Experiments with these would be most rewarding.

In the cuttlefish, *Sepia*, the young feed within a few hours

of hatching, essentially in the same way as the adults, by shoot-
ing out the two long arms at shrimps moving in the visual
field. Wells (1958) showed that the delay before attacking
decreases from more than two minutes for the first attack to
five seconds or less after about the seventh. This is not simply
a question of maturation, for young cuttlefishes starved for
several days after hatching attack at first only after long delay.
There is therefore in *Sepia* a process of learning to attack,
from the earliest days, and we may guess that this is so also in
Octopus. A curious feature, however, is that the delay before
attacking decreased as fast in baby *Sepia* that were made to
attack shrimps behind glass, as in those that could eat the
shrimps.

The process of 'improvement' in attacks at crabs by older
octopuses has been studied in detail by Maldonado (1963*a*).
When an octopus that has recently been brought into the
laboratory from the sea is shown a crab, it will attack it only
after considerable delay. Later, attacks are made more swiftly
and Maldonado has proved that this is due to a process of
learning to attack. He devised a system for recording accurately the times at which the octopus leaves its home and seizes
the crab. He distinguishes three periods: (1) a 'total time',
between the presentation of any visual stimulus and its capture
by the animal; (2) a first time-delay between presentation and
leaving the home; and (3) 'movement time', between leaving
and catching the prey. He showed that all of these three times
decrease with successive captures of the crab (Fig. 8). Moreover, the variance also decreases (Fig. 9); the animal therefore
attacks in less time and more regularly.

Maldonado analyses this situation in detail in terms of a
model in which the attacks are controlled by the values of
a 'command factor' C, submitted to a control centre (Fig. 10).
This model is of the block-diagram type but is also related to
the parts that can be recognized within the nervous system.
It is therefore an interesting example of what is involved by
an attempt to 'understand' the nervous system, and the advantages and disadvantages of a block-diagram method of doing so.

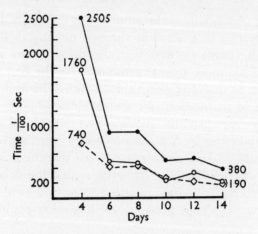

FIG. 8. Fall with learning in times taken by octopus to attack crabs. Average of ten animals, three trials a day each. Filled circles total time, open circles delay before movement begins, diamonds, movement time. (Maldonado, 1963a.)

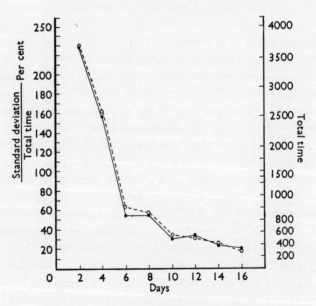

FIG. 9. Fall in variability with learning. Filled circles total time to attack, open circles represent standard deviation. Same octopuses as in Fig. 8.

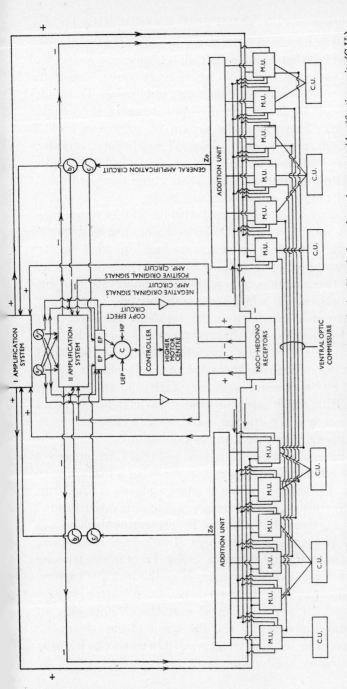

FIG. 10. Maldonado's block diagram of visual-learning circuits in the octopus brain. Signals from the retina pass to identification units (C.U.) each of which responds to a particular feature of the input (e.g. vertical or horizontal extent, degree of brightness). Signals from these pass to the memory units (M.U.), which also receive signals from the noci-hedono receptors indicating pain or pleasure (the centre of the diagram). The input from these receptors only enters those memory units whose threshold has been lowered by the identification units. These latter may thus be said to find addresses for the signals from the noci-hedono receptors.

The output of all the memory units is added in an addition unit, whose output Zo tends to produce attack or retreat. Everything so far has occurred in the optic lobes. Signals in the optic tract carry Zo to the superior frontal and vertical lobes (first and second amplification systems) whose output, the experimental parameter (EP), is one of the variables that influence the command C, to attack or retreat, which is elaborated in (probably) the subvertical lobe. Other parameters influencing C are hunger (HP) and an unspecific effect parameter (UEP) by which immediately previous experience raises or lowers the tendency to attack.

Signals from the noci-hedono receptors also pass to the amplifiers and the latter also send signals back to the memory units. Removal of the vertical lobe therefore has complex effects. Moreover, the value of EP is also sent back to the memory units (subvertical to optic tract) producing a copy effect by which the value of the command may be increased. (Maldonado, 1963b.)

We shall deal later with the stages by which the visual image is analysed by what Maldonado calls 'classification units', and recorded as 'good' or 'bad' by memory units, under the influence of receptors for 'pleasure' and 'pain'. These elements can all be located in the optic lobes of the octopus (Chapter 9). There is also a system of 'amplifiers', which adjust the effects of the pain–pleasure (noci-hedono) receptors so that they shall have the 'correct' amount of influence on the system. These amplifiers we can locate in the superior frontal-vertical lobe system of the octopus's brain.

At this stage we are concerned with the way in which these influences from the eyes and other receptors can be imagined to converge, with other influences, to build up what we may call a command (C) to attack (or to retreat).

Among these influences is what Maldonado calls the 'empirical parameter' EP, which is extracted by the analytical portions of the mechanism from the variables that have been recorded by the eyes and other receptors and the results (food or trauma) that have been associated with them (see later). Other factors influencing the value of the command will be measured by the 'hunger parameter' (HP) and an 'unspecific factor' (UEP), which raises or lowers the tendency to attack without reference to particular visual or other clues.

The supposition is that at the beginning of the training the values of EP and hence of C are low, and that C will therefore be greatly influenced by changes in the other variables, such as hunger. Thus the variations in attack time are at first large, but later decrease as EP comes to have a predominant effect on C.

That this is more than a scheme for presenting the facts was proved by an ingenious experiment. Two groups each of five octopuses were trained to attack crabs. In group A training began only two days after bringing from the sea. The training of group B began after the animals had been left for six days without food. Moreover, group B were then trained only on *alternate* days, in order to test the effect of changes in the hunger level. The results were expressed in terms of a learning index devised by Maldonado:

$$I = \frac{250}{\frac{1}{2}\left[\text{mean total time} + \left(10 \dfrac{100 \times \text{standard deviation}}{\text{mean total time}}\right)\right]}.$$

250 is the minimum total time that could be taken to attack (expressed in 1/100 seconds). This index is arbitrarily chosen but provides a sensitive measure of the 'positive learning', ranging from near zero towards 2.

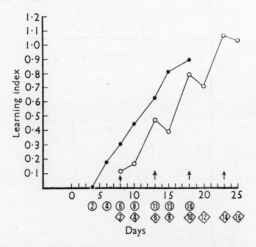

FIG. 11. Effect of hunger on learning to attack crabs by two groups each of five octopuses. Filled circles (group A) training after 2 days in tanks, open circles (group B) after 6 days in tanks without food. Abscissa, first row, days in tank, second row, days of training for group A, and third row for group B. The arrows show that at the point to which they refer the animals had been left for two days without food. (Maldonado, 1963a.)

Fig. 11 shows that the learning index for group B is not correlated with the number of days in the tank, but with the days of effective training. This shows that change in behaviour is a process of learning from experience of successful capture of crabs and is not merely due to some factor of becoming used to the tanks (Young, 1956). However, there are interesting differences in the curves, correlated with the fact that in group B the level of hunger was not constant. Whereas the

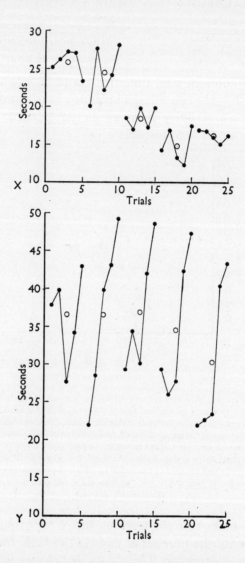

FIG. 12. Experiment to show the effect of hunger on times taken to attack crabs by previously untrained octopuses. In group X (62 octopuses) the animals were shown crabs at two sessions a day, each of five trials (10 minutes apart). They were not allowed to eat the crabs and were fed only once (5 g of fish after trial 15). In group Y (12 octopuses) the treatment was identical except that they were allowed to eat the crab when they attacked it. Filled circles individual trials, open circles mean for each session.

curve for A rises continuously, that for B rises steeply on the days after no food but then falls on the next day, when the parameter HP was less. Moreover, these oscillations become less as training proceeds and the value of EP becomes predominant.

The effect of the hunger parameter is also seen strikingly in the experiment recorded in Fig. 12. In group X the octopuses were shown crabs but not allowed to eat them. The times taken to attack became shorter in spite of the absence of reward (as Wells found with *Sepia*). Since the animals were fed only once (after the fifteenth trial) the hunger parameter was increasing throughout, which is presumably the main reason for the fall in time of attack, though other factors are no doubt involved (e.g. familiarity with the tanks).

The animals in group Y were allowed to eat the crab every time that they attacked it, and the times taken to attack became longer within each set of trials, as HP fell. The fall in the mean attack times was therefore actually less marked in those with reward than in those without it. The times to attack at the *first trial* of each set decreased in these animals that were fed at about the same rate as in the animals that were not fed but the latter tended to attack faster throughout.

The processes by which the attack is launched, and the aim and range taken, are all subjects that require investigation. Maldonado divides the whole period between appearance of an object in the visual field and seizing of it into three phases. During the 'first time-delay' the animal remains in its home. Then it comes out slowly for a longer or shorter period, the 'second time-delay'. Next it swims rapidly forwards, the 'final pattern of acceleration', and finally decelerates just short of the prey.

As an octopus learns to attack in any given situation the second time-delay becomes shorter and is finally eliminated. The first time-delay also becomes shorter as the system learns to build the command to attack more quickly. The 'final pattern of acceleration' does not change greatly with learning. During this final 'jump' the animal is acting under a programme that had been built up during the first time-delay. Maldonado was able to show this by turning out the light at various times during the attack. He found that once the jump had begun it could be completed in darkness. The successive values of the forces that are applied are, therefore, not controlled by estimation of the remaining distance by an external loop, such as the eyes. These forces must have been already determined by what we may call a 'programme', established somewhere in the brain. Similar programmes of action presumably determine many or most of the movements of animals and men. For example, a piano player does not guide his fingers to the notes by sight. He programmes each movement so that it ends at the right place. Little is known about the physiological basis for these fundamental features of behaviour. They seem to involve selecting the appropriate values for the activity of sets of motor neurons in an appropriately timed series. It is possible that in vertebrates the cerebellum is the timing device that is concerned (Braitenberg and Onesto, 1962).

Clearly there is a complex interplay of variables that influence this relatively simple process of learning to attack. A model such as that of Maldonado provides us with a means of discussing such variables and such an analysis provides a means of expressing the place of the learning process in the whole life of the animal. Thus it is clear that the value of the index in these experiments does not reach 2. That is to say, the animals never reach what might be called a 'perfect regularity'. The octopus always retains a sensitivity to other parameters and can thus restrain its behaviour to *different* times if necessary. To put it in other terms, it remains a 'machine with input', i.e. with several 'lines of behaviour'. It approaches an absolute system but never becomes one (Ashby, 1960).

The significance of this becomes very clear if we compare such behaviour with that of the Praying Mantis, which is said to be absolutely regular (under standard conditions) and would give us an index of nearly 2. Oscillations would occur for mechanical reasons, but not behavioural ones (Mittelstaedt, 1957).

3. *The reactions of untrained octopuses*

To study the reaction of octopuses in the laboratory we isolate each one in a tank, at one end of which are three bricks, where the octopus makes its 'home'. Crabs or other figures are then presented at the other end of the tank and the time taken to attack is recorded with a stop-watch.

Tested in this way with crabs an octopus at first comes out only after 30 seconds or more and attacks 'cautiously', extending the tip of an arm to touch the crab, before seizing it with several arms and the web. If the octopus is allowed to eat the crabs the latent period falls after a few trials until it reaches as little as 2–3 seconds.

Even more interesting are the reactions to figures that the octopus has presumably not seen before, such as rectangles, squares, or circles, cut out of white or black plastic. These are kept moving at the end of the tank remote from the home on a transparent plastic rod. The octopus only comes out on some occasions to attack, and always with a long delay. The animals differ greatly in readiness to attack, presumably as a result of their previous experiences in the sea and after capture. The infrequency and slowness of attack is not simply a result of handling, nor, as we have seen above, is it due to lack of hunger. Octopuses left completely alone for a week without food do not come very readily to attack strange moving figures. They may be kept for a long time by feeding with pieces of fish on a wire in the home. When shown strange moving figures such animals that have been fed in the home will then only sometimes attack them (Young, 1958). Here, however, we meet with a curious effect; shortly after they have been fed (in the home) octopuses tend to come out more frequently to attack any figure, whether or not it had been associated with the food. The nervous system of the animal is so constituted that when any object moves in the visual field an attack may be initiated. The probability that this will occur may be 50 per cent or less, but is increased if the animal has recently fed. This is Maldonado's 'unspecific effect parameter' (UEP, Fig. 10). In the sea it would have the effect of ensuring that if an octopus has attacked, say, one fish of a shoal it will be more likely thereafter to attack others (until its HP falls). However, if attacks made during this period of raised excitability do not result in food, then the frequency will decline to about the original value. Maldonado's model expresses this by showing that UEP influences the command directly but has no effect on the memory units. Such further showing of the figure after feeding does not teach. In Pavlov's terminology there is no backward conditioning. Indeed, if there is no reward, attacks by an octopus at a given object will fall away to zero by a process of habituation (extinction), though a fresh object will then be attacked (Young, 1959).

4. *Learning to attack*

Quite a different situation appears if we give a reward, a piece of sardine, shortly after an octopus has attacked a figure, say, a vertical rectangle. Later tests then show that a process of learning to attack occurs and after the reward has been given on several occasions the animal comes out quickly every time that the figure appears. This can be regarded as a process of conditioning, to use the Pavlovian terminology, but in order to investigate its neural basis we have to try to discover what form of coded representation of the figure has been established in the nervous system and associated with the food reward.

This learning to attack takes place so quickly that it is easy to get the impression that all healthy octopuses readily attack moving objects. The experiments described above show that this is not so and that learning to attack is an essential feature of the system. That it should take place rapidly is not really surprising. In the sea the octopus has to learn to attack particular types of moving object, say, crabs, while they are still available, perhaps only for a few minutes. There is no reason to expect that learning in these 'lower' animals should be slower than in ourselves. Indeed it may be faster. They learn quickly but they learn little; we seem to learn

slowly in early years, perhaps because we are then learning to
learn and as a result can later learn fast and much. But this is
speculation. The speed and simplicity of the learning system
of the octopus make this animal especially suitable for investigation. Considerable progress has been made recently in
identifying the coding system that is used. We can also begin
to understand the mechanism by which the effect of rewards
or shocks is made to produce a suitable rate of learning (p. 232).

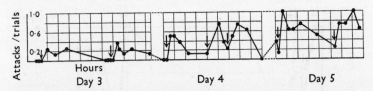

FIG. 13. Increasing responses of eight normal octopuses to feeding. At the arrows
a piece of sardine was given to each octopus immediately after showing a white
horizontal rectangle. At the other trials the rectangle was shown alone. Each
point shows the proportion of octopuses that attacked at that trial. The experiments were done on the 3rd–5th days after isolation of the animals.

In trying to discover the mechanism by which learning
takes place it is obvious, though often forgotten, that it is
important to study the effect of each single occasion on the
nervous system. In many learning studies attention is focused
on the *result*, the success achieved after learning has occurred.
But the physiologist is interested in the *changes in the nervous
system during the period immediately after each presentation*. The
increased tendency to attack after feeding has a half-life of
about 1–2 hours (Fig. 13). However, even when it has apparently completely disappeared some increased tendency to attack
must remain as the basis for learning.

5. *Learning not to attack*

It is equally important for an octopus to learn not to attack
in a situation that is likely to damage it. If attacks at an
unfamiliar object result in, say, an electric shock, delivered by
a pair of electrodes on a rod, the frequency of response will

decline so rapidly that after only one or two shocks the octopus
will not come out for several hours or even days when figures
appear at that place.

Many interesting experiments have been done in which
shocks are given following attack at a figure that had previously been 'positive', say, a crab or a rectangle that had been
the signal for food (Fig. 14). Following a single shock there is

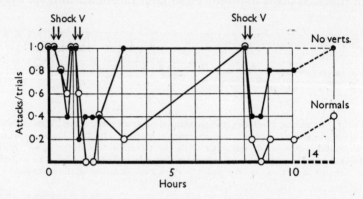

Fig. 14. Responses of five normal octopuses (o) and five without vertical lobes
(●) to a white vertical rectangle, which had previously been made a positive
figure. In this experiment the figure was shown without reward, but at the trials
marked with arrows a shock (Shock V) was given to each animal after showing the
rectangle. After the shocks the animals came out less. The effect is less prolonged, after removal of the vertical lobes (see p. 211). (After Young, 1960.)

a period during which few or no further attacks are made (the
UEP for attack is lowered) and then they gradually begin
again. After a few repeated shocks octopuses will sometimes
not attack crabs for several days. We can thus speak of the
setting up of representations that prevent attack, but it is
interesting that these do not seem to destroy or replace the
representations ensuring attack that had been previously
established. The new one seems to be distinct from the old
and if it is less well established it fades more quickly, leaving
the old tendency to attack unimpaired. This suggests that the
representations are embodied in some way in distinct sets of
cells in the nervous system.

6. *The mechanisms of retreat and defence*

It is an interesting question whether there is a process of learning to retreat. Clearly the retreat mechanism involves specific activities and is more than a failure to attack. Indeed, there are various stages of retreat. When an octopus has received a shock at the end of its attack it darkens, draws back, and swims to its home. If the stimulating electrodes are moved up towards the home the animal may suddenly change colour, turning on the display that we call the dymantic or terrifying pattern (Boycott, 1964). The animal adopts a circular outline, by curling the arms, and becomes quite white except for a dense black centre composed of the head and eyes, and a dark violet edge. The sudden appearance of this pattern is very 'disconcerting', and might well produce a startle reaction in a pursuer.

If the attack continues, however, by poking the octopus with the electrodes, a third defence mechanism is produced. The octopus withdraws as far as possible into a corner and turns the arms back over the head. The suckers towards the tips become attached to the rocks, whereas those at the base point out to the attacker. In this position there is nothing for the enemy to catch hold of and it is almost impossible to dislodge the octopus.

These defence mechanisms are initiated by pain signals, but little is known of the pathways through which they are released. Swimming backwards may be initiated by the more posterior basal parts of the supraoesophageal ganglia, especially the median basal lobe (Fig. 73). It is an attractive hypothesis that the front part of the whole supraoesophageal complex is concerned with attack (buccal lobes, anterior basal lobes) and the hinder part with retreat (median basal). However, the lobes probably co-operate in each movement, whether of walking or swimming. The dymantic reaction and defence reaction are initiated from the magnocellular lobe, lying at the sides of the brain (Fig. 22). In squids the giant cells that operate quick movements lie in this lobe (Fig. 3).

In *Octopus* 'escape' is not so much a matter of quick swimming as of switching on the devices by which an enemy is scared away or prevented from biting.

There has been little detailed study of the possibility of producing these various retreat and defence mechanisms as a result of learning. It is almost certain that 'negative' responses of this type are built up to stimuli that were at first neutral (say a rectangle). For this reason it is postulated that each neuron of the classifying or encoding system has originally two possible outputs. It may produce either 'attack' or 'retreat'. Learning consists in closing one of these channels (Chapter 9). To complete the picture proposed by Maldonado we should, therefore, have to add a second diagram of exactly the same sort as Fig. 10 for 'learning to retreat'. We shall also have to consider whether the various 'amplifiers' of that scheme operate equally in retreat. In any case it is quite clear that defence, even in an octopus, is an active process not simply the negative phase of attack.

7. *Cephalopods adapted to various environments*

Having now seen something of the feeding and avoidance behaviour of octopuses we can proceed to consider some of the variations of the pattern that are found in other cephalopods. The value of such an exercise is that it may show us the variables (e.g. in the central nervous system) and the conditions with which these variables are correlated. We cannot make a detailed experimental study of all the different cephalopods but by examining their habits and the corresponding differences in their brains we have been able to learn something of the significance of the different parts. We cannot test hypotheses by making up animals to order but we can use the great variety of animals that have appeared as a set of 'natural experiments'.

Unfortunately there is very little accurate information about the details of the life of octopuses in the sea. No doubt there are many important features that we cannot observe in the laboratory, but there is reason to believe that life in the tanks gives a good idea of at least some aspects of the animal's behaviour. Since they live in shallow water among the rocks or on coral reefs they can be observed by diving and it has long been known that they occupy 'homes', as they do in the laboratory. Outside each home is a midden heap of shells of crabs, lamellibranchs, and other animals that have been eaten by the octopus. Individual animals certainly occupy a single home for some time, essentially as in the laboratory. A major gap in our knowledge is lack of information about how often they leave the home to search for food and what distances they travel. There are probably also seasonal migrations between deep and shallow water.

Nearly all our experimental work has been with *Octopus vulgaris* Lamarck, chosen because it is a common inshore species at Naples and lives well in the laboratory. There are, of course, many other species of *Octopus* (five in the Bay of Naples, seventy-five around the world, Robson, 1929). Each no doubt has slightly different behaviour, adapted to its particular conditions of life among the rocks, sand, corals, and so on.

There are twenty-one genera other than *Octopus* in the family Octopodidae, the most familiar at Naples being *Eledone*. Unfortunately there are few reliable data about the habits of these various forms of octopus. Nor has there been any attempt to correlate the habits with differences in size or structure of parts of the brain. Such a study should be very rewarding.

Something can be said about such correlations in the related family Argonautidae. *Argonauta* and *Tremoctopus* are octopods that have left the sea bottom and live freely swimming in the water (Fig. 15). Having no home among the rocks the female *Argonauta* makes a shell by secretion from the web of the arms. The food is collected by an extended web, which is spread out, by the movements of the suckers of certain arms, over the surface of the shell. This web serves as a sensitive 'net', detecting the presence of food, which is then seized by the other arms (Fig. 15). In *Tremoctopus* there is no shell but two of the arms, with the web between them, are trailed along in the water and perhaps serve to collect food (though this has not been proved). Incidentally these arms have the strange

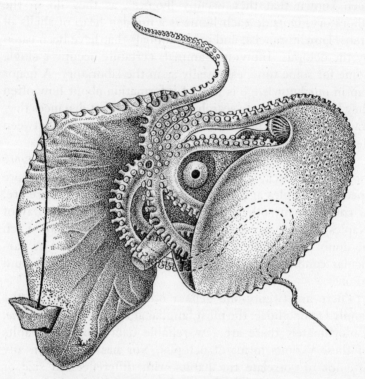

FIG. 15. Female *Argonauta* feeding. The drawing shows an experiment made when the web was made to spread out on the side of a tank. A piece of fish touched against the surface of the web elicited a backward movement of the fourth arm (dotted), sweeping the place where the web *should have been* on the shell. The arm was extended backwards, away from the food, and not over the web, which was in front of the animal. This demonstrates that the effect of contact of food with the web is to elicit a fixed action pattern, by which the fourth arm sweeps up over the shell—where the web and food would normally be found.

property of being adapted to hold fragments of the stinging tentacles of the Portuguese Man-of-War (*Physalia*). These remain alive and sting when the *Tremoctopus* is handled. They may be used for offence and as a defence (Jones, 1963).

In both of these animals the inferior frontal lobe, which in

Octopus allows the interchange of information between the arms, is very small (Fig. 16). On the other hand, the inferior buccal ganglion is large and includes thick outer layers of

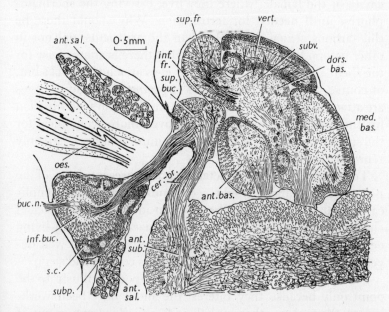

FIG. 16. Sagittal section of central nervous system of the pelagic octopod *Tremoctopus*. The inferior buccal ganglion is larger than the superior and the inferior frontal is very small.

ant.bas., anterior basal; ant.sal., anterior salivary glands; ant.sub., anterior suboesophageal lobe; buc.n., nerve to buccal mass; cer.-br., cerebro-brachial connective; dors.bas., dorsal basal; inf.buc., inferior buccal; inf.fr., inferior frontal; med.bas., median basal; oes., oesophagus; s.c., small cells of inferior buccal lobe; subp., rows of cells resembling the 'subpedunculate tissue'; subv., subvertical; sup.buc., superior buccal; sup.fr., superior frontal; vert., vertical.

small cells. As we shall see later small cells are characteristic of parts of the nervous system that are concerned with classifying complex inputs. Possibly with the great development of the web method of feeding this function has become developed in the inferior buccal ganglion.

An interesting feature of the Argonautidae is that it is only the females that grow into large animals with a shell. The males are minute creatures, hardly more than larvae, but with the arm that is used for copulation developed out of all proportion to the rest of the body (hectocotylus). These little males, or the autotomized hectocotylus alone, are found in the mantle cavity of the female, where they live, carrying the spermatophores, until needed for fertilization. Why should there be this curious sexual dimorphism in the argonauts and not in other octopods? The clue may be that there is another use for the shell. Female octopods lay their eggs attached to rocks but, of course, this is not possible for *Argonauta*. Instead the eggs are attached to the shell. Since there would be no such function for the shell in the males, it has proved more economical for the species for the males to become minute creatures with only reproductive functions.

To express all these characteristics as 'representations' of the pelagic environment might seem unnecessary and complicated. But to do so states the fact that in each species certain characteristics are selected and emphasized. In bottom-living octopods the arms and associated nerve-centres are well developed. In argonauts it is the web and its centres and so on.

I have chosen these particular cephalopods to illustrate the point only because they interest me and I have been working on them. Any other cephalopods or indeed any group of animals would provide examples. Thus the decapod cephalopods such as cuttlefishes (*Sepia*) and squids (such as *Loligo*) contain hundreds of further types, representing every part of the sea from the surface to the greatest depths. It would be possible to write a large book on the variations in their body shapes and their arms, their mantle sacks and their fins, their receptor organs and brain, their colour patterns and luminescence. Cephalopod organization includes a whole range of possibilities out of which some are selected for emphasis by each type.

8. *Mating, social and sexual life of* Octopus

These aspects of the activities of the animals show some further senses in which they may be said to represent their environments.

The octopuses that we use in Naples are adolescents or young adults of 150–600 g, probably one to two years old (Wells and Wells, 1959). The males are mature at this size and most of those that we use contain ripe spermatophores. Females of this size are all immature, with an ovary weighing at most 1–2 g. The females mature only when much larger (1 kg or more) and die after laying the eggs and caring for them (Wells and Wells, 1959; Batham, 1957; and Vevers, 1961). The endocrine mechanism that controls the onset of maturity is discussed later.

There is little exact knowledge about the social and sexual behaviour of *Octopus*. If there are several individuals in a tank they fight, and a sort of dominance order is achieved, the largest animals obtaining the best places among the stones. This fighting may be a reflection of territory holding in nature, distributing the octopuses among the rocks (see Wynne-Edwards, 1962). Fishermen and divers report that shortly after one octopus has been taken from a particular cranny another one moves in to occupy the desirable home.

No elaborate courtship behaviour has been reported in *Octopus vulgaris*. The sexes show a small difference externally in the specialized suckers and tip of the third right arm of the male, the hectocotylus. It has also been shown recently that a few of the suckers near the bases of the second and third arms are larger in the male (Packard, 1961). These large suckers are turned outwards when approaching another individual and presumably provide the display that is the basis of sexual recognition. Copulation is frequently observed in the tanks, the hectocotylus of a male being held for many minutes within the mantle of another animal. The females are probably impregnated before they are mature, the spermatophores surviving until the eggs are ripe for fertilization.

Other species of *Octopus* show different patterns of courtship. In some rather superficial observations of *Octopus horridus* on a coral reef near Singapore, I have seen a striking colour display by a male to a female, followed by copulation (Fig. 17) (Young, 1962a). A pattern of vertical stripes was displayed, similar to that shown by *Sepia* (Tinbergen, 1939). This is of great interest in the present context because, as we shall see, the nervous system is so arranged that vertical lines are readily detected. Thus the system of signals adopted for sexual recognition is itself a representation of the vertical feature of the

FIG. 17. Reef octopus (*O. horridus*, Orbigny and Ferussac). Drawing made after observation under water of the mating behaviour of two animals lasting half an hour. The male showed a pattern of vertical stripes, somewhat similar to that of *Sepia*, but not previously observed in *Octopus*. After chasing her for some time and showing this pattern he assumed the position shown and the hectocotylysed third right arm was inserted into the mantle of the female. The latter then also showed traces of the pattern of vertical stripes. The stripes on the male are more developed on the side facing the female. (Young, 1962*a*.)

world that has impressed itself so deeply upon the animals. Even such code signals cannot be entirely arbitrary in an analogue system.

Cephalopods represent their environment very strikingly in the colours they display. These are produced by the chromatophores, sacks of red, yellow, or brown pigment, each of which can be expanded by muscle fibres. These muscles are controlled by nerves and the colour patterns are changed more quickly than in any other animals.

So closely do the animals resemble their surroundings that it is often difficult to see an octopus or cuttlefish even in a clean tank when you know that it is there. The matching is achieved by switching on an appropriate combination of certain basic colour patterns and raising the loose skin into papillae, tipped with colour or white. With study it is possible to identify these patterns and to see that they are similar in all individuals. By suitably combining them the animal is made to match seaweeds, corals, smooth rocks, or sand. The patterns used vary among the different cephalopods according to the environments that they frequent.

These colour displays are interesting for analysis of the nervous system because they show that apparently complex and varied patterns of behaviour can be produced by use of a relatively limited range of built-in neural patterns. Most features of animal behaviour consist of *sequences of movements*, which are difficult to analyse. In the display of colour patterns we see the effects of neural activity spread out before us and maintained for long periods. It is therefore easier to discern that each pattern is produced by the display of a combination selected out of certain fixed components, which constitute the animals' repertoire, almost certainly inborn. Some progress has been made with identifying the parts of the brain in which these patterns are elaborated (Boycott, 1953). Unfortunately we do not know how the information provided by the eyes is so coded and manipulated as to compute the selection that makes suitable patterns.

9. *Summary of the behaviour system of* Octopus

The system used by an octopus to move itself and to manipulate the world consists in the main, then, of muscles in the mantle for swimming, muscles in the arms and suckers for exploring among the rocks, and for walking and seizing the prey, and the muscles of the chromatophores. The nervous system serves to take decisions between a relatively small number of things that the animal can do. In particular, decision must be made whether to attack or to retreat, to seize an object and bite it, or to reject it by pushing and blowing it away. Of course the nervous system must control other detailed processes, such as chewing, digestion, respiration, circulation, excretion, reproduction, and so on. Centres for all of these can be found in the brain. There are numerous nerve-cells within the arms themselves, serving for the detailed control of movements of the suckers. But the main central nervous system is concerned with deciding whether to advance or retreat, and over 90 per cent of the central neurons are concerned with this decision.

It is this relative simplicity of the action system that makes these animals so suitable for work on the coding and learning mechanisms. We can readily detect whether the result of the computation is to produce the decision 'attack'. The subsequent details of behaviour, such as seizing and eating, are then carried out largely by reflex centres within the arms themselves. This is, of course, something of an oversimplification, since intermediate forms of hesitant and cautious behaviour are seen and are of great interest in themselves (Boycott, 1954). When two representations in the nervous system conflict, as after a shock has been received from an attack on a crab, the fluctuating effects of the two appear, e.g. an arm is put out, but is withdrawn before it touches the crab.

A further valuable characteristic is that there is little fluctuation in the motivation of the animals by the rhythm of day and night or even by hunger and satiety. They are ready to attack if a crab appears at any hour. There have not been detailed studies to determine whether this tendency is exactly equal all round the clock and there is some indication that it is weaker in the early morning (Young, 1958).

As we have already seen, the immediate effect of food is to *increase* the tendency to attack. However, an octopus that has not fully learned to attack in a given situation may cease to do so after catching two or three crabs (Fig. 12). Animals that have been trained for some time to take crabs in the laboratory have been seen to come out on twenty or more trials at two-minute intervals to attack crabs, killing them, and storing them in the web until the animal becomes so laden as to be hardly able to move. After consuming all these crabs the octopus will attack somewhat less regularly and more slowly in the subsequent hours, but this effect of satiation soon wears off.

Conversely the effect of hunger is only to increase some-what the responsiveness or speed of attack. Presumably in the sea the 'hungry' animal would leave its home and search for food, and starved animals sometimes wander about the tanks. Octopuses can live for weeks without food, probably using reserves in the 'liver'.

The feeding system is thus adjusted to the life of an animal that, being unprotected when in the open, sits hidden in one place until food appears, and then dashes out and quickly returns. It can wait a long time without losing its food-gathering capacity and if food is abundant will eat all it can obtain. A 500 g octopus will double its weight in a month, given sufficient food.

6

THE ORGANIZATION OF THE
NERVOUS SYSTEM OF *OCTOPUS*

1. *The Receptors*

THE greater part of the information by which decisions are
made by an octopus whether to attack comes from the eyes and
chemotactile receptors of the arms. Experiments with training
have been made with both of these systems and will be considered later. The eyes are probably the most important distance receptor. The chemoreceptors of the arms can detect
food only at a distance of a few centimetres. There is a so-
called olfactory pit, with its own nerve and centre, but the
apparatus is very small and of unknown function. It certainly
does not allow detection of food at a distance. This can be
shown by studying octopuses that have been blinded by sever-
ance some days previously of the optic tracts distal to the
olfactory lobes (Fig. 23). If a piece of sardine is placed, say
10 cm from such an animal, there is no reaction even after
many minutes. Only when the food is placed quite close (2 cm)
does the animal stretch out an arm towards it. Often then,
if the food has not been taken, the whole animal rises up and
swims forward.

We can be fairly sure, therefore, that octopuses can be
described as microsmatic, a condition that is often found in
animals with well-developed eyes (e.g. higher primates). It is
interesting that in the Pearly Nautilus, which is probably not
very far from the ancestry of all modern cephalopods, there is
a large olfactory pit and olfactory lobe. The animal is presumably macrosmatic and, of course, its vision must be limited
by the pin-hole image-forming system and long optic nerves
(p. 116).

2. *Plan of the receptor organs*

All the known receptor cells of cephalopods consist of 'primary sense cells' in the epidermis, from which an axon proceeds inwards (Fig. 18). The same plan is found for the chemotactile receptors of the arms and in the cells of the eyes,

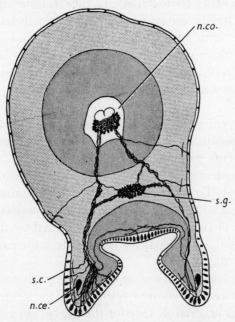

FIG. 18. Diagram of transverse section of the arm of an octopus, showing one sucker. n.ce., nerve cell near the surface; n.co. nerve cord; s.c., sensory cell; s.g., sucker ganglion. (After Graziadei.)

statocysts, and olfactory organs. Many, perhaps all, the receptor systems allow for interaction between neighbouring receptor cells. Thus although the retina differs from that of vertebrates in containing no ganglion cells, it is more than a simple conducting pathway, as the retinal cells carry collaterals, by means of which they presumably influence each other (p. 114). In the statocyst and in the skin there are nerve-cells immediately below the receptor surface.

Such arrangements probably indicate an important feature

of nervous organization, although the details of its functioning are not known. The detector points are characteristically spread out over relatively large areas. Each transducer point (cell) responds to a change in its immediate neighbourhood ('stimulus'). But the whole assembly of points serves to signal some other characteristic of the 'stimulating complex'. This characteristic capacity to signal certain selected characteristics of the 'form' of a situation (its *'gestalt'*) has given rise to many difficulties of interpretation. The words 'response to stimulus' can be ambiguous if used both for the point event at the detection surface and for the response to the whole complex.

It is convenient to say that these peripheral mechanisms serve to transmit in code information about certain characteristics of events around them. A code is a set of physical changes whose significance for the system is arbitrarily determined (p. 20). To speak of the receptors as encoding messages thus emphasizes that the process is one of selection among a repertoire of possible messages determined by the previous history (usually the heredity) to provide information that is relevant for the animal.

A further characteristic of several cephalopod receptors is that they receive efferent fibres from the central nervous system. This is certainly true for the eye (p. 46) and probably for the statocyst and skin. There are several possible ways in which such efferents may influence the process of encoding. They may bias the sensitivity (as the gamma efferents do to muscle spindles in vertebrates). They may serve to condition and determine the nature of the information transmitted. Their existence thus further emphasizes that the whole significance of the receptor system is to tell the organism what it needs to know. Homeostats have no means for recording an 'unbiased' view of 'reality'.

3. *The statocysts*

The most conspicuous receptors other than those for sight and touch are in the statocysts, a pair of sacks below the brain

(Fig. 19). These provide interesting parallels with the vertebrates in the way they 'represent' the environment. Each contains three main types of receptor: (1) a macula, vertically

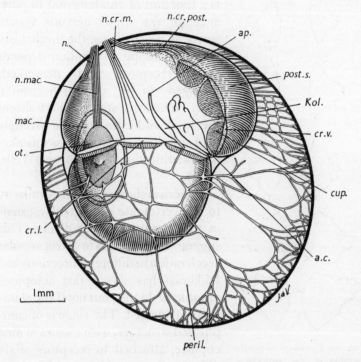

FIG. 19. Left statocyst of *Octopus vulgaris* viewed laterally. Drawing made
from a thick slice preparation. The cupulae and statolith are shown diagram-
matically.

a.c., anticrista; ap., internal aperture of Kölliker's canal; cr.l., longitudinal
crista; cr.v., vertical crista; cup., cupula of crista; Kol., Kölliker's canal; mac.,
macula; n., nerve bundle; n.cr.m., middle crista nerve; n.cr.post., posterior
crists nerve; n.mac., macular nerve; ot., statolith; peril., perilymph; post.s.,
posterior sac. (Young, 1960*b*.)

placed and carrying a statolith; (2) a ridge of cells with long
hairs, the crista; (3) numerous isolated hair cells scattered in
the wall of the sack (Young, 1960*b*). Removal of the statocysts
produces abnormalities of posture and movement, especially
if the animals are blind (Boycott, 1960). Something is now
known of the function of the various parts of the statocyst

(Dijkgraaf, 1961). It is likely that the macula is a static-dynamic receptor, providing continuous information about

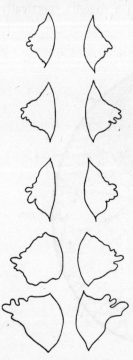

the position of the head and eyes. This is a function of fundamental importance for the whole nervous system since, as we shall see, the mechanism for visual shape recognition depends upon receptors and nerve-cells arranged in a vertical–horizontal array. When the statocysts are absent the head and eyes may be wrongly held and there are then gross mistakes in identification of figures (Wells, 1960).

The crista shows a striking similarity to the vertebrate semicircular canals in that it runs in three planes. This suggests that it serves to detect angular acceleration in different directions and Dijkgraaf has shown that octopuses are able to do this, but not if the statocyst is damaged. The ridge is of complicated structure, with a series of nine cupulae, attached to receptors of six different types, asymmetrical above and below the ridge. This presumably allows signalling of direction of movement in each plane. By recording from individual fibres of the static

FIG. 20. Drawings of whole mounts of the anticristae from the two statocysts of five octopuses to show the variations in shape but general similarity between the two sides of each animal.

nerves it has in fact been shown that the various parts of the crista respond to angular acceleration in the appropriate directions (Maturana and Sperling, 1963).

A curious feature is that in front of the vertical section of the crista is a ridge of cartilage, the anticrista (Fig. 20). It is suggested that this protects the receptors of this section from activation that would give false information, for instance during sudden forward acceleration or stopping. The effect on the resolution of the system is thus similar to that produced in vertebrates by the enclosure of endolymph in canals. In *Sepia*, which can spin about its own axis with its fins, there is a more elaborate set of anticristae, making almost complete canals. Thus the detectors of each species represent faithfully the conditions of its life. Indeed, variations between individuals may be reflected in the structure of their statocysts, as the anticristae differ considerably in shape between individual octopuses, though those of the two sides of one individual are alike (Fig. 20). This might be due to heredity, but the cartilages only develop after hatching, perhaps under the morphogenetic stimulus of the fluid movements. So it is likely that an octopus carries a record of its past activities in its anticrista. This would be useful to it since, if the particular circumstances of its life require active movements, the statocyst would not tend to signal these as rolling, as a smaller anticrista would allow. In *Octopus macropus*, a species that lives buried in the sand, the anticrista is very small, as it is also in the argonautids, which drift at the surface.

There is no information about the function of other hair cells that are scattered in the wall of the statocyst, perhaps they are pressure receptors, detecting changes within the body of the animal as it squeezes itself among the rocks. Octopuses are able to vary their shape remarkably in this way, but there must be some limit to the extent to which the powerful arm muscles can be allowed to drag the head and mantle through a cranny! It may be significant that the octopus statocyst is separated from the cartilaginous wall by perilymph, not present in decapods, which do not change their body shape. There is a real danger that an octopus may kill itself by the strength of its arms. An octopus kept in a tank sometimes lifts the heavy lid and begins to crawl through but then drops the lid on to its mantle and dies horribly crushed.

If the tank containing an octopus is tapped the animal draws in its head and changes colour, but this response persists after removal of the statocysts. It has not been possible to train the animals to respond to single tones (Hubbard, 1960; Dijkgraaf,

1962) but further experiments are needed before it is certain that they do not respond to sound at all. It is strange if this is indeed so. The information available from sound in water has been used by so many other animal groups, either for detecting enemies or prey, or for signalling. Crabs moving on the bottom of a tank produce sounds that can be readily heard with a hydrophone, but blinded octopuses make no response to running crabs unless they actually touch them. By recording with electrodes in the wall of the statocyst it is possible to show responses to vibrations of quite high frequencies (Lettvin and Maturana, personal communication). It is not clear whether these have any significance for the life of the animal.

4. *Parts of the brain*

A characteristic of all nervous systems beyond the very lowest level of complexity is that they are divided into numerous distinct parts, ganglia, lobes, centres, or whatever we are pleased to call them. This fact is undoubtedly one of the clues, subtle though obvious, that we may use for understanding how brains work. Cephalopods and vertebrates have been evolving separately for 500 million years at least, and their common ancestor probably had very little central nervous tissue. Yet in both these groups, and also among arthropods, we find nervous systems based on similar plans and with even some surprising similarities of detail. Many types of animal need the same information about, say, gravity or light, and they evolve similar equipment to detect it. We can learn much from the similarities and differences in the instruments that they develop for measuring, coding, and computing this information.

The octopus's nervous system is less completely centralized than that of vertebrates. Many of the important reflex centres remain separated at the periphery, for instance within the arms and in the stellate ganglion of the mantle (Gray, 1960). Indeed the nerve centres in the arms make up much the greater bulk of the whole nervous system. Out of the total of some 500 million nerve-cells in the animal more than 300 million are in the arms. There is an elaborate ganglion at the base of each sucker and these ganglia can work together to produce quite complicated movements. Thus when an isolated arm touches food the suckers move in a co-ordinated manner to convey the food towards the end where the mouth would have been. The suckers at the end of each arm serve more for sensory functions than for seizing, as the delicate tip feels its

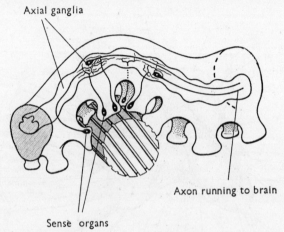

Axial ganglia

Axon running to brain

Sense organs

FIG. 21. Diagram of part of the arm of an octopus touching a plastic cylinder. The pathways from the receptors are inferred from physiological and degeneration experiments. (After Wells and Wells, 1957*b*.)

way over surfaces and into crannies. The centre of the terminal region is occupied almost entirely by nervous tissue, including many very small cells. These presumably serve for computational rather than motor functions. The octopus might be said to 'think with its arms'.

The true central brain itself is based on a system of much shortened, ganglionated cords, with cells at the outside whose fibres extend into a neuropil at the centre (Fig. 73). Here they make synaptic contacts by collateral 'dendritic' branches and then continue as axons to some other destination. The ganglionated cords of the arms are still of this type (Fig. 21).

In the central nervous system we can recognize cords, running transversely above and below the oesophagus, but they

are much subdivided and it is disputed whether they should
be considered as derived from three simple transverse cords
(cerebral, pedal, and viscero-pleural) or from a more complicated system of longitudinal and transverse cords. The
cephalopods have been separated from other molluscs for so
long that detailed comparisons are difficult.

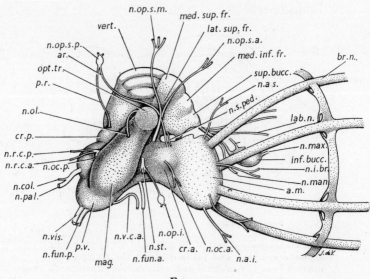

FIG. 22

In order to have a clear nomenclature the central nervous
system is divided into some fifty named lobes and lobules
(Figs. 22 and 23; Boycott and Young, 1965). The nerve centres may be grouped into five sets, having interesting functional similarities with the vertebrate centres (Boycott, 1961):
(1) lower motor centres, e.g. arm ganglia, stellate ganglia;
(2) intermediate motor centres, suboesophageal ganglia;
(3) higher motor centres, the basal supraoesophageal centres; (4) receptor analysers and memory stores, optic lobes,
perhaps brachial, and probably posterior buccal lobes; (5) systems for control of motivation and assessment of rewards, the
inferior and superior frontal, vertical, and subfrontal lobes
(Young, 1963c).

Separation into classes in this way is obviously an arbitrary matter, since many lobes collaborate in any action. Because of

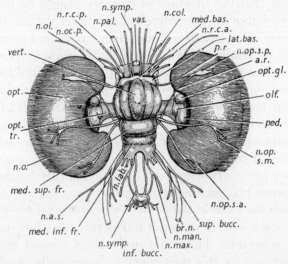

FIG. 23

FIGS. 22 and 23. Lateral and dorsal views of the brain of *Octopus vulgaris*.
a.m., anterior suboesophageal mass; a.r. anterior root of the posterior superior ophthalmic nerve; br.n., brachial nerve; cr.a., anterior chromatophore lobe; cr.p., posterior chromatophore lobe; inf.bucc., inferior buccal lobe; lab.n., labial nerve; lat.bas., lateral basal lobe; lat.sup.fr., lateral superior frontal lobe; mag., magnocellular lobe; med.bas., median basal lobe; med.inf.fr., median inferior frontal lobe; med.sup.fr., median superior frontal lobe; n.a.i., inferior antorbital nerve; n.a.s., superior antorbital nerve; n.col., collar nerve; n.fun.a., anterior funnel nerve; n.fun.p., posterior funnel nerve; n.i.br., interbrachial nerve; n.lab., labial nerve; n.man., cerebro-subradular connective; n.max., maxillary nerve; n.o., optic nerves; n.oc.a., anterior oculomotor nerve; n.oc.p., posterior oculomotor nerve; n.ol., olfactory nerve; n.op.i., inferior ophthalmic nerve; n.op.s.a., anterior superior ophthalmic nerve; n.op.s.m., middle superior ophthalmic nerve; n.op.s.p., posterior superior ophthalmic nerve; n.pal., pallial nerve; n.r.c.a., anterior head retractor nerve; n.r.c.p., posterior head retractor nerve; n.s.ped., subpeduncular nerve; n.st., static nerve; n.symp., sympathetic nerve; n.v.c.a., anterior vena cava nerve; n.vis., visceral nerve; olf., olfactory lobe; opt., optic lobe; opt.gl., optic gland; opt.tr., optic tract; p.r., posterior root of the superior posterior ophthalmic nerve; p.v., palliovisceral lobe; ped., peduncle lobe; sup.bucc., superior buccal lobe; vert., vertical lobe; vas., vaso-motor lobe.

this essential unity of animal organization some theoretical objections can be raised to any system of analysis. These are usually raised by people who, for some reason have decided that they do not wish to make an analysis. For example, those who believe that the brain is controlled by some outside agent, will argue that the function of memory cannot be localized anywhere within it. Alternatively they will emphasize that it is everywhere. As we shall see later there are indeed great difficulties in determining the site of memory changes. However, valuable clues to understanding are provided by the fact that brains are not homogeneous masses of cells. One of the most important facts about nervous systems is that distinct lobes exist, each with an input and output. Moreover, the various lobes contain neurons of very different forms and physiological properties. It seems certain that in any satisfactory analysis of behaviour (or 'psychology') consideration of this division into centres must play an important part.

Though the lobes of the octopus's brain are clearly marked off from each other it does not follow that their functions are sharply separable. Thus, the optic lobes control much of behaviour and for this they contain 'motor' cells. Again, the actual representations that constitute the visual memory system probably lie in the optic lobes. But this record cannot be established without the vertical lobe circuit, nor, once established, can it be used if that circuit has been damaged (Chapter 13). We have, therefore, to try to define the part that each lobe plays in controlling the behaviour of the whole animal. To do this we may study its input and output and the form of the cells and connexions within it. Such anatomical investigation provides an essential 'blue-print' with which we can then proceed to physiological analysis by stimulation and recording through electrodes, and by other means. With all this information available we should then be able to explain the effects of removal of the part or interruption of pathways to or from it. The practical value of this for medicine and surgery is obvious enough. Equally important from our present point of view is that the knowledge of the 'functions' of the lobes, even of a nervous system such as that of the octopus, provides a system by which we can 'understand' animal and human behaviour.

5. *Intermediate motor centres*

These lie in the suboesophageal lobes and from them axons proceed to the effectors, either direct or after a single synapse in lower motor centres. The cells of lower and intermediate motor centres are few and large and the neuropil shows a characteristic tangle, generally with no pattern that can yet be discerned by us, although it must embody the detailed connexions that make the action systems possible.

Electrical stimulation of these centres produces movements of the parts innervated, usually movements of an unpatterned type. Thus, after stimulation of the posterior chromatophore lobes all the chromatophores of the mantle expand. With electrodes in the middle suboesophageal mass (pedal lobes) there are uncoordinated movements of the arms and funnel. The posterior suboesophageal mass (palliovisceral lobe) controls the mantle and respiratory and visceral apparatus. After removal of one of these motor centres the part concerned is totally and permanently paralysed, even though the muscles are not necessarily denervated. Thus, after section of the mantle connective, which runs from the brain to the stellate ganglion, the mantle makes no further 'spontaneous' movements. Its muscles are still innervated by fibres proceeding from the ganglion, whose cells indeed show interesting hyperexcitability to mechanical and other stimuli (Sereni and Young, 1932; Gray, 1960).

An animal from which all the brain except the suboesophageal lobes has been removed lies on the bottom of its tank, an immobile mass without posture, giving only certain isolated reflexes when stimulated. Clearly these motor centres are thus in some ways similar to the spinal cord of vertebrates. The animal left only with them is even less active than, for example, a spinal fish, perhaps because there is less proprioceptive feed-back to the brain in an octopus. This is another feature that helps analysis of behaviour. Sequences of action, once set off by the higher computing centres, are then completed by reflex actions at the periphery. In this respect indeed the cephalopod organization differs somewhat from that of vertebrates. There are, as it were, two lower levels, the intermediate and lower motor neuron, but the details of their actions still require further studies.

6. *Higher motor centres*

The main action patterns of the animal are generated by a series of basal lobes in the lower part of the supraoesophageal mass (Boycott, 1961). These have cells of smaller size than the suboesophageal lobes, to which they send their axons. The actions with which we are especially concerned are those of attack and retreat and in a general way these are produced by the anterior basal and medial basal lobes respectively. Electrical stimulation of the anterior basal lobes causes the animal to rise up, turn its head, and walk towards the side stimulated. The action may persist for some seconds. Stimulation of the medial basal lobe produces movements mainly of the mantle and funnel, also of the arms.

After removal of these basal lobes many abnormalities of movements are seen. If the lesion is asymmetrical the animal may walk or swim in circles, sometimes for many hours, especially shortly after operation. The action of these centres is not fully understood and it would certainly be too simple to say that the anterior basal lobe initiates and directs attack, and that the medial basal initiates retreat. Nevertheless, the data are sufficient to suggest that these lobes are organized so that when they receive a relatively simple input, such as is imitated by electrical stimulation, they can set up complicated and enduring patterns of attack or retreat.

An animal in which these lobes are intact, but from which all of the superior frontal and vertical lobes have been removed, maintains a good posture and can walk and swim, though it will not attack normally or keep within a home. It sits on the side of the tank, not wandering or seeking food. Nevertheless, its posture and responses to stimuli mark it off from the still more inert animal with only suboesophageal lobes. The difference is an indication of the function of the higher motor centres.

The colour patterns are controlled from a distinct pair of lateral basal lobes. Stimulation of these produces colour changes, though rarely with the patterns normally seen. Such patterns appear more frequently after stimulation of the centre of the optic lobe. There can obviously be no sharp distinction between the later stages of the receptor analysers (optic lobes) and the higher motor centres. The cells at the centre of the optic lobe presumably form various sets, each able to switch on a particular pattern, through appropriate connexions in the basal lobes. Similarly, stimulation of the optic lobes may produce movements of attack or retreat, by the fibres that lead from them to the anterior and medial basal lobes. The nerve-cells in the optic lobes that initiate these various patterns are, however, presumably all intermingled and close together within the optic lobes, so that distinct patterns of action would not be expected from stimulation with large electrodes. Nevertheless, the identification of such cells whose connexions produce particular actions is a most important task. They control the set or alphabet of responses out of which 'choice' is made by the signals arriving from the receptors and appropriately directed by the memory units (p. 155). In the visual system the cells in question occupy the cell islands towards the centre of the optic lobes (p. 152).

7. *Receptor analysers and memory stores*

The description of the functioning of the parts of the brain by which incoming information is analysed and stored has not yet been successfully achieved. There is a vast amount of information about the sensory pathways of vertebrates and their cerebral centres, but it is not really possible to say that we understand 'how they work'. This is partly due to the difficulty of formulating a scheme that defines the operations to which we must attend. To do this is part of the value of block diagrams such as that suggested by Maldonado (p. 73). The attempt to study the chemotactile and visual learning

systems of *Octopus* has helped to bring out some of the principles with which such analysing and storing systems operate.

On the pathways from the chemotactile receptors and the
retina lie centres that play a large part in the coding systems.
There are chemoreceptors in the lips, and fibres from these
pass to the superior buccal lobe and thence to the posterior
buccal. Here they meet fibres from the arms that are known
to signal both touch and chemical composition (Wells, 1963).
These fibres pass through the anterior suboesophageal mass,
where some of them end, and this may be an important analysing centre. However, many of the chemotactile fibres run
up without interruption to the posterior buccal and inferior
frontal lobes. These, with the subfrontal lobes, are certainly the
main centres for these receptors. The details of their activities
will be considered in connexion with the experiments by
Mr. and Mrs. Wells on tactile and chemical discrimination.
Here we need only notice that they contain numerous small
cells, some 5 million in the subfrontal lobes, which are associated with the inferior frontal lobes. In the latter there are also
numerous interweaving bundles, probably allowing for interchange of information between the eight arms.

The optic lobes form the greater part of the mass of the
whole central nervous system and contain 120 out of the 130
million nerve-cells in the centres. This is a measure of the
importance of vision for the animals and of the extent of the
equipment required to allow such discriminations of visual
shape as are possible for an octopus.

The lobes are connected with the rest of the brain by large
optic tracts, containing numerous bundles of fibres running
from the optic lobes to all parts of the supraoesophageal and
many parts of the suboesophageal systems. The lobes also
receive fibres from many parts of the higher motor centres and
from the tactile and gustatory pathways.

It is in these lobes and their connexions that we must look
for the coding, learning, and computing systems of the visual
input. It will be shown that they are the seat of visual memory
stores, though in this respect they operate only imperfectly in

the absence of the vertical lobe system. On the other hand, the inferior frontal and vertical lobe system can store chemotactile representations in the absence of the optic lobes, which are thus only concerned with vision.

On the stalk of the optic lobes are two further lobes and the optic gland (p. 293) (Fig. 23). The peduncle lobes receive mainly optic input, but send fibres to a large number of supra- and sub-oesophageal lobes. Their functions are uncertain but may be concerned with movement control, perhaps especially of the eyes. It may be noticed that no timing mechanism for afferent systems is present in an octopus. Is this a result of the absence of sound detectors, or have the latter not developed because they would be of little use in the absence of a means of detecting time differences?

8. *Centres for motivation and addressing of rewards*

The 'highest' parts of the octopus's brain, the superior frontal and vertical lobes, are concerned with the proper application of signals indicating reward, a most important function for an exploratory, self-teaching homeostat. Though these lobes are the highest, in the sense of being on top of the brain, we must be careful about the implications of the term. In mammals the corresponding centres are probably those of the limbic system and basal ganglia (p. 235). These lie anatomically below the thalamo-cortical systems, which represent the receptor analysers and memory stores of our system.

It is not easy to specify the functions of lobes of this type, or to give them suitable names, because no exactly similar units are to be found in even the most ambitious experimental man-made computers. Calculating machines go to work when they are started, using the programmes given to them by their masters. Animals must be provided with the right degree of exploratory drive to probe the environment and learn from the rewards and penalties that it provides in various situations. The successful creature will be the one that uses the clues thus provided in an optimal way to alter its tendency to attack. It will be encouraged by success—but not to the extent of rashness, and be made cautious by pain—but not so much as to lead to depression. Obviously the achievement of this optimum is one of the outstanding features of an exploratory homeostat. The median superior frontal and vertical lobes seem to provide the system by which this is achieved during visual learning in an octopus. Together with two underlying lobes, the lateral superior frontal and the subvertical, they provide the means by which the few nerve impulses that signal the results of action, pleasure or pain, that is positive or negative rewards, give rise to a suitably weighted action, distributed through a sufficiently large mass of tissue to ensure that learning changes occur and future behaviour is appropriately altered. These lobes may have a further equally important function, to bridge the interval between the initiation of an action and the receipt of a reward or penalty. In any learning situation where distance receptors are concerned there is a delay between the moment when, for example, an image falls on the retina and when the process of pursuit has led to capture and consumption of the prey. If the animal is to attach the correct reward signals to the coding elements that recorded the situation, the address of these elements, as we may call it, must be kept in the nervous system until the signals for pleasure and pain arrive. There is reason to think that the circuits in question provide the means of bridging this time gap.

After removal of these lobes the octopuses show no gross defects of receptor or motor functions. They cannot be distinguished from normal animals by any superficial observation. But anyone who studies them closely finds a subtle change of 'personality', or 'motivation', a greater or lesser degree of caution. Moreover, without these lobes the animal's powers of making effective learned responses is grossly impaired.

In all these respects these centres show some close analogies with some of the higher parts of the vertebrate and human nervous system. The palaeocortical centres and basal parts of the forebrain are also concerned largely with 'motivation' as well as being involved in learning. It would be unwise to press the comparison too far at this point but undoubtedly much can be learned from these highest centres about how to study and describe these subtle features of animal and human life. Incidentally these centres have probably been evolved relatively recently in octopods (perhaps in 10 million years) and are rather differently arranged in decapods such as cuttle-fishes and squids.

7

SOME PROBLEMS IN THE DESIGN
OF EYES AND OPTIC PATHWAYS

1. *Problems in the transmission of detailed visual information*

THE eyes and other receptor organs are designed to encode efficiently the relevant features of surrounding changes. By following the implications of this rather obvious though neglected fact in the case of visual form discrimination, we can begin to understand some otherwise obscure features of the optic pathways. It would be possible to discuss many details from this point of view. For example, effective form discrimination requires an optically adequate lens and focusing system. We shall be more concerned with the fact that it also requires a system capable of handling the intractable problems presented by the transmission of detailed information by the numerous slow and 'noisy' channels of the nerve fibres. We shall try to show that some strange features such as the apparently inefficient inversion of the vertebrate retina may be related to the design required to meet this need.

Speculations about such matters are difficult to test, but they are worth putting forward to call attention to the characteristics of the system and to stimulate investigation of features often neglected. Moreover, there are some bizarre aspects of the layout of the pathways, which throw much light on the mechanisms involved. Thus interpretation of the chiasma system by which the retinal information is re-inverted suggests a whole train of thought on cerebral mechanisms in general.

In dealing with these problems of design we constantly have the opportunity to consult the results of the array of experiments that evolution has provided in the visual or other systems. Our power to use this source is limited by our ignorance as zoologists. Its value is also apt to be decried by some biologists, apparently from a certain unwillingness to credit experiments that have been done by someone else, even when the someone is mother nature herself; an attitude unbefitting—to say the least—for a biologist.

2. *The retina of* Octopus

Even in the structure of the eyes of an octopus there is evidence of the importance of the horizontal and vertical directions that we shall later show to be all-important. The eyeball itself is elongated antero-posteriorly and the pupil is a horizontal slit when narrow. The optic lobe behind the eye is a bean-shaped structure, elongated in the antero-posterior direction.

The elements of the retina are arranged in a rectangular array that is normally held in the vertical/horizontal axis (Fig. 24). The retinal receptors are not altogether comparable to vertebrate rods, though they contain a rhodopsin-like pigment, displayed on an extended surface that is revealed by electron-microscopy (Wolken, 1958; Moody and Robertson, 1960). The surface consists of a series of tubules, probably comparable to the microvilli that make up the rhabdomes of arthropod eyes. In *Octopus* eye the tubules are arranged in paired sets (rhabdomeres) on either side of each retinal cell body, which contains black pigment. The sets of paired rhabdomeres are arranged at right angles to each other, in fours, making squares that can each be called a rhabdome. There are between ten and twenty million retinal cells in each eye, with an average density of about $50,000/mm^2$. There may be several sorts of rhabdomes, perhaps allowing for differential wavelength sensitivity (Young, 1962c). However, attempts to train octopuses to respond to particular colours have not been successful (Muntz, 1964).

The part of the receptor that carries the photosensitive pigment is thus directed towards the light. This seems to be a more logical design than that of the vertebrate eye, where the light must pass through the thickness of the retina before reaching the pigment. The cephalopod retina differs from that

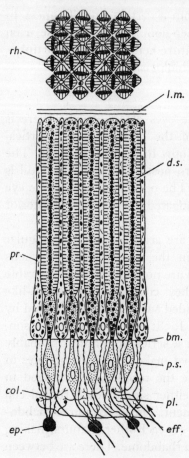

FIG. 24. Diagrams of the structure of
the retina of *Octopus*. Above, as seen in
tangential and below in radial section.
bm., basement membrane; col., collaterals of retinal cell processes; d.s.,
distal segment of retinal cell, directed
towards the light; eff., efferent fibres
ending in the retina; ep., 'epithelial' cell
of retinal plexus (a glia cell); l.m., limiting membrane; p.s., proximal segment
of retinal cell, containing the nucleus;
pl., retinal nerve fibre plexus; pr., process of supporting cell of retina; rh.,
rhabdome, composed of numerous fine
tubules arranged tangentially.

of vertebrates in an even more fundamental respect in that it contains no ganglion cells. Each retinal cell has a proximal segment containing the nucleus and is then drawn out into a nerve fibre that proceeds through an optic nerve to the optic lobe of the brain (Fig. 24). There is therefore no interruption by a synapse between the photoreceptor and the optic lobe. Paradoxically, however, the retina does contain synapses. The retinal cells are provided at the base with short collateral branches before they enter the optic nerves. These branches interweave in a retinal nerve plexus with the endings of fibres that arise from cells in the optic lobes (p. 146). This has all the appearance of a centrifugal pathway and indeed Lettvin and Maturana have shown that when a retinal area is illuminated nerve impulses can be detected proceeding from the optic lobes into the optic nerves (personal communication). We do not know how this centrifugal pathway operates but it is likely that it serves in some way to reduce the redundancy of the information that is recorded, perhaps by lateral inhibition of the firing of cells by their neighbours. This would accentuate contours, and reduce the amount of information about the inside of illuminated or dark areas.

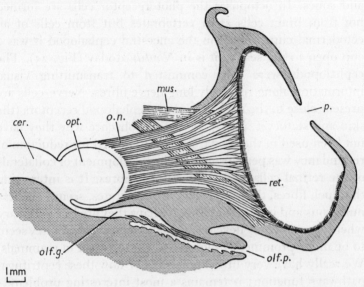

FIG. 25. Transverse section of *Nautilus* to show the pin-hole eye, retina and optic nerves without chiasma.

cer., cerebral cord; mus., muscles of eye-stalk; o.n., optic nerves; olf.g., olfactory ganglion; olf.p., olfactory pit; opt., optic lobe; p., pupil; ret., retina.

Hartline and his colleagues (1961) have shown that a mechanism for lateral inhibition exists in the eye of the king crab (*Limulus*). This animal has a not very elaborate compound eye but it transmits the visual information over an exceptionally long optic nerve (up to 10 cm) to the brain. Even in an octopus the nerves are about 2 cm long and it is presumably of great importance that the optic nerve fibres should not have to transmit every detail of the pattern of activity of the retinal cells. This is no doubt the design principle that has operated to place the elaborate ganglionic apparatus of the vertebrate retina so close to the photosensitive elements. By constructing the eye from an evaginated part of the brain the morphogenetic processes necessary to provide elaborate neural machinery were made available in the right place. The efficiency of this aspect was sufficient to overcome the disadvantage of passing the light through the nervous layers before it reaches the rods and cones. In octopuses the photoreceptor cells are formed not from brain cells as in vertebrates but from cells of an ectodermal cup. Indeed in the ancestral cephalopod it was a cup open to the sea, as it is in *Nautilus* today (Fig. 25). The cephalopods were thus committed to transmitting visual information along relatively long nerve fibres. Nerve-cells are present close to the surface in some cephalopod receptors (the skin and statocyst, p. 95). It remains obscure why they have not been used in the retina. Instead, the need for reduction of redundancy was perhaps met by the development of collaterals of the retinal cells and by centrifugal fibres. It is interesting that such fibres, though present in vertebrates, seem to be less numerous and important there, perhaps they are less necessary where there is a fully developed ganglionated retina. They seem to be more prominent in lower vertebrates than in mammals. We really have very little knowledge of how these centrifugal pathways function; it remains a most interesting problem.

3. *Differentiated regions of the retina of* Octopus

The retinal cells are not identical throughout the visual field. Those occupying a strip along the equator are longer and thinner than those in either the dorsal or ventral part of the eye (Fig. 26). The equatorial strip is thus a central area, whose small visual elements give the potentiality of higher resolution than elsewhere. But the strip itself is not everywhere the same. The rhabdomes at the front and the back of it are taller and more closely packed than those at the centre (Fig. 27). There are thus two special areas within the main horizontal area. This agrees with the fact that the octopus may attack by swimming either forwards or backwards to its prey. An analysis of photographs of a series of attacks showed that in the majority of them the octopus moves forwards with a small angle between its axis and the direction of the prey. However, if the

prey enters the hind part of the visual field the octopus may
swim backwards, holding the target in the extreme back

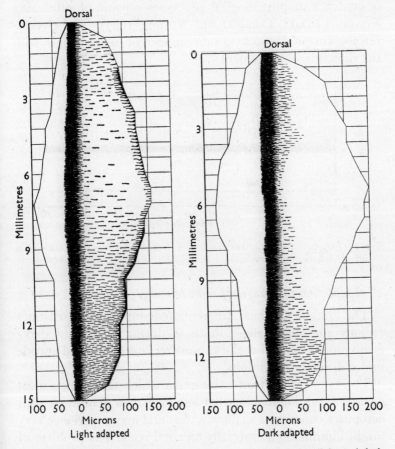

Fig. 26. Changes in the retina of *Octopus* in accommodation to light and darkness. The measurements were made on transverse sections across the centre of
the two eyes. The ordinates show distance from the dorsal border of the retina,
and abscissae, lengths of the retinal cells. Figures to the right of the zero are
lengths of rhabdomes, and to the left, of the proximal (nucleated) segment. Both
parts expand in the dark. The pigment migrates to the distal part of the retina
in the light—especially ventrally. (Young, 1963*b*.)

portions of both visual fields (which overlap). The eye is
provided with elaborate extrinsic eye-muscles, which produce
conspicuous flick movements in the horizontal plane as the

octopus turns. Although the details are not fully clear it seems likely that some processes of fixation take place. Indeed there is evidence of physiological processes capable of producing fixation (Tasaki, Oikawa, and Norton, 1963). The electroretinogram produced by a moving spot of light changes with the direction of movement.

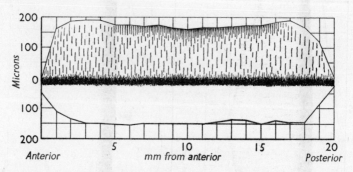

FIG. 27. Length and distribution of pigment in the rhabdomes of an octopus as seen in a horizontal section along the equator of the eye. Light adapted.

4. *Adaptation to changes of light intensity*

The retina is thus differentiated into several distinct regions and the changes in these during light- and dark-adaptation suggest that the various regions detect and encode under different conditions.

The range of light intensity under which the animals must operate is no doubt somewhat less in the sea than in air. But octopuses enter quite shallow waters and may experience very bright illumination, especially on coral reefs. The problem of arranging for the receptors to operate over a range of intensity of many thousand times is probably one of the most serious that living homeostats must meet. The cephalopods have developed all the three means of adjusting visual sensitivity that are found in the vertebrates. The amount of light entering the eye is controlled by an adjustable pupil, which narrows to form a horizontal slit. Secondly, there are granules of melanin pigment in the retinal cells and supporting cells and these move distally (towards the light) under illumination but

retract in the dark (Fig. 26). Thirdly, the rhabdomes shorten
under illumination, presumably reducing their sensitivity.

There are conspicuous differences in these changes in the
different parts of the retina (Figs. 28 and 29). The pigment
retracts most rapidly from the
cells in the central strip, more
slowly dorsally and still more
slowly ventrally. Conversely it
comes out fastest in the light in
these ventral cells. These movements are somewhat puzzling
since they suggest that the central
cells are the most sensitive, but
they are also the shortest. The
pigment seems to lie over the
distal ends of the cells in the
ventral region but *between* them
centrally (in the light). It is
possible that in this position they
have some collimating action. It
remains for experiment to show
how these various cell types are
used. The fact of their presence
shows that the coding for different
conditions is largely performed
simply by using different nerve fibres.

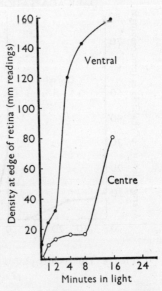

FIG. 28. Time courses of light
adaptation in *Octopus*. The ordinate is densitometer reading in
arbitrary units at the distal edge
of the retina. (Young, 1963*b*.)

The eye can thus adjust itself so as to be able to 'represent'
a variety of conditions. Similarly in animals that live in different ways we find differing conditions in the retina. The squids
(*Loligo*) live in more open water and have no strip, indeed
their retina is like a saucer, with longer cells all round the edge
(Fig. 30). They must look up and down as well as forwards and
backwards. In the deep sea squid, *Chiroteuthis*, however, there
is a 'fovea' of specially long cells in the *ventral* part of the retina
presumably because they look mainly upwards (Glockauer,
1915). The cuttlefish (*Sepia*) has a horizontal strip, like the
octopus but the retinal cells are much more closely packed in

an area at the back of the strip (100,000 mm²). *Sepia* catches its prey (prawns) by turning until the image falls on the back of both retinas. The long arms are then shot out to seize the prey.

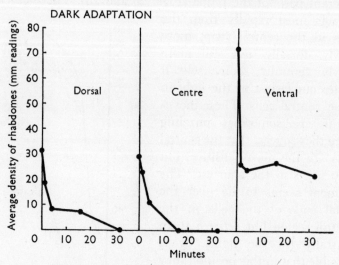

FIG. 29. Time course of dark adaptation in *Octopus*. (Young, 1963*b*.)

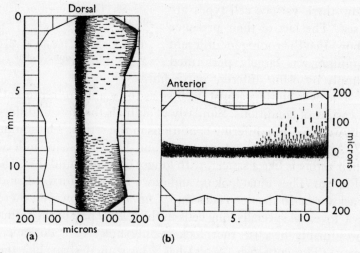

FIG. 30. Saucer-shaped retina of *Loligo*. Length and distribution of pigment in a light-adapted retina as seen in transverse (*a*) and horizontal (*b*) sections.

5. *The optic chiasma and the retinal map*

Each retinal cell is connected by a single nerve fibre to the optic lobe, after passing through a plexus behind the retina. The optic nerve fibres then cross in an interweaving chiasma, such that the more dorsal fibres reach a ventral position on the

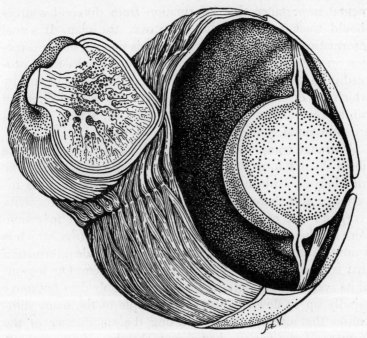

FIG. 31. Drawing of a dissection of the eye and optic lobe of *Octopus*. Young, 1962*e*).

surface of the lobe and vice versa. The display of information is thus inverted between the retina and the optic lobe as regards its dorsal-ventral but not its antero-posterior relations (Fig. 31). This inversion presents fascinating suggestions. First, it recalls the fact that the information is conveyed along a great number of parallel channels and that there is an importance in the topographical relations of these channels. Then why is the inversion in one direction only, that of gravity? Again, we get the hint that in this system the vertical/horizontal directions are of some special importance. The predominant influence of the direction of gravity may be the factor that produces inversion of the image only in the up/down plane. Our thesis is that the performance of the system depends at least in part on its operation as a model or map. If the course of events is to be appropriately traced on a map, it is obviously of fundamental importance that information from different sources should track in similar directions over the map. If visual information indicates that a crab, say, is moving in one direction on the map, then the indications from gravity must proceed in the same direction. The fact that there is a chiasma by which the display is reinverted in the dorso-ventral direction can be regarded as a demonstration that the system operates on approximately these principles.

A strange complication is that in *Nautilus* the optic nerve fibres do not form any such chiasma (Fig. 25). If the eye functions as a pin-hole camera presumably its image is inverted, and if there is to be an interrelation with the gravity receptors one of the pathways must contain an inversion. Perhaps the answer is that the statocyst of *Nautilus*, which is a simple sack filled with crystals, does not provide information that is in any way relevant to the visual system. On account of its system of gas flotation *Nautilus* probably does not move rapidly up or down. This is an example of the many difficulties that one meets in assessing the significance of the features of the various homeostats that have been evolved. This is no reason for discontinuing the search for methods adequate for the problem.

It may be that similar considerations apply to projections on to the optic lobe of lower vertebrates. Here there is an elaborate mapping of the retina on to the opposite tectum (p. 33), and the map is reversed with respect to the retina, so that the dorsal part of the visual field is projected to the dorsal (median) part of the tectum. There is thus the possibility of correct interaction of visual and stato-acoustic information, these being the two chief systems that project to the midbrain roof.

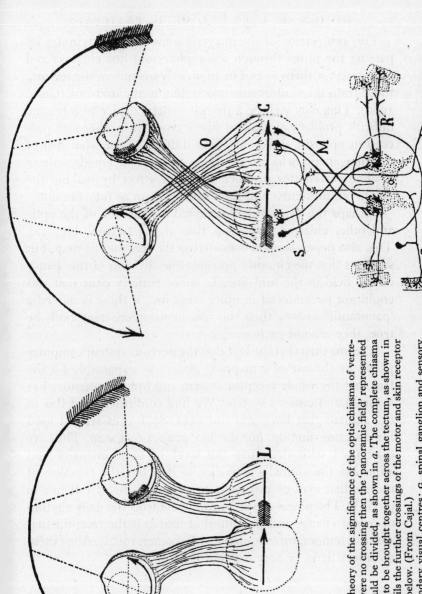

Fig. 32. Cajal's theory of the significance of the optic chiasma of vertebrates. If there were no crossing then the 'panoramic field' represented
by the arrow would be divided, as shown in a. The complete chiasma
enables its parts to be brought together across the tectum, as shown in
b. This then entails the further crossings of the motor and skin receptor
systems shown below. (From Cajal.)

c and L, secondary visual centres; G, spinal ganglion and sensory
roots; M, crossed pathway of motor cells; R, motor nerves crossed; o, optic nerves crossed; R,
motor roots of the spinal cord; s, sensory central crossed pathway.

This reinversion of the image is achieved in vertebrates by passing the fibres through a complete mid-line chiasma and arranging for them to end in an orderly manner in the tectum, those from the ventral side proceeding to the mid-line (Gaze, 1960). This may well be a morphogenetic device to solve the difficult problem of making fibres cross each other and proceed in opposite directions. It is difficult to see what sort of morphogenetic field can do this, yet the cephalopods achieve it. The vertebrates produce the same effect by making the whole bundles cross and then sorting them as they fan out.

Perhaps the most widely accepted explanation of the optic and other chiasma systems is that of Cajal (1911, Fig. 32). This also depends upon considering the tectum as a map, but suggests that the chiasma prevents the division of the 'panoramic' field in the mid-line. It is not entirely clear that this could not be achieved in other ways but, if there is indeed a 'panoramic' vision, then the two explanations may both be true, they are not exclusive.

It seems then that the fact that the nervous system computes partly by the use of a mapping system is responsible for the fact that the whole receptor system and brain is organized as a paired and crossed system. We find confirmation of this in the animals that have mid-line eyes. Such eyes are not used for direction-finding, nor do they project to a map. They are concerned with detecting the level of light intensity and adjusting the animal's activities to it. Thus the function of the median eyes of insects is to stimulate flight, but not to guide it. The pineal eye of lampreys controls the daily rhythm of colour change and the pineal of lizards is the receptor that controls temperature regulation (see Young, 1962b). All of these receptors lie in or near the mid-line.

8

MODELS IN THE BRAIN

1. *Some uses of models*

THE late Kenneth Craik of Cambridge taught us to say that
we learn by building models in the brain (1943). I shall try to
push the idea to the extent of describing in an octopus brain
the units out of which the model is built. There is enough
evidence to make us suspect that we shall find them in other
brains, including our own.

If this approach is to be useful it must be specific. We must
define clearly what we mean by a model in this connexion
and show how the conception may be developed and made
quantitative. Like most other words, this one has the advantages and disadvantages of many shades of meaning, but the
only alternative to using it is to adopt some word with no
particular connotations at all. For example, if we say that a
brain that has learnt contains an engram, we are, in effect,
only repeating that there must be in it some entity representing the situation. What more is meant by saying that the brain
contains a model?

A model is certainly a representation of something else,
and many representations, as we have seen, use some kind of
conventional code. Thus, at one extreme, a set of equations
may be a mathematical model, using suitable symbolism to
define the operations of a physical system, say a new rocket. A
working model or a child's toy imitate some, but not all, the
features of larger systems, by assembling parts made of other
materials. Analogue calculating machines, such as a differential
analyser, can obviously be described as models.

Like all representations in codes, models in the nervous
system are used for transmitting, storing, or manipulating
information that helps in making predictions by which

homeostasis is ensured. In particular, the conception often, though not necessarily, contains the idea of something that 'works'. An engineer makes a model of the structure he proposes to build, so that he may test it, on a small scale. Similarly the idea of a model in the brain is that it constitutes a toy that is yet a tool, an imitation world, which we can manipulate in the way that will suit us best, and so find how to manipulate the real world, which it is supposed to represent.

To recapitulate, when we say that the brain contains a 'model' we intend to emphasize the following points about the 'engrams' that are built up in the brain by learning. (1) They are formed by appropriate selection among a set of code units, predetermined, probably mainly by heredity. (2) They are used in making predictions that are useful for homeostasis. (3) The usefulness, at least of more elaborate models, is that they can be made to conduct, as it were, small-scale experiments within the head.

Perhaps you will see already that this concept can be quite powerful in describing how we use our brains and showing how they go wrong, for example if the model inadequately represents the environment or is inappropriately used for 'wishful thinking'. But we must not be too ambitious, certainly not at this early stage; our job is to see whether we can find any such model, and in particular to show what component elements it is made of. For the characteristic of models that I would particularly stress is that they are often constructed out of unit parts, components that are individually unlike those of the structure represented but can be assembled to make the finished, working model. I shall venture the hypothesis that the varied cells of the brain provide sets of such components, and that these are assembled during learning to make the model. The characteristics of each component are specified in the main by the forms of their dendritic branches.

The evidence for this hypothesis, slender as it is, comes from study of the brains and behaviour of octopuses and cats. In order to find the sort of model that is constructed in these brains we must first find out what the animals can do. We may then be able to discover what information they transmit and store in their nervous systems.

2. *Visual discrimination by octopuses*

Octopuses readily learn to come out to attack when one visual situation occurs and is followed by a food reward, but to stay at home for another that has in the past been associated

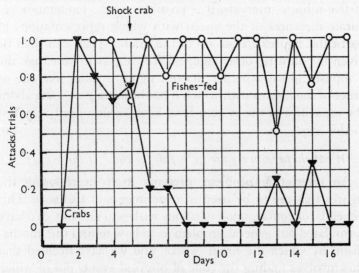

FIG. 33. Teaching an octopus to attack fishes (circles) but not crabs (triangles). For the first five days the octopus was allowed to eat either type of food when attacked. From the fifth day shocks were given for attacks at crabs but the octopus was allowed to eat the fish. Five trials with each form of food were given each day. The ordinates show the proportion of attacks on each day. (Boycott and Young, 1955.)

with a shock. Thus they can be trained to attack moving crabs but not fishes or the reverse (Fig. 33). In early experiments Boycott and I showed at alternate trials, first a crab alone, which the octopus was allowed to eat, then a crab with a white square, which produced a shock if it was attacked. The animals readily learnt this discrimination, although it is a complicated situation since the positive figure (crab) enters into both presentations. We were able to show that retention in the memory lasts well for several days, and that performance is still correct after prolonged anaesthesia with urethane, or electrical stimulation of the brain in various ways. After removal to a different tank the animals showed retention, but the accuracy of performance was reduced.

Using figures that the animals have presumably not seen before allows much greater flexibility in choice. By having sets of, say, ten animals, each shown a figure and given reward at five-minute intervals, it is possible to take moderately accurate measures of the speed with which representations of particular figures are set up in the brains. Tests can then be given by showing other figures. We can, as it were, ask the octopuses to say whether the test figure is more like one or other of the figures with which it has been trained. Data about the capacities of the system have been accumulated very fast in this way.

3. *What shapes can we use to 'break the code' of the brain?*

An interesting problem presents itself in choosing the figures that are to be used in experiments of this sort. This depends, of course, upon what one wishes to find out. We have formulated our general problem as to how to find the 'mechanism' by which the brain 'works' and we have decided that this involves finding the code of physical events out of which selection is made for transmission and storage within the nervous system.

In the procedures for code-breaking adopted by cryptographers the problem is to discover the relevant features of, say, ink-marks or electrical signals that are being used for communication. We are in a somewhat similar position as regards communication in the nervous system, since we know that the information is transmitted in a code of pulses, the nerve impulses. But this does not help so much as might be thought, because we have to deal not with one channel carrying the pulses, nor even with many similar ones, but with a large number of nerve fibres, which perhaps vary greatly in their properties. Moreover, there are only few data about the actual frequencies in given types of nerve fibre in response to a range of visual stimuli. Work such as that on coding in the visual system of the frog has shown what can be achieved by such an analysis (p. 32). This work indicates that the code structure is provided by the presence of a variety of channels, rather than by specific impulse frequencies.

We are, therefore, in the position of not knowing exactly what physical elements constitute the code for transmission, or the 'script' in the memory. There are various ways in which this situation can be met. Clearly a first requirement is to find out what the code is about. Experiments in which the powers of discrimination of the animals are tested are very well suited for this. It is relatively easy to test the response to a wide range of variables in animals kept under controlled conditions in the laboratory. Observations under natural conditions are, of course, extremely valuable in telling us what situations the animal responds to, but such observations are hard to control. At the other extreme, laboratory experiments in which responses of individual nerve fibres are used also tell us a great deal, but it is hard to make the presentation of the 'stimuli' to single units realistic and repeatable (though in some situations it can be done).

Discrimination experiments, then, may serve chiefly to tell us what properties of the world around are encoded by the nervous system. This is perhaps an obvious conclusion and still does not tell us very much about how to set about choosing which shapes to show to an animal. We can, of course, use those that seem to resemble the objects that the animal reacts to in its natural habitat. Thus, Boulet (1954) has studied the responses of cuttlefishes to a variety of 'prawn-like' objects. There is much to be said for this approach with a species that reacts to a small range of objects and perhaps mainly on an inherited basis. Crabs are perhaps the most important food objects for *Octopus vulgaris*, but there is little detailed information as to which features of a crab serve to release an attack. The visual analysing system is probably especially concerned with responding to movements of vertical and horizontal edges (p. 151), such as are provided by the moving legs of a crab and perhaps by its whole body. It has long been noticed that a crab (*Carcinus*) is in general not attacked as it falls through the water (when its legs are usually still). As soon as it touches the bottom the crab begins to run and it is then that the octopus pounces upon it.

Unfortunately study of the 'natural' prey does not carry us very far with the problem of what shapes to present to an animal such as an octopus that can learn to react appropriately to a wide variety of visual or tactile situations. No general solution to this problem seems to have been made. In our own work we have all the time been feeling our way by 'empirical' or 'intuitive' guesses as to what questions to ask the octopus. Indeed, we have found that the nature of the problem has only appeared as we proceeded.

We used at first figures with the same area and the same extent of outline, in order to avoid situations in which the discrimination could be made by estimating the amount of light reflected from the figures or the amount of stimulus given by their contours. Moreover, in nearly all the early experiments each figure was shown separately. Octopuses can be made to choose between one of two figures shown simultaneously (p. 174), but it has always seemed to me to be easier to consider the matching of each figure separately with its representation in the brain than the more complicated situation in which both are shown together. This may be only a peculiarity in my way of thinking about the process of matching that is involved in recognition.

The octopuses readily learned to attack vertical and not horizontal rectangles or the reverse, though if the figures were moved up and down the latter discrimination was slightly the more difficult. This was the first hint about the nature of the model that we were later to find in the brain—it has something to do with vertical and horizontal directions.

4. *Discrimination of shapes not differing in area or outline*

We were particularly concerned to demonstrate the possibility of discriminations based strictly on the 'shape' of the figures and not, for instance, on area. If one figure has a larger reflecting area than another they can be distinguished simply by the differences in total reflected light. Figures with different extent of outline may be discriminated by that factor and so on. It is not easy to discover a series of figures such that neither of these variables could be used. For example, no square and circle can have both the same area and same outline. This difficulty can, of course, be got over by testing, after training, with larger or smaller figures (p. 171).

However, we chose to study at first rectangles, all of the same area, but bent at right angles at either one or both ends, or straight (Table 2). Discrimination proved to be readily possible between any pairs of these and this cannot be based upon estimates of area or outline. There are, of course, differences in the number of angles as well as in what we may call the 'distribution' of the reflecting surfaces, which is one way of defining 'shape'.

TABLE 2

The results of training octopuses with various pairs of figures. In every case, except 6, the figures have the same area and extent of outline (Young, 1961).

	Figures		Errors (actual)			
Octopus	Positive (Food reward)	Negative (Shock)	Positive (60 trials)	Negative (60 trials)	Total (120 trials)	Errors (Percentage)
1	⌐	—	14	3	17	14·2
2	—	⌐	1	13	14	11·6
3	—	⌐	1	11	12	10·0
4	●	○	1	11	12	10·0
5	●	○	11	6	17	14·2
6	○	o	9	19	28	23·3
7	L	⌐	23	9	32	26·6
8	⌐	L	5	30	35	29·2
9	⌐	L	7	27	34	28·3
10	□	◇	34	13	47	39·2
11	oo	o o	37	15	52	43·3
12	••	• •	49	10	59	49·1

5. *Discrimination of other shapes*

In further experiments with a wide range of shapes, Boycott and I made a general exploration of the capacities of octopuses. More recently Sutherland and others have designed many experiments to test particular hypotheses about the coding system that is at work. Crosses are distinguished from squares and open from filled figures. Triangles and squares are distinct,

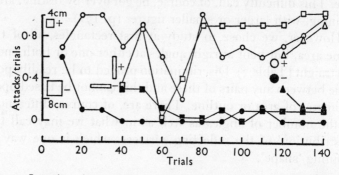

FIG. 34. Learning of several discriminations by an octopus. For the first thirty trails a small square was given with food and a large square with shock (if attacked). Then alternate trials with vertical and horizontal rectangles were introduced. This produced disturbance of the previously learned response, but by the 80th trial responses were mostly correct. Finally, reactions to black and white circles were also learned. (After Boycott and Young, 1957.)

also a square with its base horizontal and the same shown as a 'diamond'. The level of accuracy of response is lower with these more difficult discriminations and lower still for a circle and a square, which though very unlike to us, are nearly similar for an octopus. Results in simple experiments with various pairs of figures are shown in Table 2.

6. *Discrimination of several pairs of shapes*

Preliminary work has been done on the learning of several pairs of figures, showing an interesting interference, for example, in responses to large and small squares when vertical and horizontal rectangles are interspersed (Fig. 34). Clearly the representations for these figures in some way overlap or interfere. This might happen for various reasons; we shall suggest that it is due to the use of partly the same set of cells to encode the measurements of the figures to make the models that represent these situations. In the continuation of the above experiment addition of training with black and white circles interfered little with the other two discriminations, presumably because these differences are recorded by another set of cells, constituting what we may call a different section of the memory.

7. *Analysis of shapes along vertical and horizontal axes*

An important advance in understanding of the mechanism was Sutherland's demonstration that the animals are unable to recognize rectangles shown in oblique positions, although those that are vertical or horizontal are easily distinguished. This must indicate that some feature of the system is especially related to vertical and horizontal directions. Sutherland suggested that the analysing system counts horizontal extent of a shape at each point on the vertical axis and vertical extents on the horizontal axis. Each shape is thus converted into its horizontal and vertical projections (Fig. 35). He suggested that the analysis then proceeds by a mechanism that extracts some value such as the ratios of maximum horizontal and vertical extents to square root of area. With these ratios it is possible to explain the relative difficulties of some of the discriminations that the animals have been shown to make. Thus, vertical and horizontal rectangles are easily distinguished, as are triangles from squares or circles. Squares and diamonds and squares and circles are discriminated with greater difficulty and oblique rectangles little, if at all. Certain curious transfer results are also well explained. Animals trained to attack a square but not a horizontal rectangle, when shown a vertical rectangle treated it as a square. This seems at first to our way of thinking to be a failure by the animal to generalize, because all rectangles are not treated alike as we might think they should be. But this is to misunderstand the nature of the mechanism that the octopus uses, which measures vertical and horizontal extents. Consider the ratios of vertical and horizontal rectangles and squares (Table 3). The vertical rectangle differs from the horizontal in the same

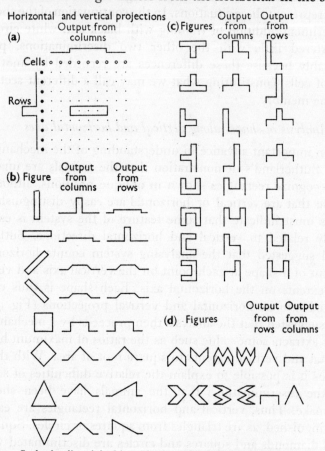

FIG. 35. Sutherland's original hypothesis of shape discrimination.
(a) the small dots represent the retinal array with a horizontal rectangle projected onto it. Open circles at the top represent cells specific to each column, filled circles at side cells specific to each row. The cells for the rows and columns are supposed to be connected to distinct outputs (Sutherland, 1957a). (b) the outputs produced by various rectangles, squares, diamonds, and triangles (Sutherland, 1958). (c) mirror images (Sutherland, 1960a). (d) figures that should be confused. (Sutherland, 1959.)

direction as the square does, but to an even greater extent. It is, as it were, more square than a square, as recorded by this system. This would be a bad defect in a machine designed to do geometry, but the brains of octopuses nevertheless help to make their possessors some of the most successful animals in the sea. As Sutherland points out, the octopus (or any other animal) must discriminate between figures by measuring along some dimensions, in this case vertical and horizontal extents. We, in a sense, confuse ourselves by speaking of comparisons between 'shapes', without specifying the dimensions along which they are measured.

TABLE 3

The form of various figures, expressed as vertical and horizontal extent in relation to area.

Figure	Horiz. extent $\sqrt{\text{area}}$	Vert. extent $\sqrt{\text{area}}$
□	1·0	1·0
◇	1·4	1·4
○	1·1	1·1
△	2·1	1·8
▯	0·4	2·2
▭	2·2	0·4
╱	0·5	0·5

8. Outline solution of the problem of the visual coding system

Sutherland's original scheme has met with some interesting criticisms. Alternative explanations by Deutsch and Dodwell will be discussed later. Sutherland himself has carried out further experiments to test the consequences of his theory. Many of its predictions have been verified but some have not, and accordingly he has produced a modified version (p. 185). However, many of the results found with octopuses have later been shown to be true also of rats, goldfishes, monkeys, and children. That a hypothesis should be much discussed and should stimulate experiment is the best evidence of its vitality. The present example illustrates well the thesis that advance in 'understanding' of the brain proceeds by the process of building models of it.

Sutherland's demonstration that the octopus is unable to discriminate oblique rectangles led to the suggestion that detectors of vertical and horizontal extent are of special significance for the coding (1957a). It was soon possible to link this suggestion with the anatomical studies of the optic lobes that I was making. These showed that the fibres of certain layers do not turn and twist and run hither and thither, but follow single directions for long distances. Stimulated by Sutherland's results I measured the frequencies of fibres in different directions and found more in the horizontal and vertical than in other directions. Looking then with the Golgi technique I found that many of the cells have orientated dendritic fields and this suggested that they could serve as detectors of lines of excitation in particular directions. Meanwhile, fields of this sort were discovered by microelectrode recording in the cortex of the cat (Hubel and Wiesel, 1959).

Such orientated dendritic fields may thus provide the code elements from which selection is made in at least some sorts of visual pattern discrimination by octopuses and other animals. In subsequent chapters I shall try to show how these fields provide the units out of which the model is constructed in the brain. To show this it is necessary to give a reasonable account of how particular responses to given shapes could be built up. We shall try first with the single example of discrimination between vertical and horizontal rectangles. To explain this would already be a considerable advance. Further studies of other shapes, especially by Sutherland (1963b), have shown that, as might be expected, other factors besides horizontal and vertical extent are important, even in octopuses. We shall discuss these later and also the possibility that the animal has to learn which analysing mechanisms to use in a particular case.

We shall also have to show that the model proposed is able to deal with the other complications that are met with in learning experiments. It will be shown, for example, that it can explain the phenomena that are seen when cues are reversed or when cues that interfere with each other are introduced (Chapter 10). We shall also have to deal with the most important phenomena of generalization—by which animals that have learned to discriminate between two figures of, say, a particular size, are able to recognize similar shapes at other sizes.

Most difficult of all will be the attempt to show that a model made out of such elements in the brain could be used as a toy or experimental tool, that it could be the basis of what we commonly call 'thinking'. This clearly could not be done on a basis of experiments with octopuses, but speculation about it may be worth while (Chapter 19).

Whether or not this approach succeeds in dealing with these more difficult problems, its real value is that it is rooted in certain indisputable facts about the structure of the nervous system, which must now be described.

9

THE OPTIC LOBES,
THE SEAT OF THE MODEL

1. *The plan of the optic lobes*

IN the optic lobes of an octopus we meet the first great section of the visual computing system, a mass of some 50 million neurons behind each eye (Fig. 36). The output from the optic lobes proceeds through the optic tract essentially to two sorts of centres: (1) the higher motor centres, which determine that particular behavioural acts shall be performed, and (2) the superior frontal and vertical lobe system, which sends its output back to the optic lobe, and is concerned with distributing the signals that indicate food or trauma and in determining the level of motivation to attack or retreat (Chapter 12). The optic lobes themselves can be regarded as the classifying and encoding system and as the seat of the memory.

In order to perform these functions they receive not only visual impulses but also signals from the taste and pain receptors, both directly and after multiplication and distribution by the superior frontal and vertical lobes. Since such signals are an essential part of learning, interfering with these lobes greatly influences the performance of learned reactions. Nevertheless, the evidence is that the actual memory record is in the optic lobes.

In trying to discover 'how the optic lobe works' we may do well to look at it first as a whole, as seen in a section at a low magnification (Fig. 36). At the outside are two regular layers of cells, the inner and outer granule layers, separated by a plexiform zone of fibres, elaborately layered. This outer region of the lobe, known as the deep retina, immediately recalls the nervous layers of the vertebrate retina. The similarity in arrangement can surely not be accidental. If we can find anything about the coding system that operates here in an octopus we may find something at least of the principles used in ourselves.

From the deep retina bundles of fine nerve fibres proceed toward the centre, at first more or less parallel and then interchanging with ever more widely distant parts of the lobe, so that the cells at the centre must come under the influence of

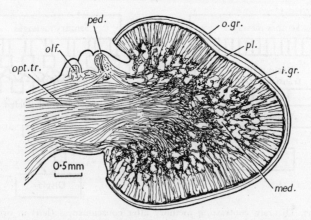

FIG. 36. Drawing of a transverse section across the optic lobe of an octopus. i.gr., inner granule cell layer; med., medulla; o.gr., outer granule layer; opt.tr., optic tract; olf., olfactory lobe; ped., peduncle lobe; pl. plexiform zone.

impulses from almost all parts of the retina. They in turn then activate the motor centres.

The plan of the lobe thus allows first for interaction between near neighbours and then between those farther and farther apart. Some plan of this sort must surely be the basis of all systems that allow response to 'formed stimuli'. Millions of words have been written on this problem of *'gestalt'*. In essence it becomes simply the problem of how the mechanism sets up a response appropriate to the stimulation of a particular array of points on the receptor surface. The most important equipment for doing so is a system such as the optic lobes that allows signals from points on many parts of the surface to interact. We can almost 'see' the solution to the *'gestalt* problem' by looking at a section of the optic lobe. It is interesting to compare this plan with a scheme devised by Barlow (1959) to express a possible means of producing a memory system with storage before display, giving what the engineer calls an optimum coding (Fig. 37). This essentially involved rejecting the redundancy of the information at a series of stages. The system of filtering at each stage must, of course, be so designed as to remove only those items that are

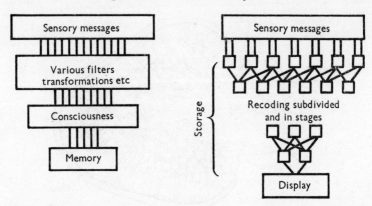

FIG. 37. Diagram contrasting memory after consciousness (left) in orthodox scheme with storage before display (right) in optimal coding scheme. (From Barlow, 1959.)

irrelevant for the system of coding that is to be adopted. Taylor (1957) has discussed how this may be done and constructed a model to do it, operating essentially as we believe the octopus does.

This, however, we shall discuss later. The approach we are using in this chapter is to look at the general layout and try to obtain an idea of the plan on which it is built. When one thinks of the various patterns of all the nerve centres that one has looked at it is perhaps rather shocking not to have thought more about this before. Perhaps this has been because there have been so few man-made models of comparable complexity with which to make comparison. Also, perhaps, biologists have been given too little opportunity to train themselves to understand the principles of design of known machines.

Even if it is stimulating to try to guess how a machine works by looking at its general arrangement we certainly shall not get very far without further knowledge of its individual parts. Fortunately there is a good deal of information about the anatomy of the cells and fibres of the optic lobes of cephalopods, though unfortunately almost none about their electrical activities. Much was provided by Ramon y Cajal, working with *Sepia* and basing his analysis on the earlier studies of Lenhossék (1896) and Kopsch (1899). Further studies of *Octopus* itself have suggested that certain of the cells provide the units out of which the models that produce the coding are built (Young, 1960*a*, 1961).

The optic nerve fibres pass through the outer granule cell layer to a plexiform zone. Here most of them end and come into synaptic relationship with fibres of at least four types. The zone is elaborately stratified (Fig. 38). We may recognize four layers in which the fibres run mainly in the tangential plane, that is, at right angles to the entering optic nerve fibres. Between these tangential layers the fibres are mainly radial, including, of course, the optic nerve fibres themselves. The fibres that the optic nerve fibres meet in the plexiform zone include: (1) short branches of the amacrine cells of the outer and inner granule cell layers, (2) collateral branches of cells with efferent fibres proceeding to the retina, (3) dendritic branches of cells whose axons carry excitation onwards deeper into the lobe, (4) endings of axons conducting centrifugally from cells placed more centrally, either in the same or the opposite optic lobe or in the vertical lobe system or from the centres for the fibres for taste and pain.

2. *Endings of the optic nerve fibres*

The endings of the optic nerve fibres have been classified into three types (Fig. 39). About half of them end in swellings in the outermost radial layer. A second type shows swellings in this layer but also passes on to end with terminal bulbs in the inner tangential layers. The third type has branches but no swellings in the plexiform zone and then passes on to end in the inner granule cell layer.

The swellings in the outer radial layer form a system of closely packed bags, filled with synaptic vesicles (Fig. 40).

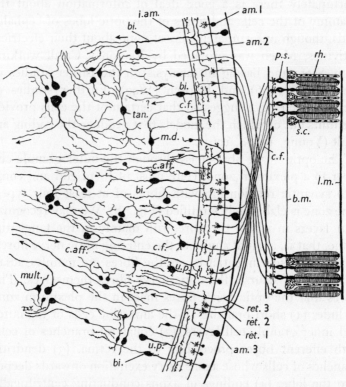

Fig. 38. Diagram illustrating the connexions of the outer part of the optic lobe. The connexions with the retina are also shown.

am., 1, 2, 3, amacrine cells of the outer granule cell layer. These cells have no axons; b.m., basal membrane; bi., bipolar cells, these cells probably conduct away from the plexiform zone; c.f., centrifugal cell of the inner granular layer; c.aff., afferent to the plexiform layer from the central regions; i.am., amacrine cells of the inner granular layer; l.m., limiting membrane of retina; m.d., cell with many dendrites proceeding outwards; mult., small multipolar cells; p.s., proximal segment; ret., 1–3, retinal nerve fibres of three types; rh., rhabdome; s.c., supporting cell; tan., tangential cell of outer medulla; u.p., unipolar cells with a fibre running to the plexiform zone and axons running from this zone. The arrows indicate the probable direction for the conduction of nerve impulses within the cells (Young, 1962*d*).

Into these bags penetrate twigs from other cells, presumably including the amacrines. The twigs carry the thickenings that

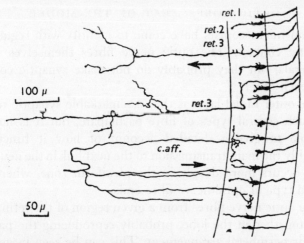

FIG. 39. Drawings of the three types of endings of the retinal nerve fibres in the optic lobe, as seen after Golgi–Kopsch staining. The type labelled ret. 1 ends only in the first radial layer; ret. 2 extends to the deeper parts of the plexiform zone, and ret. 3 passes beyond the plexiform zone to end in branches more deeply. A fibre reaching to the plexiform zone from a central source is also shown (c.aff.).

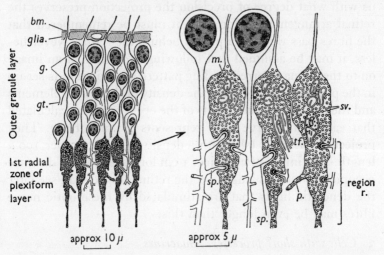

FIG. 40. Outer layer of optic lobe of *Octopus* as seen by low-power electron-microscopy. Scales approximate. The optic nerve fibres enter between the cells of the outer granule layer and then swell out into bags full of synaptic vesicles. These then make contact with the dendritic spines of the granule cells. (Dilly, Gray, and Young, 1963.)

bm., basement membrane; g., granule cells; gt., granule cell trunk; m., mitochondria; p., projecting twig from one bag to another; region r., region of spine contacts with optic axon presynaptic bags; sp., spine contact with presynaptic bag; sv., synaptic vesicle; tf., tunnel fibre.

electron-microscopists have come to identify with regions of synaptic contact. The optic nerve fibres themselves carry collaterals, but they probably do not make synaptic contact with each other.

The outer radial layer is thus a remarkable synaptic region in which several types of fibre participate, but it is not yet possible to give a detailed account of how it functions. Probably the main transmission to the next link in the neuronal chain occurs more deeply in the plexiform zone, where the second type of optic nerve fibre ends.

The optic nerve fibres from a given region of the retina end close together in the lobe, probably reproducing the pattern of their peripheral arrangement. This can be seen in general from the fact that after section of a few optic nerves there is a sharp boundary in the plexiform layer between normal fibres and those that have degenerated. However, this does not tell us with what degree of precision the projection preserves the retinal arrangement. Moreover, it must be remembered that the fibres pass through a plexus behind the retina. Nevertheless, it may be assumed that following projection of an image on to the retina a corresponding pattern of excitation is set up in the plexiform layer. From the density of the retinal elements and the dioptric arrangements of the eye it has been calculated that each optic nerve fibre represents 1 min. of arc. They project to the optic lobe with a density of some 30 per 100 μ length. The image of an object 1 cm long seen at 1 m distance occupies about this length on the retina. As we shall see later the dendritic fields that are stimulated by these optic nerve fibres may be even longer than this.

3. Cells with short processes. Amacrines

The cells on either side of the plexiform layer are perhaps concerned with the emphasizing of contours or rejection of some redundant features of the output. The outer granule cells have fibres that proceed to varying depths in the plexiform layer, but do not extend beyond it. The innermost and smallest of them have a very few branches, limited to the outer radial layer (Fig. 41). No single one of these branches seems to constitute an 'axon'. They thus resemble the amacrine cells that are so numerous in the retinae of some vertebrates.

Proceeding outwards the granule cells become larger, with branches that spread to greater depths and over wider extents within the plexiform layer. Many of them have twigs in the outer radial layer, as well as their deeper branches, but some have one main trunk dividing only in the deeper parts of the plexiform zone.

The function of these cells with many equal branches can hardly be to conduct digital signals by action potentials. Presumably the fact that those proceeding deeper also spread more widely is a significant feature for their functioning. It might perhaps produce the effect that contours at greater distances apart produce excitation at greater depth in the plexiform layer. Thus the three inner tangential layers could possibly be detectors for three ranges of length (see

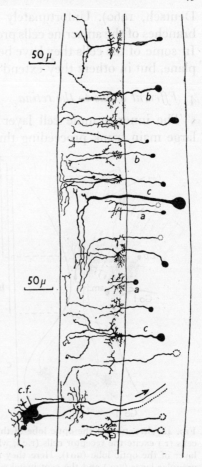

FIG. 41. Drawings of cells of the outer granule layer as seen after Golgi–Kopsch staining.

a, cells with processes limited to the first radial layer; *b*, small cells with two branches; *c*, larger cells spreading widely in the deeper tangential layers; c.f., centrifugal fibre.

This picture is a composite from many drawings. The scale covers a slight range, as shown by the changing thickness of the plexiform zone. The two scales shown indicate the range (Young, 1962.).

Deutsch, 1960). Unfortunately it is not known whether the branches of the amacrine cells proceed equally in all directions. In some of the cells they have been seen to lie mainly in one plane, but in others they extend (? equally) in all directions.

4. *Efferent axons to the retina*

The inner granule cell layer contains many cells with a large main trunk proceeding through the plexiform layer to

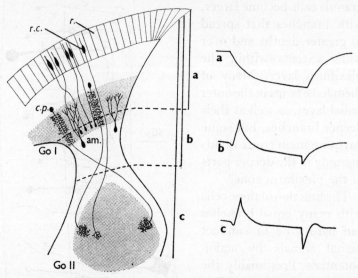

FIG. 42. Structure of the optic lobe of the blow-fly (*Calliphora*). The retinula cells (r.) excite the receptor cells (r.c.), whose axons conduct to the outermost layer of the optic lobe (GO I). Here they meet the amacrine cells of the inner granular layer (am.) and the centripetal cells of the outer granular layer (c.p.). The axons of the last-named run to the second optic ganglion (GO II).

At the right are shown the action potentials recorded on illumination (*a*) from the isolated retina, (*b*) from the retina and outer optic lobe (GO I), and (*c*) the whole optic system. (After Autrum.)

the optic nerves and thus to the retina (Fig. 41). They have numerous collateral branches in the plexiform zone, often in several of the layers. They sometimes, also, carry several short dendrite-like branches close to the cell body and there may be a second axon-like fibre proceeding a short distance towards the centre of the optic lobe.

Presumably these cells are excited through the collateral branches in the plexiform layer and carry impulses to the plexus at the base of the retinal cells. Nothing is known of the details of their synaptic endings there, but there is good reason to suppose that they are also concerned with the sharpening of the effects of contours. Similar cells occur in the optic lobe of insects and Autrum (1958) has shown that the time course of retinal potentials becomes longer if these cells are removed (Fig. 42). They are conspicuous in insects that can follow a high flicker rate (bees, blow-flies), but absent in those that cannot (cockroaches). It is interesting to speculate on the significance of the second, axon-like, fibre that proceeds inwards from some of these cells in octopuses.

5. *Cells conducting inwards from the plexiform layer. Classifiers of orientation and length*

The shapes of the cells that carry excitation onwards from the plexiform zone probably play a fundamental part in the coding system. The cell bodies lie at various depths within the lobe and send dendrites up into the tangential layers of the plexiform zone and axons deeper into the lobe. The shapes and sizes of their dendritic fields probably constitute the means by which the orientation and length in different directions of figures are measured. Hence they may be called classifiers of orientation and length. The dendritic fields vary greatly both in extent and form. They are not arranged at random but show signs of an orientation mainly in the vertical and horizontal directions.

The simplest of these cells are bipolar (Fig. 38) with a thick apical dendrite (20 μ), branching out in one or more of the tangential layers of the plexus. The axon is thinner (5 μ) and proceeds inwards to break up into relatively few beaded terminal branches. These axons proceed to a depth that is probably roughly proportional to the extent of the superficial dendritic field of the cell. Thus the axons of the smaller cells, lying near the surface, end more superficially and those of the large cells deeper. However, it has proved very difficult, for obvious reasons, to obtain good estimates of this relationship, which unfortunately, therefore, remains uncertain.

Other cells have numerous dendritic branches streaming up towards the surface, so that they are influenced from a number of distinct points in the plexiform zone (Fig. 38). Still others are unipolar cells, with a trunk that turns into one of the tangential layers and carries collateral dendritic twigs there before turning inwards again to produce one or several axons leading towards the centre of the lobe. This apparently strange course is in fact that of a typical invertebrate unipolar nerve-cell—sending its trunk into the neuropil (plexiform zone).

The tangential layers thus contain the dendrites that are excited by the incoming optic nerve fibres. They therefore remain intact after previous surgical interruption of the optic nerves. Tangential sections of the plexuses show that these dendrites run nearly straight for surprisingly long distances. They may bend a little, but seldom turn through a sharp angle. Moreover, they do not run equally in all directions. The greatest number of individual branches run in the vertical direction. They are numerous also in the horizontal direction, but there are fewer obliques. In the relatively thin sections of material stained with Cajal's silver method it is not possible to say which are the major trunks of the dendritic fields and which are minor branches.

The arrangement of the dendrites of individual cells can be seen in Golgi-stained sections cut tangential to the surface of the lobe (Fig. 43). The dendritic fields vary but many of them are oval, with the long axis mainly in either the horizontal or vertical direction. Unfortunately it is rare to find exactly suitable sections and the sample that has been studied is not large enough to allow any more detailed statement about these fields. They are certainly very large, some of them extending as much as 400 μ away from the main trunk. They thus cover areas as large as those likely to be influenced by the discharges of optic nerve fibres produced by the contours of the images even of large objects on the retina.

The fields vary greatly in extent, but no accurate measure of their sizes and numbers is available. There are 10–20 million optic nerve fibres entering the surface of the optic lobe. The latter contains a total of 50 million cells but most of these are small. The centre of the lobe (all of it that is except the outer granule layer) contains 2·2 million cells with nuclei greater

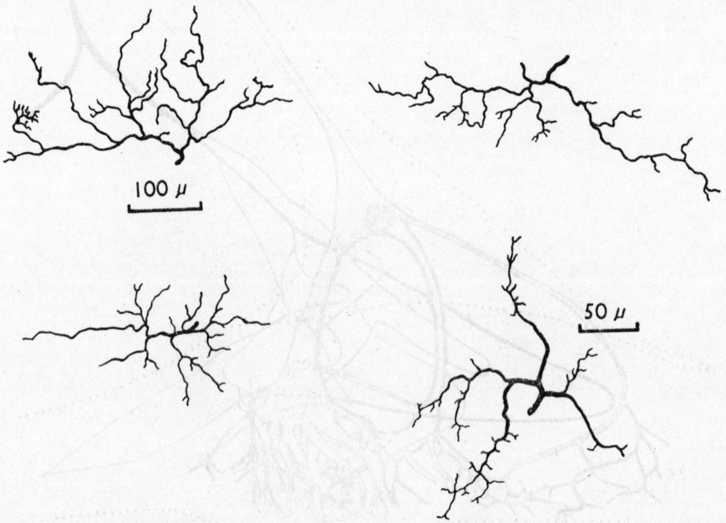

FIG. 43. Drawings made from photographs of dendritic fields of cells in the plexiform zone of the optic lobe of *Octopus*. Three of the cells shown have oval fields with their main axis in the horizontal plane. At bottom right is a part of one field at higher magnification to show the collateral twigs at the tips of the branches. Golgi stain and tangential plane of section.

than 5 μ in diameter. This number includes all these classifying cells as well as many of the memory storage cells later to be described.

The dendrites of the classifying cells, spreading in the tangential layers of the plexiform zone, carry collateral twigs at intervals, which it is reasonable to suppose are related by synaptic contacts with the optic nerve fibres that end in these layers. The twigs are more numerous towards the tips of the branches and it is presumably here that generator potentials are set up and conducted electrotonically down the dendrites

to initiate action potentials in the axons. Although there are
no data about the electrical characteristics of these cells it
is probable that they are similar to those of dendrite-like
systems elsewhere. Thus Kuffler (1958) has shown that in the

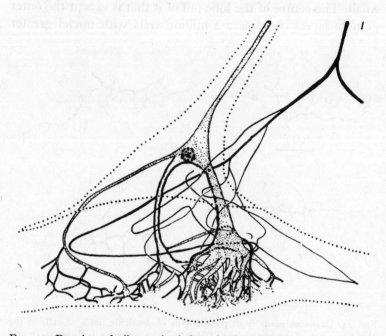

FIG. 44. Drawing of silver-stained fast-adapting receptor cell in crayfish.
1, inhibitory nerve. (From Kuffler after Florey and Florey.)

branches of the stretch-receptor cells of Crustacea (Fig. 44)
the tips of the dendrites are the transducers, generating up
to 40 mV potential when stretched. The inside of the cell
is at a potential of 70 mV, and 10 mV depolarization at the root
of the axon releases an action potential. This is provided in
life by the summed potentials conducted electrotonically from
the dendrites, which are not themselves excited by the potentials they produce.

Bullock and his colleagues (1958) have shown similar
phenomena in the much-branched dendritic systems of the
ganglia of crustacea, which were described, as were the stretch

receptors, by Alexandrowicz. As Bullock remarks, several different sets of pacemaker, generator, and local potentials are known to exist in such dendritic systems and may summate to produce what he calls 'integrative phenomena'. In the present terminology it is these graded additions (and subtractions) that provide the operations of encoding and computing in the analogue.

The details of the distribution of synaptic points on the dendritic tree, and of the diameters and electrical characteristics of the latter, must be essential features of the system. Little can be said about this at present. The dendritic twigs are most numerous near the tips, where the potentials they produce are presumably less effective at the axon. It may be that the synaptic points are arranged logarithmically or exponentially, proceeding away from the main trunk. Such plans could ensure the encoding of length into frequency of nerve impulses in a way highly suitable for additions or subtractions. In the present account, however, it is simply assumed that each cell acts as a detector for length in one direction. The crowding of the synaptic contacts at the tips suggests a mechanism ensuring the response of each cell to a particular length (presumably with a reasonable safety factor).

There is as yet no information about the discharge characteristics of these classifying cells. It may well be that, as Hubel and Wiesel put it, they 'look at' oval visual fields, perhaps with excitatory centre and inhibitory periphery, or the reverse (p. 162). For the present discussion we shall assume only that each field is caused to discharge impulses when a contour of the right orientation and length falls upon it. The 'alphabet' or code-set thus consists of a set of these fields, with various orientations, and lengths, and perhaps also breadths.

An especially significant feature of these dendrite systems in the octopus is that they are orientated mainly in the vertical and horizontal directions, which are known already to be the directions especially concerned in the coding of the visual input. There are various ways in which such dendrites may be used to act as detectors of the extent of contours in specific directions and even of the ratio between these. Many of the dendritic fields spread out at two different depths in the plexiform zone. It has not so far been possible to discover whether these fields at different depths extend in different directions (this is obviously technically very difficult to discover, since the direction of the field can only be seen in tangential sections). If the fields have different orientations at different depths the cells could serve as detectors of particular horizontal/vertical proportions.

6. *Failure of recognition after alteration of the position of the eyes*

If the mechanism for the recognition of shapes operates in the way suggested there are certain corollaries that can be tested experimentally. Perhaps the most obvious is that the capacity to recognize shapes correctly should depend upon the position of the eyes. This could be tested by surgical rotation of the eyes after training, but a more elegant method has been adopted by Wells (1960). The position of the eyes is controlled by the statocysts; if the latter have been removed the position of the eye varies with that of the head. It is therefore possible to train animals to discriminate vertical and horizontal rectangles and then, after removal of the statocysts, to test performance with the eye in various positions (Fig. 45).

When the animal sits on a horizontal surface the eye is held normally, as can be seen from the pupil, and responses to the rectangles are in the main correct. When the octopus sits on the side of the tank the eye is held at right angles to its normal position and responses are incorrect, or, as would be expected, actually 'perverse'. This experiment thus provides striking proof that discrimination is performed by a system that has a definite orientation in relation to the vertical and horizontal directions.

7. *Cells at the centre of the optic lobe. Memory storage cells and motor cells*

The centre of the optic lobe is occupied by a mass of islands of nerve-cells, separated by tracts containing dendrites, axons, and synaptic junctions. In each island of cells there are a few large ones with many spreading dendrites, and many small cells with numerous short branches but with no obvious axon. The axons of some of the large cells proceed into the optic

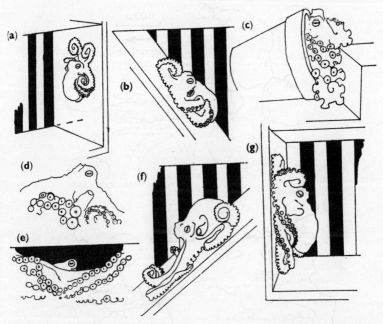

FIG. 45. Orientation of the eyes before and after bilateral statocyst removal. In unoperated animals the slit-like pupil normally remains horizontal or very nearly so (*a–e*), whatever the position of the octopus. After removal of both statocysts this ceases to be true, and the orientation of the retina, as indicated by the position of the pupil, thereafter depends upon the position in which the animal is sitting (*f–g*). (Wells, 1960*a*.)

tract and are presumably the efferent fibres, reaching to the higher motor centres of the basal lobes. Many have axons that end within the lobe itself. A further important set are those that send impulses to the superior frontal-vertical lobe system. Others proceed in an optic commissure to the opposite optic lobe. Unfortunately there is no evidence at present to help us to identify these various types of cell within the lobe.

The large cells of the medulla of the optic lobe have dendritic trees of very varied form (Fig. 46). Some of them send many branches up towards the surface, others spread mainly tangentially. It will be a long time before it is possible to define the shapes of these fields adequately, which is, of course,

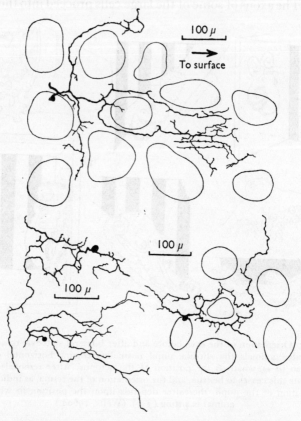

FIG. 46. Cells from the centre of the optic lobe of *Octopus* to show various forms of dendritic tree. (From Young, 1962*d*.)

very difficult to do since they spread so widely, and at various depths. If, however, the trees (or some of them) have branches of different extents in different directions and at different depths then they might serve as detectors of particular vertical/horizontal ratios, if it is true that the cells conducting away from the plexiform layer send axons reaching to depths that are proportional to the extent of their dendritic fields.

This is only one of many ways in which these cells at the centre of the lobe may allow for computations with the data encoded by the more superficial cells. We are handicapped so much by ignorance that further speculation is not profitable. We do not know whether the representation of length is in the form of projection to different depths, as has been suggested here for simplicity. It may be that there is also some form of pulse-frequency modulated code in the axons of the classifying cells, these deeper cells of the lobe serving to add (or subtract). Moreover, we do not know how much the dendrites of these deeper cells influence each other, nor the effect upon them of the numerous accompanying multi-polar cells.

8. *A possible learning system in the optic lobes*

For the sake of discussion it may be useful to suggest that a very simple scheme such as that of Fig. 47 operates. The large cells at the centre of the lobe are considered to provide the mechanism responsible for storage of a record that figures with particular horizontal or vertical extents (or other characteristics) have been associated with conditions that were 'good' or 'bad' for the octopus. Three types of cell are involved. Those immediately deep to the classification cells are memory storage cells, which have alternative outputs to what we may call motor cells, or command cells, lying still nearer to the centre of the lobe. The process of learning consists in closing one of the output pathways of each storage cell. The third cell type, multipolar cells, provide the source of inhibition of that pathway.

Although much is hypothetical we know that storage is a function of the optic lobes. Electrical stimulation shows that they also constitute a motor centre, from which various action patterns can be elicited (Boycott, 1961). The multipolar cells are there in large numbers. The components for a system such as that proposed are therefore all known to be present.

The final outcome of the calculation is to be a decision whether to attack or retreat. Therefore all through the system the cells must be potentially capable of exciting the axons that produce both of these movements. The diagram is arranged to show learning to attack a horizontal but not a vertical figure, or the reverse. Classifying cells at the surface, with the form

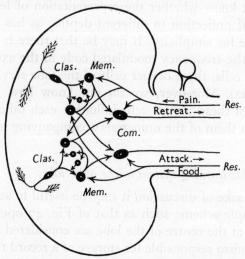

FIG. 47. Diagram to show the method suggested for encoding and storing information in the optic lobe of an octopus. There are systems for rejecting redundancy in the retina and plexiform layers to the left of the figure. The large classifying cells (Clas.) shown with spreading dendritic trees, then record the extent of vertical and horizontal contouring. Each of these has access to higher motor (command) cells (Com.), producing either attack or retreat, through the memory storage cells (Mem.). These pathways only operate if the 'results indicators' (Res.) are active. The operation of any one pathway closes the alternative, through the inhibitory collaterals and small cells.

of bipolar cells, have spreading dendritic fields with synaptic connexions more numerous at the tips. For the sake of simplicity it is considered that there are two sets of cells, detectors of varying horizontal and vertical extents according to the sizes of their dendritic trees. No cells are included that extract the ratios of horizontal to vertical, though these may well be present. Instead it has been considered that each detector has access to both 'attack' and 'retreat' pathways, through the storage cells associated with them.

The system must be initially biased with some tendency to attack any object that moves in the visual field. As we have seen, an 'unsophisticated' octopus makes such attacks, though with long delays. Whether the attack is repeated when a similar object again appears must obviously be made to depend upon the outcome. If food is obtained, then the probability that the 'attack' channel will be used on the next occasion is to be increased. If there is no food, or if there is pain, then the channel that leads from the particular classifying cell to a command neuron for retreat should be made more probable.

These effects are, of course, produced by the receptors that signal 'food' or 'pain'. The details of the operation of this system are discussed later. We say that these receptors collectively indicate 'results' or 'rewards' (if we are prepared to consider that a 'reward' may be negative, p. 197). An important point to emphasize is that the signals of results arrive a long time after the classifying, memory, and command cells have initiated the attack. Therefore, in order that the signals of results shall be fed into the right channel, the 'address' of the latter must somehow be kept in the system during the delay period. We shall suggest that this is one function of the superior-frontal/vertical lobe system.

If this analysis is correct, the question that we should most like to have answered is 'How do the signals of results change the probability of use of the channels in the future?' It may be by facilitating transmission along one of them, and/or by inhibiting transmission along the other. As a further variant, the facilitation may be by removal of a pre-existing inhibition (see p. 284). There is so little to tell us the answer that speculation is of little value. However, the analysis at least begins to tell us what to look for and where to look. We shall consider this further in Chapter 17.

In Fig. 47 the signals of results are shown as if fed to the memory storage cells. Collaterals of the axons of each of these memory cells are able to inhibit the action of the opposite member of the pair. It is assumed that this inhibition involves the small cells that accompany the larger ones in the islands. These small cells may possibly act as commutators, producing the appropriate inhibitory mediator, perhaps by presynaptic inhibition (see Eccles, 1961).

Supposing that a classifying cell for 'large horizontal' is activated shortly before food reward occurs. When the food reward signals reach the storage cells, besides activating the connexion that increases the tendency to attack they will close by inhibition the pathway for 'retreat'. This closure is supposed to be the action that constitutes the memory change. For simplicity it may be considered to occur immediately, and completely, after occurrence of suitably prolonged activity in the memory cell in question. One of the two possible outputs of the corresponding classifying cell is thus blocked and that cell becomes a predictor that attacks following visual stimulation of large horizontal fields will be followed by food.

If this were the mechanism it would not, of course, follow that 'learning' would instantaneously appear complete. Upon each occasion of presentation certain classifying and storage cells would be activated and hence 'selected'. The gradual process of learning would consist in the accumulation of sufficient of them to ensure a reliable response. The effective 'strength' of any memory would thus depend on the number of neurons whose output had been determined (see Wells and Wells, 1957b). However, it may well be that the closure of any given unwanted pathway is not an all-or-nothing event on one occasion of learning. In many ways it is attractive to consider that learning is a form of growth process, increasing or decreasing the probability of conduction in a given pathway. The fact that we do not know whether to look for an all-or-nothing event emphasizes again the ignorance that persists about the nature of the changes that occur on each learning occasion.

In our scheme there must also be some mechanism for ensuring that storage neurons other than those immediately stimulated are altered, that is for 'generalization'. Discriminations that have been learned with only one eye can be performed with the other (p. 167). The possible mechanism for this and other forms of transfer and generalization is discussed later. It may well be that following the immediate receptor event a process occurs that stores the essential features of it in a 'dynamic' or cyclical form and at the same time serves to spread it to reach further units (p. 213).

Whatever form the conditioning effect takes it must consist in a change of the probability of conduction in particular pathways. The question of the physiological or anatomical nature of this change is perhaps the greatest of all problems in learning. We are approaching it now by trying to discover where in the system it is likely to occur. In the scheme presented this might be supposed to be at a relatively small number of synapses in the storage systems. By looking closely at the actual forms of the cells that are involved we begin to see two of the principles that the coding system uses. Cells with long spreading dendrites provide the encoders. They make the classification by the spatial distribution of their branches. The numerous small cells among the large ones perhaps essentially provide the switching system between alternative pathways, by inhibiting one of them.

Of course a system as simple as this could only serve to learn the simplest of responses, for example to attack when classifying neurons of a particular type are activated. If an animal is to learn to recognize more complex features there must be means of allowing for interaction between the activities of various combinations of the classifying cells. The problem of how such combinations are allowed for in the nervous system has occupied many workers (see Uttley, 1961). We shall later consider the particular solution that has been suggested by W. K. Taylor. In order to allow for many possible combinations it would be necessary for learning changes to occur in numerous cells. We should not be able to pin-point it as we can at least in principle, in the simple example of learning to attack (or avoid) a figure with one particular characteristic. This emphasizes the advantage of studying in the first instance the very simplest possible example of learning, namely to perform some single act. Even this as we have seen is a less simple affair than is usually supposed. Learning to perform one action involves learning not to do the opposite one. Until we can make testable hypotheses about the physiological mechanism of simple conditioning we are not likely to understand how more complicated logical operations are performed. These are elementary principles that should have been clear at least since Pavlov's work. Yet there has still been very little investigation directed to finding the change that occurs at each occasion of learning.

9. *Evidence of similar analysing mechanisms in vertebrates*

It is obviously of the greatest interest to consider whether a mechanism like that suggested for *Octopus* might operate for the recognition of visual forms in other animals. There is some evidence available about the orientation of the cells in the vertebrate retina, and elsewhere in the visual system. It is usually supposed that mammalian cones are arranged in a random pattern, but many of the photographs given by Polyak (1957) show them arranged in sets of parallel rows, perhaps with some sort of spiral pattern. They do not form a regular hexagonal array, but it certainly cannot be assumed that they are at random. In fishes the arrangement is much more regular and in some follows a rectangular pattern, orientated in the vertical and horizontal axes as in *Octopus* (Lyall, 1957).

Nearly all the investigation of the dendrites of the bipolar and ganglion cells of the retina of vertebrates has been made on radial sections. These, of course, cannot show whether there is any orientation in the directions at right angles to the light path. In the primate fovea the cones are connected by midget bipolars, each with a single parasol ganglion cell and optic nerve fibre, so the question of orientation hardly arises.

However, the larger parasol bipolars and garland and giant ganglion cells make contact with hundreds or thousands of bipolars and thus cones (and rods) of the fovea and perifovea (Fig. 48). These dendritic trees cover areas equivalent to quite large portions of the visual field (350 μ spread for a giant ganglion cell). It is generally assumed that their summative

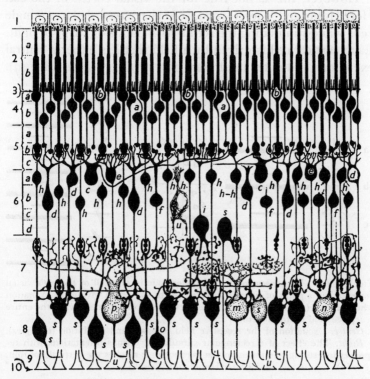

FIG. 48. Scheme of the structure of the primate retina as revealed by the Golgi staining method. Light enters from the bottom of this diagram.

The layers and zones are: 1, pigment layer; 2a, outer zone of rod and cone layer; 2b, inner zone of rod and cone layer; 3, outer limiting membrane; 4a, b, outer zone, inner zone of the outer nuclear layer; 5a b, c, outer, middle, and inner zones of the outer plexiform layer; 6, inner nuclear layer with its four zones; 7, inner plexiform layer; 8, layer of ganglion cells; 9, layer of optic nerve fibres; 10, inner limiting membrane; a, rods; b, cones; c, horizontal cells; d, e, f, h, bipolar cells; i, 'reverse bipolars'; m, n, o, p, s, ganglion cells; u, 'radial fibres' of Müller. (From Polyak, 1957.)

functions are in some way concerned with intensity or colour rather than form discrimination. Although there is no anatomical information about the orientation of their fields, investigation with microelectrodes shows that the fields 'looked at' by cells either of the retina or lateral geniculate are circular (Hartline, 1938; Barlow, 1953).

However, this is not true for the visual cortex of the cat. Here Hubel and Wiesel (1959, 1962) have recorded from single cells while stimulating the retina with points or strips of light. Each cortical cell is driven by a field that has either a central excitatory and outer inhibitory part or the reverse (Fig. 49).

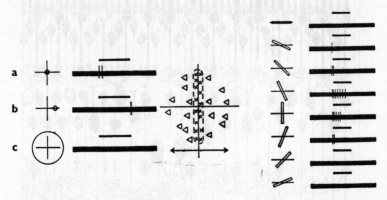

FIG. 49. *Left.* Responses from a microelectrode in one cell of the cat's visual cortex when a point of light is directed on to the retina giving (*a*) excitation when central, (*b*) an 'off' response when peripheral, and (*c*) none when the entire receptive field is stimulated.

Centre. Excitation of the receptive field (crosses) and inhibition (triangles).

Right. The effect of a rectangular stimulus in various orientations with responses increasing to a maximum as the rectangle reaches the vertical position. (After Hubel and Wiesel.)

Moreover, the fields are usually ovals, orientated in various directions. A cell with a given field thus acts as a specific detector for a reflecting object elongated in that direction.

These findings may well depend upon orientation of the dendritic trees of the cortical cells. Hitherto no detailed studies have been made of sections cut tangential to the surface. The first results of such an investigation show that the fibres in the cat's striate cortex run straight for long distances, as they do in the optic lobe of an octopus. They do not twist and turn, as would be expected in a 'random' system. Moreover, they run predominantly along the horizontal face of the gyrus. Golgi preparations show cells with oval fields (Fig. 50) (Colonnier, 1962). More recently still the stellate cells of the striate cortex of the monkey have been shown to have oval fields (Colonnier, personal communication).

We may therefore entertain the hypothesis that in the visual system of the cat as in the octopus, measurement of vertical

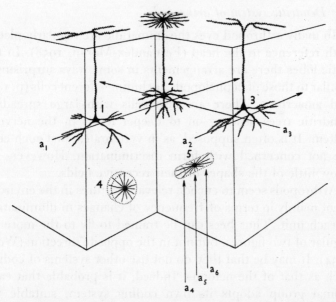

FIG. 50. Diagram of a portion of the visual cortex of the cat, showing the orientations of the dendritic fields of some cortical cells and fibres. (Colonnier, 1963.)

a 1–6 show incoming axons, 1–3 being association and intracortical axons; 4–6 lateral geniculate axons; 1 is a pyramidal cell with the basal dendritic field in the form of a cross and an elongated terminal in layer 1; 2, pyramidal cell with circular basal dendritic field and circular terminal in layer 1; 3, elongated basal dendritic field and elongated terminal in layer 1, the two being at right angles; 4, disk-shaped stellate cell; 5, cylindrical stellate.

and horizontal extents provides an important part of the coding system. Obviously the interlocking fields of a column of cortical cells with suitably orientated dendritic fields would provide a most subtle analogue computer. However, there are many problems to be considered. The visual images must cover numerous overlapping cortical fields. Without further information it is difficult to forecast what net outputs this would produce. Hubel and Wiesel have used rectangular slits for stimulation and shown that a given cortical cell gives its maximum output when the rectangle is in one particular orientation. Further experiment will almost certainly show that the visual system analyses figures in this way.

10. *Dendritic system of arthropods*

In many arthropod eyes the ommatidia are regularly placed with reference to the head (Fernández-Morán, 1958). In the optic lobes there are arrangements in some ways surprisingly similar to those of cephalopods, including efferent cells (p. 146) and amacrines. There are also cells with large spreading dendritic trees, leading on to deeper levels in the nervous system. It is often supposed, as in vertebrates, that such cells are not concerned with form discrimination. However, we know little of the shapes of their receptive fields.

Arthropods seem to encode relevant features in the environment mainly in terms of frequency of changes in illumination of each unit. Thus bees can be trained to fly to the more irregular of two figures, but not in the opposite direction (Wolf, 1934). It may be that they do not use other systems of coding such as that of the octopus. Indeed, it is probable that each animal group adopts its own coding system, suitable for detecting those features of the environment that are relevant for its life.

11. *Conclusions. The model in the brain*

The combined evidence from histology, physiology, and training experiments shows that there is some connexion between the shape of the cells of a nervous system and the things that can be learned by it. This at least suggests that the form and activity of the dendritic trees may be of fundamental importance in this coding system. There are so many ways in which this principle could be used that it is all too easy to speculate. The general idea is that each cell leads to two possible outputs and that learning consists in closing one of these. This may seem an absurd parody of the immense possibilities of learned behaviour, especially in man. But nearly all the complex actions of animals are produced by a few pairs of muscles. Even in learning to write or speak we have to learn the proper sequences of contractions of 'antagonistic' muscles. In the octopus, we have supposed each storage cell to lead directly to the two command cells. But suppose the storage and command cells are arranged in layered patterns, as in the cerebral cortex. The possible combinations even from a few layers are very numerous. Before we can even consider them we must have further information about the shapes of the dendrite fields and how they overlap.

It must inevitably seem that the model discussed is too static. It is unlikely that any animal system waits in a state of rest, ready to be activated. I have presented it in this way simply because one must begin somewhere. Once we have the information about the properties of these cells it should be possible to discover how they interact when the whole system is attentive and when it is put into action as, for example, in vertebrates by the reticular system. Bullock(1958) has emphasized that spontaneously active pacemakers may play a part, with the receptor and generator potentials fed into a ganglion. He was dealing, however, with ganglia responsible for the regulation of the rhythmic activity of the heart. It remains to be seen how such rhythmic activities are concerned with the building and operation of models in the brain. It may be that internal systems for activation, perhaps in relation to diurnal cycles and sleep, are among the special and significant features of higher vertebrate brains. Perhaps if they are absent from invertebrates we can take advantage of the greater simplicity (while, of course, being correspondingly cautious in making comparisons).

A further question is the extent to which the networks representing the various situations that have been learned interact to form one model. As formulated so far they would do so already within narrow limits. It is likely that in the higher animals there are opportunities for parts of the model to act together so that the results of training with different situations influence each other. Indeed, in our own human learning there is evidence that we put all the individual items together to make a very general scheme with which to predict the likely course of events, even in the world far beyond our own individual receptors. One great value of a model is that it can be turned around and so operated and examined as to produce forecasts about situations not yet experienced in real life.

10

TRANSFER, GENERALIZATION, REVERSAL, AND FORGETTING

1. *Transfer to different parts of the receptor field*

ACCORDING to the scheme of learning by suppression of alternative pathways only the memory storage units connected with those classifying cells actually stimulated are changed during each occasion of learning. In Fig. 47 each storage cell is shown receiving stimulation from only one classifying cell, but in practice each may well receive from many, which may be dispersed throughout the visual field. The effect of impulses from, say, a large horizontal object in one part of the field associated with shock would thus be to reduce the probability of attack on large horizontal objects presented anywhere in the visual field of that eye.

We do not know to what extent transfer in this way within one visual field occurs. Experiments could be made with presentation, say, only in the front of the field during learning and then testing in the back of the field. Interpretation might be difficult, however, until more is known about eye movements and fixation in octopuses. The equatorial strip (p. 116) presumably functions to some extent as a special area, but it is not known whether there are corresponding special arrangements of bipolar and other classifying cells within the optic lobe.

2. *Transfer results of training from one visual field to the other*

There is some small overlap of the visual fields at the front and back but octopuses can, nevertheless, be trained in a discrimination in such a way that the images fall only on one eye. They then show good discrimination when the objects are presented to the untrained eye (Muntz, 1961, 1962b). Accuracy with the two eyes is equal for easy discriminations, but if the task is harder or the performance is for any reason imperfect on the trained side, then identification will be even less correct with the untrained eye.

The mechanism of transfer thus shows interesting weaknesses. There has been some further investigation of its properties. First, there is the demonstration that the representation that links the particular shape with food or shock is truly transmitted across the mid-line. This is shown by removing the optic lobe from the trained side. After this operation the animals proved able to continue to make correct responses with the untrained eye. Response was as accurate as after removal of the lobe from the untrained side. The correct responses to tests given to an untrained eye do not, therefore, depend simply on the use by the untrained side of the representation set up on the trained side.

Muntz has made some study of the pathways necessary for transfer. There is a large, direct, optic commissure between the lobes, and in addition many fibres cross in the superior frontal to vertical tract (Fig. 51). The vertical lobe system plays a part in learning that will be discussed later. Animals in which the vertical circuit is interrupted learn slowly and in particular have difficulty in learning a reversal—for example, not to attack a crab. Muntz demonstrated that normal octopuses, when trained by shocks not to attack a crab shown in one visual field, will not attack it in the other (Fig. 52). After removal of the vertical lobe, or mid-line bisection of its input tract, this transfer does not occur, although the large direct optic commissure is left intact after either operation. The vertical lobe is not, therefore, concerned only to assist the setting up of the representation on the trained side, but also in the actual communication of the representation to the other side. Muntz also showed that in training octopuses not to attack crabs, the side to which the shock was given was irrelevant. This was so even in animals without vertical lobes.

For the discussion of the hypothesis of learning by suppression of alternative pathways the question is 'How is the visual

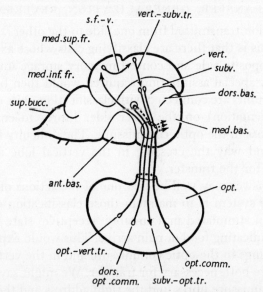

FIG. 51. Diagram of the brain of *Octopus* showing the lobes and tracts. The top half of the figure represents a medial sagittal section of the supraoesophageal lobes, the bottom half represents the optic lobe which has been displaced downwards.

ant.bas., anterior basal; dors.bas., dorsal basal; dors.opt. comm., dorsal optic commissure; med.bas., median basal; med.inf.fr., median inferior frontal; med. sup.fr., median superior frontal; opt., optic lobe; opt.comm., optic commissure; opt.-vert.tr., optic to vertical tract; subv., subvertical; subv.-opt.tr., subvertical to optic tract; sup.bucc., superior buccal; s.f.-v., superior frontal to vertical tract; vert., vertical; vert.-subv.tr., vertical to subvertical tract. (After Muntz.)

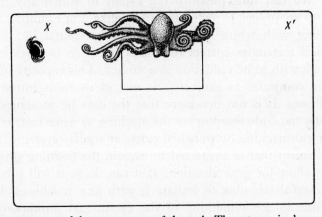

FIG. 52. Diagram of the arrangement of the tank. The octopus is shown in its 'home' exhibiting 'cautious behaviour' towards the crab at *X*. If the crab had been presented at *X'* the other eye would have been used in attacking it. (After Muntz.)

information transmitted from one side to the other?' A simple hypothesis is that there are classifying cells whose axons cross to the opposite side and control memory storage units there. The only special assumption required would then be that all memory units are connected with classification units of similar type (orientation) on the other side. Fibres to ensure this might cross in the optic commissure. The difficulty is then to understand why the crossing in the vertical lobe system is essential for the transfer.

The answer may well be that one of the actions of the vertical lobe system is to maintain those classification cells that have been stimulated in a suitably 'receptive' state until the signals indicating food or pain arrive. This would explain why the crossings in the optic commissure and in the vertical lobe system are both necessary for transfer. We might say that the optic commissure fibres find the right address and the vertical lobe fibres then hold it for the period between stimulation and reward.

3. *Generalization*

As test figures are made to depart more widely in shape from those used in training, more errors are made in responding. We can thus measure the extent to which any given figures are judged by octopuses to be alike. For example, after training with white figures to attack horizontal but avoid vertical rectangles correct responses are given to black ones, though with some reduction in accuracy. This capacity of the living computer to *generalize* is one of its most important attributes. It is not necessary that the data be presented on exactly the same receptors of the machine, as when instructing a logical machine by punched cards or similar systems. Any mechanism that is suggested to explain the learning process must allow for generalization. If it can do so it will provide a powerful stimulus to imitate it with new machines. It is possible to see something of the extent and limitations of generalization by octopuses.

After training with figures of a given size octopuses are able to give approximately correct performance with figures either larger or smaller (Fig. 53). The fact that discrimination was nearly always better for figures of the size used in training than for any other suggests, however, that we must be cautious in supposing that generalization is a capacity that is automatically conferred during learning. Further experiments showed that the very reverse is true and that the apparent generalization depends upon the fact that the animal has learnt to see the figures at various retinal sizes. If the octopus is sitting at the back of its tank and comes forward to attack a figure, images of a large range of sizes fall upon its retina. By keeping the animals fixed either at the back of the tank, or at the front near to the figures, we were able to ensure that they experienced each figure *only at one retinal size.*

In our experiments we compared the capacity to generalize between larger and smaller figures by animals allowed to move, with others who were trained in fixed positions. These latter were given food or shock immediately they made the appropriate response. They thus saw the training figures only at a single retinal image size. Some animals were fixed near to the training figures, others far from them (Parriss and Young, 1962).

A series of tests with figures of sizes other than those used in training showed that the octopuses that had been allowed to move discriminated figures of twice the linear dimensions nearly as well as those used in training, and of half size rather less well. Figures four times or one-quarter those used in training were recognized less well (Fig. 53). The animals that had *not* been allowed to move during training recognized figures of twice size as well as did the moving animals, but were much less accurate in all other tests.

This effect of retinal experience appeared even more clearly when the homes of the animals were moved, so that an octopus that had been trained with the figures far away now saw them close to and vice versa. Animals trained in only one position now showed very little recognition (Fig. 54). Octopuses that had been allowed to move during training were, however, little disturbed when their homes were moved from the back to the front of the tank.

It seems, therefore, that there is not really much true 'generalization' for size changes, in the sense of recognizing

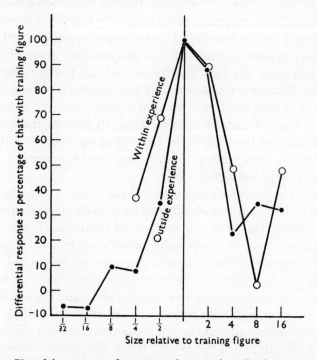

FIG. 53. Plot of the accuracy of response to larger and smaller figures than those used in training. Open circles are for figures that gave retinal images within the size range that had been seen during training. Filled circles, the images of the figures were larger or smaller than any seen in training. (Parriss & Young, 1962.)

figures of sizes never seen before. It is true that animals fixed at a considerable distance from the figures will recognize figures of twice the linear size of any that they have seen during training. This is perhaps to be expected from our hypothesis. Retinal image sizes of distant objects do not differ greatly. The finer dendritic branches of the classifying cells spread over a considerable distance, and stimulation of them by figures rather larger than those seen in training is to be expected. Smaller figures are less likely to be effective and it is the general experience of those who have studied size transfer that smaller figures are recognized less well than larger ones.

These findings, therefore, do not disagree with our hypothesis of form classification by the shapes of dendritic fields.

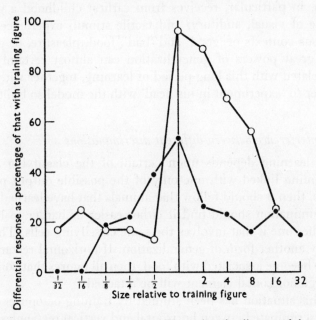

FIG. 54. Experiments similar to that of Fig. 53 but the distance of the animal from the figure was different from that used in training. (Parriss & Young, 1962.)

They also emphasize how much more anatomical and physiological evidence we need about these fields. Presumably there is a whole array of them of different sizes and orientations. But there is little evidence as to whether the receptive areas are limited in the sense that the cell can be activated only by stimulation of a field of a particular size as well as shape.

Experiments with other forms of generalization have, of course, been numerous in various animals and man. It would be impossible to survey the subject adequately here. Our hypothesis predicts that the stimulus situation used for training could be varied only within certain limits without impairing discrimination. There seem to be few cases in which the possibility that the animal had experienced the essential features of the transfer situation can be excluded. Indeed, it is very difficult to do this (some of these octopuses may well have experienced horizontal food objects of various sizes). Man, in particular, receives from earliest childhood a great range of visual, auditory, and tactile stimuli experienced in various contexts of 'good' and 'bad', food, pleasure, or pain. His great powers of generalization can almost certainly be correlated with this long period of learning, together with the power to 'experiment in his head' with the model so built up.

4. *Interference between different discriminations*

If learning depends upon certain of the classifying cells becoming linked with one only of the possible output pathways, then it should follow that animals that have learned one discrimination should find it either easier or harder to learn another one if that involves the same classifying cells. This is really another form of generalization. If horizontal rectangles have become associated with food, then all figures that contain a large horizontal element will be attacked.

This situation has been studied by training octopuses first to discriminate between horizontal and vertical rectangles and then between figures such as Z and V, each shown either in the vertical positions or on their sides (Fig. 55). The results agreed with the expectation that the level of learning of the second set is dependent upon the similarity or dissimilarity of the horizontal/vertical ratios of the two positive and two negative shapes respectively (Parriss, 1964).

Evidence of interference is found even when there are no differences in the proportions of the figures in the two discriminations. Thus the difficult discrimination of 'square' against 'diamond' (Table 2, p. 131) was learned less well following previous training with the easy horizontal and vertical rectangles than when it was learned as a first discrimination (Parriss, 1963c). On the other hand, the training with the

harder discrimination did not interfere with the performance
of the easier one.

If the animals had been previously operated upon to reduce

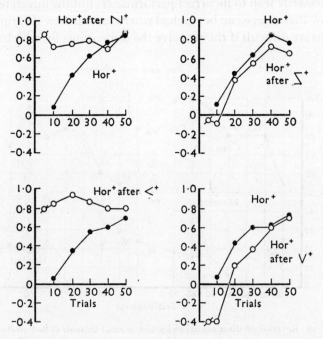

FIG. 55. Interference as a result of learning different sets of figures. The ordinates
show an index for discrimination obtained by calculating:

$$\frac{\text{attacks at }+ve\text{ figure}-\text{attacks at }-ve\text{ figure}}{\frac{1}{2}\text{ total trials}}$$

Each point represents the mean score for either 4 or 5 animals. Octopuses were
trained to make two different visual discriminations, the one following the other.
They were then re-trained on the first discrimination. Filled circles represents
the learning of the first discrimination between horizontal and vertical rectangles
(Hor$^+$). Open circles represent the re-learning of this discrimination following
a discrimination between either V^+ and Z^- or V^- and Z^+.

the amount of optic lobe tissue available, however, learning
the more difficult discrimination was found to make inroads
on performance with the easier one.

All of these results suggest that there is a common pool of
cells used in these discriminations. Presumably it is possible

to reach a state in which all the classifying cells for, say, large horizontal have become linked only with 'attack'. The facts of reversal learning in the next section show that this does not necessarily lead to incorrect performance, but the interferences show that a stage can be reached where further new discriminations are difficult if they involve the dimensions for which all of

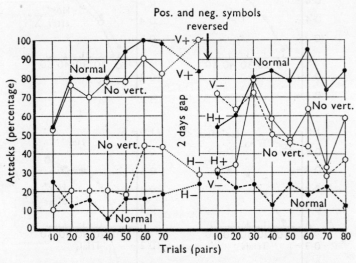

FIG. 56. Reversal of discrimination by five normal animals (filled circles) and five with 94 per cent of the vertical lobes removed (open circles). Trials at 5-minute intervals. Points show percentages of attacks at the positive and negative figures for each ten trials. Circles with a stroke (⊘ and ◉) indicate trials without reward. (Young, 1962f.)

the coding elements have been used. If this hypothesis is true, then the learning of discriminations involving other coding systems should not be impaired by these previous situations of interference.

In Miss Parriss's experiments, when the animals were unable to learn to discriminate horizontal and vertical rectangles, they readily learned to distinguish black and white circles. The interference thus affected only the coding of information about horizontal and vertical, and the learning power in general was not impaired.

5. *Reversal of learned discriminations*

Complete reversal of cues will obviously produce representations that interfere with each other particularly strongly. If shocks are given when an octopus attacks crabs that have previously been its food, then it will cease to attack crabs for a while. But after some days attacks will begin again. Similarly, if training with two rectangles is reversed signs of the original responses remain apparent for a long time. Thus in the experiment of Fig. 56 attacks at the previously negative figure remained rather irregular and were always slow, even after 120 trials in the new direction.

Such reversal experiments suggest that the effect is produced not by attaching a new condition (shock) to the old representation, but by establishing a wholly new representation associating, say, a crab with shock. Being weaker than the original one this representation soon fades and the other is again revealed intact.

Experiments in which the cues were repeatedly reversed provide further insight into the problem. In the experiment shown in Figs. 57 and 58 a black circle was the positive figure on the first day's training and the negative a white one. The rewards were then reversed on each successive day. After each of the earlier reversals there were numerous errors and the animals then learned during that day. As judged by the percentage of errors the performance deteriorated to a random level. However, many of the errors were due to the increasing failure to attack either figure. Analysis of the occasions on which attacks were made shows that the proportion that were correct declines over the first few reversals but then rises consistently. However, the effect was not very marked and was not seen in all experiments. The interpretation in terms of our hypothesis is that equal numbers of memory cells representing, say, black, are switched to produce 'attack' and 'retreat'. The animal therefore tends to do nothing until a small amount of food reward (given at each trial with the 'positive' figure) tips the scale in one direction. It is interesting that this did

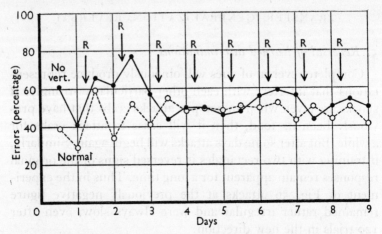

FIG. 57. Repeated reversal of the direction of training. The octopuses were given two sets of trials daily, with five positive and five negative trials given alternately in each set. A piece of sardine was given for attacks at the positive figure, a shock for attacks at the negative. The cues were black and white circles. On the first day black was positive. Thereafter the cues were reversed each day.

The open circles are the results with ten normal animals. The filled circles are for nine without vertical lobes. The normals improve in performance during each of the first three days. Thereafter they appear to perform at a random level of errors. (Young, 1962g.)

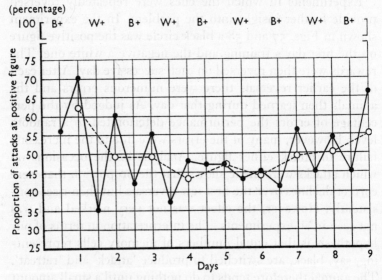

FIG. 58. The same experiment as Fig. 57. The results for the normal animals plotted to show the attacks at the positive figure as a proportion of all attacks. Filled circles show individual sessions, open circles show means for each day. By this criterion there was some improvement in ability to reverse.

not happen after removal of the vertical lobes. It may well be the sign of a relatively short term effect associating the reward with one set of memory units.

Using a simultaneous discrimination situation Mackintosh and Mackintosh (1964) showed rather more definite signs of

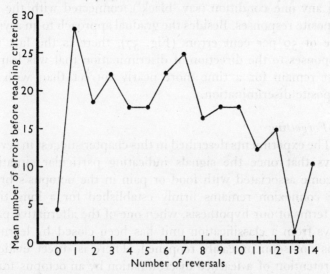

FIG. 59. Improvement in learning to reverse in octopuses is shown as the animals proceed towards the end of a long series of reversal experiments. Positive and negative objects were presented together, which made simultaneous dis-crimination necessary. After the animals reached a criterion of 8/10 correct responses the positive and negative objects were reversed.

The whole reversal series was spread over about 4 days and the number of animals used was five except for reversal 13 where only one animal was available.

improvement in learning to reverse (Fig. 59). They made their reversals after training the animals to a criterion of 8/10 correct responses in a day. Towards the end of their series there was one occasion on which most of the animals made the correct responses at nearly every trial of the day.

Marked improvement in performance on successive reversals has been shown by Harlow (1949) and others in mammals, but not, in general, in other animal groups. Most of these experi-ments differ from the above in that the animals were trained with reversal of a succession of different pairs of cues rather than with repeated reversal with one pair. In order to explain the phenomenon of learning to reverse it seems to be necessary to postulate some special mechanism. However, the series of reversals in the octopus show several features that seem to follow from the progressive accumulation of cells representing any one condition (say 'black'), connected with the two opposite responses. Besides the gradual approach to an asymptote of 50 per cent errors (Fig. 57), there is the fact that responses to the direction of discrimination that was learned first remain for a time more nearly correct than with the opposite discrimination.

6. *Forgetting*

The experiments described in this chapter suggest in several ways that once the signals indicating particular situations become associated with food or pain in the octopus's brain, the connexion remains firmly established for a long time. In terms of our hypothesis, when one of the alternative pathways from a classification unit has been closed by learning, it is not soon or easily reopened. There is direct evidence of retention of a learned discrimination by an octopus for 27 days (Sutherland, 1957*b*). Experiments on forgetting have not been very actively pursued because they keep tanks occupied for a long time to give rather little information, and, in the short seasons available for work, tank time is a limiting factor.

Examples of recall after long periods by animals and man are too familiar to need emphasis. There is much to suggest that once a representation associating particular signals has been established, it persists perhaps for a lifetime. The question of how the connexions are made is dealt with in Chapter 17. It may well be that the essential feature of the process is the 'switching off' of pathways that are not required. This change may occur for each cell quite rapidly during the period following each occasion of learning. The gradual process of learning then consists in the accumulation of cells that are suitably connected. If the process is irreversible once achieved, we have to explain the phenomena of forgetting with which we are all only too familiar. Interference between representations can be a potent factor even in an octopus, as we have shown above. Equally important must be the onset of conditions which make it impossible for the representations that have been established to be properly used. In other words, forgetting may be due to the failure to 'read out' properly from the memory.

A simple example of this sort can be seen in octopuses from which the vertical lobe has been removed. They seem at first sight to have 'forgotten' what they had learned before operation. Thus, an octopus trained by shocks not to attack crabs begins immediately again to attack them after operation. Again, a simple discrimination between horizontal and vertical rectangles is no longer correctly performed after operation. Further analysis shows that what is now lacking in these animals is the proper balance between attack and restraint (Chapter 13). The representations are still present (in the optic lobes) but are not effective, mainly because of a failure to inhibit any tendencies that there may be to attack. The proof of this is that under some circumstances (absence of food or shock) the animals may make entirely 'correct' responses (Fig. 77).

In the much more complicated situation of a mammalian brain there are, no doubt, many similar reasons for failure to use the model that has been set up by learning. The forgetfulness of old age may be due to the onset of pathological deficiencies of this sort in the mechanisms for 'reading out' from the memory. However, the memories of the aged for well-recorded events of long ago is usually excellent. It is recent events that are 'forgotten' and this is probably due more to a failure of the mechanism for 'reading in' to the memory store than of that for reading out.

11

FURTHER STUDIES OF
SHAPE ANALYSING MECHANISMS

1. *Developments from Sutherland's early model*

INVESTIGATIONS of the capacity for discrimination of shapes have suggested that estimation of vertical and horizontal extents of figures is of special importance for the encoding system. In Chapter 9 a mechanism was suggested by which the cells with oval dendritic fields that are known to exist in the optic lobes of octopuses may accomplish this. Sutherland, after his early experiments, suggested a somewhat similar system, in which the vertical and horizontal projections are counted and related to the area (Chapter 8).

It would obviously be a great mistake to suppose that estimation of vertical and horizontal extent was the only coding system at work. Indeed, the principle we are insisting on is that there is a set of encoding units present, ready to respond to various features of the visual input. In the block-diagram scheme suggested by Maldonado these are called classifying units (Fig. 10). We may list, as examples, units responding to various degrees of brightness, of movement, of horizontal and vertical extent, perhaps of contour, number of angles, and so on. According to Maldonado's model the various classifying units are connected with memory units and information from the classifying units is 'addressed' to appropriate members of this set by the lowering of their threshold by signals from the receptors for pain or food. A corresponding quantity is stored.

The processes to which Sutherland and Maldonado refer correspond approximately to those considered to be the functions of the classification cells and memory storage cells in the model of Chapter 9. The various models give somewhat different emphasis on the various types of data, anatomical, psychological, and physiological that are involved. All of them suggest problems for solution and will be judged in the fruitfulness of the hypotheses that these answers in turn suggest.

It is therefore of special interest to consider some of the further developments that have already followed from Sutherland's hypothesis. Some of the findings that have been pre-

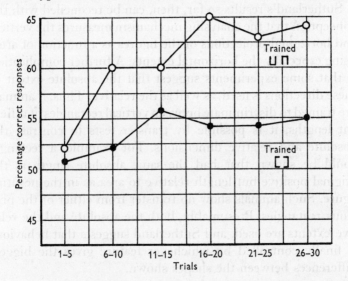

FIG. 60. Results of training with up/down (open circles) and right/left mirror images (filled circles). Three animals in each group. (Sutherland, 1960a.)

dicted or explained by this model have been discussed in Chapter 8. As a result of other experiments it has been necessary, as expected, to introduce some complications. Thus the octopuses proved to be able to distinguish between figures that are mirror images, though less easily in the right/left than in the up/down directions (Fig. 60). Sutherland interprets this to show that the projections of horizontal and vertical extents may be 'differentiated', so that they can then be analysed in terms of the direction and size of changes, and the animals will be able to distinguish between figures giving different distributions of vertical extent along the horizontal axis or vice versa. It is not clear by what neural mechanism this would be done.

To explain the difference between up/down and right/left Sutherland assumed that shapes differing only in their horizontal projections are more readily discriminated than the reverse. For this there is direct experimental evidence, since differences of length were found to be more accurately estimated along the horizontal axis (Sutherland, 1960a, 1961).

Sutherland's results so far, then, can be reconciled with the conception that the analysing mechanism measures the vertical and horizontal projections of the figures as a function of area, using especially the horizontal extents. A further complication is that some experiments suggest that the absolute extent in these directions is used, as well as the relative. Thus, if animals are trained to discriminate between vertical rectangles of different lengths, it is possible by transfer tests to contrast the absolute and relative dimensions. For example, a rectangle could be shown that had the same absolute length as the original positive but length relative to area as in the negative figure. Such animals show no transfer from either of the previous rectangles. Presumably, both the absolute and the relative extents are used, and Sutherland suggests that behaviour is finally controlled by whichever feature gives the biggest differences between the shapes shown.

2. *Some facts not explicable by Sutherland's first model*

Certain further results that have proved especially interesting may now be considered.

(a) *Reduplicated patterns.* The horizontal and vertical projections given by the patterns in Fig. 61 are identical, nevertheless, they are more easily discriminated by an octopus than are single vertical and horizontal rectangles of the size of the elements of the pattern (Sutherland, Mackintosh, and Mackintosh, 1963). This is, however, the result that would be expected from the simple theory suggested in Chapter 9. Clearly the first pattern will fire many vertical fields and the second many horizontal ones. Transfer experiments with different sizes of rectangle might be interesting in determining which size of neuronal field had been used for coding. In this example the sophistication involved in extracting horizontal and vertical projections of the figures is evidently not needed. It may be needed to explain other discriminations, but the simpler alternative is more likely to be correct, especially since no specific mechanism for counting the 'projections' has been suggested.

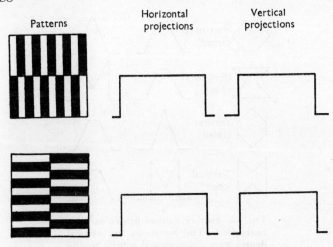

FIG. 61. Patterns of replicated rectangles which give identical horizontal and vertical projections but nevertheless can be discriminated by octopuses. (Sutherland, 1963b.)

(b) 'Open' and 'closed' figures. Sutherland has recently provided an addition to his hypothesis considered especially in relation to the possibility that the coding system involves analysis by oval fields. According to his original hypothesis the figures called 'horizontal open' and 'horizontal closed' of Fig. 62 should be more readily discriminated than the corresponding vertical figures. It was found that the discrimination between the pairs was equally easy (Sutherland, 1960b). Moreover, tests showed that the animals responded correctly even when the figures with which they had been trained were rotated through 180°. Evidently in this case discrimination must depend upon measurement of some dimension other than horizontal or vertical projections.

Investigation of a series of shapes showed that they can be arranged in an order such that members at one end have the quality that Sutherland describes as 'open' and at the other end as 'closed' (Fig. 63). An octopus is trained with one of the pairs shown at the left of the figure and then in transfer tests the figures to the right are shown. Those nearer to the top will

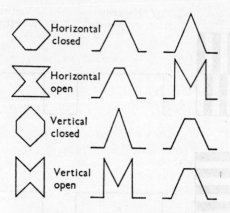

FIG. 62. Further pairs of figures used by Sutherland. The horizontal and vertical figures were discriminated equally readily by octopuses. Animals trained with vertical figures recognized them when horizontal and vice versa. (Sutherland, 1960*b*.)

be considered more 'open' than those lower down, that is, they will be reacted to as more similar to the odd-numbered than to the even-numbered training figures.

This result has been confirmed for several of the possible combinations, so that we can say that within each block of figures on the right of Fig. 63 the upper members are more 'open' than the lower. This is also approximately true between the blocks (i.e. for the whole series) but some further experiments are needed to be sure of this.

Similar results have also been obtained with rats and with goldfishes, and it seems that the 'dimension' concerned, whatever it may be, is one of considerable importance in visual shape discrimination. In trying to discover more about this

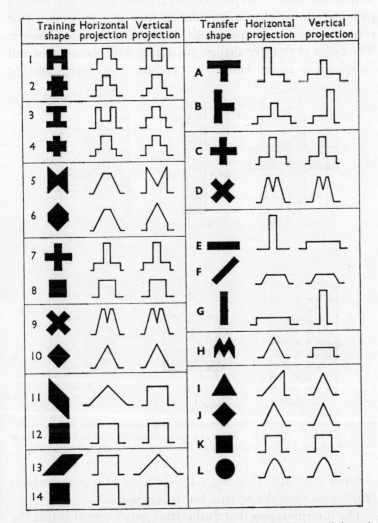

FIG. 63. Open and closed shapes. Octopuses are trained with one of the pairs shown at the left. When tested with any of the groups of figures to the right the upper members are treated as more like the upper (more 'open') training figure. Thus A–L is approximately a series from most open to most closed. (Sutherland, 1963*b*.)

dimension Sutherland pointed out that the more open of each pair of training shapes includes at least one projection that contains more or sharper peaks than that of the closed figure. The order of transfer shapes also agrees with the number and sharpness of peaks. However, there are some exceptions, for

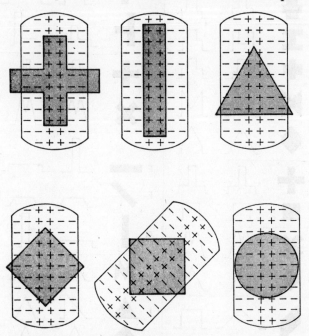

FIG. 64. Possible coding system provided by oval dendritic fields with excitatory centre and inhibitory margin. There is a characteristic balance of E (+ = excitation) and I (− = inhibition) for each figure. (Sutherland, 1963b.)

instance the circle (Fig. 63, L) gives more of a peak on both projections than the square, but is less open.

The interpretation that Sutherland puts forward is that the position on this dimension is determined by the number of oval receptive fields that it fires. An open shape fires many, a closed one few. If we consider fields such as those found by Hubel and Wiesel, with excitatory centres and inhibitory peripheries, we might get results such as those of Fig. 64. Sutherland assumes that the firing rate will vary with E−I, where E is the number of excitatory units (? synapses) stimulated and I the inhibitory. The values of E−I for the figures if placed in the positions shown would be for the cross 8, rectangle 20, triangle = diamond = square 0, circle −5. With different positions relative to the receptive fields the values would be different, but would lie in the same order. Changes in the relative sizes of the excitatory and inhibitory parts of the field will also influence the values but not the order. However, as Sutherland points out, fields composed of equal numbers of E and I units could be fired strongly by almost any shape placed slightly off centre, and, would therefore be less useful as coding units.

Whether or not the experiments on 'openness' of figures can be explained as due to rates of firing in this way the discussion is interesting for our purposes as showing how investigation proceeds from a model (hypothesis) to experiments to test it, which may then suggest other investigations. The results of these, in connexion with observations and experiments made with other techniques lead to still further experiments and so on. The process of discovering 'how the brain works' cannot be perfectly systematic, because we cannot say precisely what it is that we want to find out. We are searching all the time for questions as well as for answers. The abundance of models that are suggested in this situation may be an embarrassment to clear explanation but it at least serves to emphasize that the situation is neither simple nor well understood. To emphasize this we may now consider two further hypotheses that have been put forward to 'explain' the facts of visual form discrimination by octopuses.

3. *Alternative hypotheses of form discrimination*

(a) *Dodwell's hypothesis.* Systems of coding quite different from those of Sutherland's have been suggested to explain his findings in *Octopus*. The scheme put forward by Dodwell (1957) assumes that the excitation produced by the contours of shapes is scanned by impulses sweeping horizontally and vertically across the array of cells on to which it is projected.

The impulses are slowed, where they cross the excited area, by
an amount depending on the direction of the contour in relation to that of the sweep. The output is characterized by two
factors: (1) the sizes of the impulses, and (2) the temporal
pattern in which they occur. Figures that give differences in

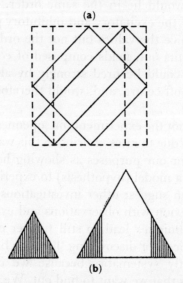

FIG. 65. Some implications of hypotheses about shape discrimination. (a) If
the animal analyses by measuring the oblique contours of a figure it should
confuse a rectangle and a square set on edge (Dodwell). It does not do so. (b) In
doubling the dimensions of a triangle the ratio of horizontal contour to reciprocal
of vertical contour is changed (Deutsch). In practice, transfer to small triangles is
as good as to small rectangles.

either of these will be discriminated and Dodwell produces
estimates of values that would be produced by various figures.
In effect these are measures of the amount of oblique contouring. Sutherland pointed out that if this were so oblique rectangles and squares should not be discriminable (Fig. 65). He
showed that these figures can be distinguished by octopuses
and he believed that this disproved Dodwell's theory. Subsequently the latter agreed that this was a critical test but held
that Sutherland had not sufficiently controlled for the fact that
the square was larger in area. To this Sutherland in turn replied

that he had made the necessary control by transfer tests with smaller squares, proving that the discrimination was not being made only on a basis of brightness.

The controversy is an interesting example of the complexity of such studies. Several mechanisms can plausibly be suggested to explain a given result. The problem is to devise experiments that can show decisively what mechanism is at work. Perhaps only in recent years is it reasonable to hope that this will be possible by combining behavioural, anatomical, and physiological studies.

It is not easy to see what detailed neural system would extract the values suggested by Dodwell, nor how the storage and comparison with the store would proceed. Scanning systems such as he suggests seem to demand a greater reliability and precision than nervous tissue provides. But it would be hazardous to reject a suggested mechanism only on these grounds. Scanning systems have often been suggested for the vertebrate brain and the presence of rhythmical phenomena such as brain waves might encourage us to look for scanning.

(b) *Deutsch's hypothesis*. Deutsch (1960) suggests that the figures are discriminated by the octopus making what seems at first a relatively simple measurement, namely of the reciprocal of the distances between contours in the vertical direction, summed for all points along the horizontal axis. In effect this is a measure of the length of the horizontal contour multiplied by the reciprocal of the vertical extent. There is thus a single figure for each shape along this 'dimension'. A horizontal rectangle is high and a vertical one low on it. Oblique contours that approach each other will obviously tend to give infinite values for the reciprocal of the distance between them, and there must be some special device to prevent this, limiting the count on close approach.

If this theory is correct there must be a horizontal or vertical rectangle equivalent to any given figure and it would be interesting to test this. A difficulty for this theory is that a broken vertical rectangle should be treated as if horizontal, since a count of the reciprocals of distances between vertical contours would be high. Experiment shows that the broken vertical rectangle is treated as vertical.

One of the great advantages of Deutsch's theory is that it gives a possible explanation for transfer to larger or smaller size. For example, if the linear dimensions of a vertical rectangle are halved the horizontal contour is halved, but the reciprocal of the vertical distance is doubled, the product thus remaining unchanged. However, the same would not apply to triangles, which would change on this dimension with change in size (Fig. 65). In practice, transfer to smaller triangles is as good as to smaller rectangles and the theory is not supported. Actually, the transfer to smaller figures is always less good than to larger ones and it remains a question whether there is any specific mechanism for size generalization (p. 171).

A further difficulty with Deutsch's theory is that it would not predict any discrimination of mirror images. Moreover, it would not predict that length differences should be more readily detected in the horizontal than the vertical direction, as we have seen them to be. The theory is no more successful than Sutherland's in providing an explanation for the possibility of discrimination of the shapes shown in Fig. 63.

4. *The search for the elements of the model*

This survey of the results of experiments with different shapes and of the theories based on them is an interesting example of the possibilities and limitations of working in this way, without direct reference to the nervous system. By discovering what figures the animals can and cannot discriminate it is possible to assess which features are being measured, and this is clearly a first step in the search for the mechanisms that measure them. The task of examining the nervous system with the microscope and microelectrode must then continue the work if the mechanism is to be understood. This analysis should, in turn, suggest further experiments on the possibilities and limitations of the capacity of form discrimination. It is difficult to see that there is any advantage in pursuing any of these types of study in isolation, or any justification for claims of precedence for psychological, anatomical, or physiological methods. The problem is that all are technically difficult but yet anyone seriously working in the field must have knowledge of at least the results of each of them. It should not be impossible to arrange to undertake work for a while in parts of the field other than one's own. Such work may not provide startling results immediately, but its effect in producing an informed point of view is very great.

These investigations of the capacities of the animals give us some indication of the sort of messages that we may expect to find encoded by the octopus. The system produces different responses (attack or retreat) according to the extent of figures in the visual field in the vertical and horizontal directions (perhaps mainly the latter). It also takes account of the area of the figure and its contour. Figures are thus distinguished by combinations of measurements along these various 'dimensions', and no doubt others as well. We shall therefore expect to find in the eyes and brain means for measuring and recording these variables and perhaps also for selecting which of the variables is likely to provide the most useful clues. In other words, the model is constructed out of coding elements that represent these variables.

12

SOME REQUIREMENTS OF AN EXPLORATORY COMPUTER. MOTIVATION AND ADDRESSING OF THE SIGNALS OF RESULTS

1. *Some specifications for a self-instructing computer*

ENGINEERS are beginning to design adaptive machines that improve their own instructions by exploring the environment and learning from it. The concept of a computer with no instructions either built in or given to it may seem an absurdity. What would it be *for*? This problem certainly raises fundamental philosophical questions; it might be considered as a way of attacking the whole question of the origin and significance of life. Living organisms have indeed found their own instructions, basically by the processes of variation and natural selection. It has taken some thousands of millions of years to acquire the information that is now stored in the population of animals and plants of the world. Yet such very slow methods, making continual small random changes, are exceedingly powerful means for providing very delicate adjustments. For example, the most perfectly flat or spherical surfaces are obtained by grinding systems that allow random adjustment (see Platt, 1958).

We are not for the present concerned, however, with these most fundamental biological processes, but with the special problem of how the nervous system acts as an exploratory learning computer. Yet there must, of course, be a relationship between the 'exploration' conducted by recombining genes and the investigations conducted by the nervous system. We shall return in Chapter 18 to this question, which involves the relationship of rates of reproduction to brain size.

The nervous system of each individual animal is provided by heredity and is by no means devoid of built-in instructions. Nevertheless, it is able to undertake a great deal more exploration and learning than any man-made artefact can yet achieve. Since we have no models with which to compare these aspects of the organism, we are apt to become confused when talking about such subjects as motivation and the evaluation of rewards and results. Indeed, the poverty of our knowledge and language in these fields is a major source of philosophical difficulties. Fortunately by observation and experiment the fog of words is beginning to be dispersed from this aspect of nervous function, as from the coding system. From clinical observations of physicians and surgeons and from experiments with animals it has become clear that there are 'centres' in the brain that are active in the evaluation and indication of the results of action, producing what we call pleasure or pain. These centres are only dimly understood in vertebrates, but we may acquire some insight into them by once again looking at the simpler but comparable centres in an octopus. Here the inferior frontal/subfrontal and superior frontal/vertical lobe systems seem to control what may be called motivation and assessment of results or rewards.

Before describing these lobes and the experiments with them it may be convenient to consider some features that seem to be needed to make a satisfactory exploratory computer, though some of these have only become apparent during study of the octopus system itself. Clearly the 'explorer' must take action, for example an octopus must emerge to attack unfamiliar objects, otherwise it will learn nothing. This is what we mean by being motivated. There must be receptors that indicate the 'needs' of the animal, e.g. for food. Little is known about the hunger mechanism of *Octopus*. Fig. 66 shows an experiment in which after a large meal the octopuses showed a reduced tendency to attack. It is not known whether this period of satiation is related to the fullness of the crop, nor by what pathway the relevant impulses pass to the brain.

However much the animal needs food, exploratory actions

in unfamiliar situations should not be undertaken with the full potential available. It would not pay the octopus to dash out at full speed to attack every new moving object.

Supposing that a given action achieves 'success' (e.g food), how much change should be made in the tendency to repeat the action? Clearly the animal must be 'encouraged' by suc-

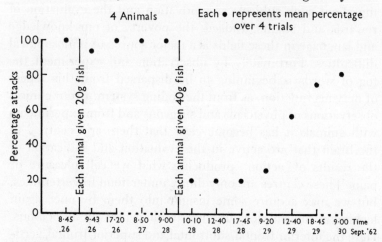

FIG. 66. Four octopuses were tested by showing crabs and recording whether they attacked. They were not allowed to eat the crabs. Attacks were made on almost every occasion. Each octopus was then fed with 20 g of fish and the tests were resumed. There was little reduction in attack. However, after giving 40 g of fish the attacks were much reduced for 24 hours and had not returned to the original level in 48 hours.

cess; but not too much. Conversely, any situation that proves traumatic should be avoided; but a small prick should not deter exploration for a long time. One of the functions of the vertical lobe system seems to be to ensure that proper balances of this kind are achieved, and there must be comparable mechanisms in other animals and in man.

Any such exploratory system depends upon detectors that record the results of any action and promote further action according to whether the outcome was 'good' or 'bad'. It is curious that no words are available to name these detectors as a class. There seems to be a resistance to recognizing that good and bad, pleasure and pain, need to be considered in one category.

A convenient terminology is to speak of 'reward detectors', reward being considered either positive or negative. With regret I have not adopted this use, because for many psychologists it is firmly established that 'reward' is positive. 'Nocifensor' and 'hedonoreceptor' are available, but are hideous and 'nocihedonoreceptor' is worse still. Moreover, 'hedono-' is used by some to indicate positive reward and by others to indicate *any* reward. I shall therefore use 'detectors of results', which is simple, not inelegant, and at present arresting by its unfamiliarity. We can, of course, speak of these signals as providing 're-inforcement', but this is a somewhat different concept.

The basis of these detector systems must be provided by heredity, though they may, of course, be modified by use. The population would become extinct if the detectors of results failed in their work, and by reshuffling of genes it is ensured that the detectors are kept appropriate to the environment of the race.

The signals set up by these detectors may be said to have three functions. (1) Firstly, they operate the consummatory mechanisms that appropriately end each action; food must be eaten, the hand must be snatched away from the flame. For these purposes we find that such receptors have what may be called reflex connexions.

(2) Secondly, the signals of results must appropriately change the probability of response. In this respect they co-operate with what we may call the signals of need, for example hunger. With increasing hunger level the exploratory tendency is increased, but it does not follow that signals indicating that food has been obtained lower it. Indeed during the minutes immediately after taking a small amount of food an octopus is more likely to make an attack, even at unfamiliar objects (Fig. 13). After larger amounts of food the tendency to attack is decreased for some hours (Fig. 66).

Evidently there is a complicated interaction between signals indicating what the organism needs and those indicating the results of its actions. Unfortunately we still have little knowledge in the octopus or any other animal of how these signals producing 'drive' and 'drive reduction' interact in the brain and control the level of 'motivation' of the organism.

(3) These general changes of tendency are reversed after a relatively short time. Under most conditions there would be little advantage from a permanent, unspecific raising or lowering of exploratory potential. But the third function of the signals of results is to increase or decrease the tendency to take action when the *specific* condition that was indicated by, say, the eyes, at the time of action recurs. The animals must learn to attack figures that have yielded food, but to avoid those that do not, or that result in trauma.

These signals of results thus have the special function of making the selection among the elements of the code (p. 156), producing the prediction that it will be advantageous to repeat the action, or not to repeat it, as the case may be. For this third purpose the signals must presumably be allowed to reach to all the elements of the alphabet. This may perhaps be considered as a dispersal, though it is an amplification in the sense that impulses in relatively few nerve fibres are spread out into a much greater number of channels. The plexiform arrangements to be described in the superior frontal and vertical lobes are indeed such as to allow just this mixing and dispersal.

A specially important consideration arises from the fact that the signals of results may arrive at quite long intervals after the classifying and memory cells (the elements of the alphabet) have been activated by the receptors. Obviously the signals of results must act to ensure that precisely those cells or systems that were in operation at the time of a given action change their probability of response according to whether the results were good or bad. This seems to require that these particular cells be maintained in such a state that the signals of results shall affect them and not others. We may express this by saying that the address of the systems activated by the stimulus must be maintained until the signals of results arrive and can be delivered to them.

It may well be that an important function of the higher

centres is this maintenance of addresses in the memory. Of course the cells stimulated by the receptors might by their own properties remain addressed for sufficient periods (e.g. by lowering of threshold). However, for distance receptors the delay period is quite long (seconds, minutes, or in the highest animals and man even days).

An alternative possibility suggested by Sommerhoff (personal communication) is that the brain learns by formulating a series of hypotheses and then testing them. The particular classifying systems operating on any occasion are thus as it were pre-addressed. Various combinations of them are made sensitive in turn, and learning proceeds as each combination that is ineffective is rejected. This would certainly avoid the necessity to bridge a delay but requires a special mechanism to select the hypotheses.

There is little evidence concerning this problem, but we can get considerable help from looking at different brains and parts of brains. Various special circuits appear when distance receptors come to provide clues for learning. We shall describe these circuits, first in the visual system of *Octopus*, then in the tactile system, and finally in other cephalopods. From the comparisons we can obtain hints as to how to begin to experiment about these matters.

The plan of attack on the problem that we shall adopt is to study these systems *within* the organism rather than from outside it. Millions of words have been written about 'drive' and its 'reduction'. The firm knowledge about it has come from studies with electrodes implanted in the brain (Olds, 1958). We shall try to find the pathways by which the signals that operate these processes are conducted. We shall find centres by which the signals are multiplied and appropriately spread so that they can 'teach' large masses of tissue in the nervous system. Moreover, we shall compare the form of these centres for assessing the results of action in animals with different habitats. In such ways it should be possible to provide objective facts about the mechanisms that control the exploratory tendencies of a learning homeostat.

2. *Balancing by tiers of paired circuits*

The three functions of reflex control, change of motivation, and classification, are all related, the last two especially closely so. It is partly the presence of these various functions of the system for assessing results that makes the study of the higher nervous centres so difficult. We find it hard to make distinctions between parts of the brain concerned with consummation, motivation, and learning. Each region seems to participate in many activities but not to be the exclusive seat of any one of them. This elusiveness becomes less confusing if we realize that the whole system depends upon maintaining a balance between tendencies to do and not to do a given action. It has been possible to find evidence that the attack system of *Octopus* is controlled in this way by paired centres and there are hints that the same principle applies to the much more complicated behaviour of vertebrates.

A system of interlocking centres each producing positive or negative effects is bound to be difficult to disentangle, especially if the centres are so connected as mutually to excite and/or inhibit each other. The proper balancing and assessment of probabilities is produced in the nervous system by pairs of centres with opposite effects, arranged in circuits placed in parallel, in tiers, each acting upon the one below it. There are three such levels in the octopus's visual system (Figs. 67 and 68).

3. *The basic circuit*

A large tract passes from each optic lobe to the anterior basal lobe, this latter being the centre mainly responsible for setting off the attack mechanism (p. 106). An octopus that has been deprived of all the centres above the anterior basal lobe is not blind. It will put out an arm to seize a crab if this is within its immediate reach. But it cannot be induced to follow if the crab moves away, nor will it ever attack a distant moving object. Unfortunately little is known of the direct influence of either food or pain rewards upon this primary optic lobe system.

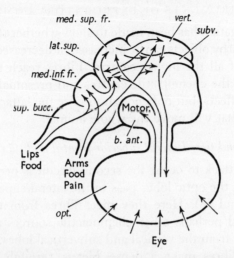

FIG. 67. Diagram of the connexions of the optic lobe with the higher centres of the supraoesophageal lobes.

b.ant., anterior basal; lat.sup., lateral superior frontal; med.inf.fr., median inferior frontal; med.sup.fr., median superior frontal; opt., optic lobe; subv., subvertical; sup.bucc., superior buccal; v., vertical. (Young, 1964b.)

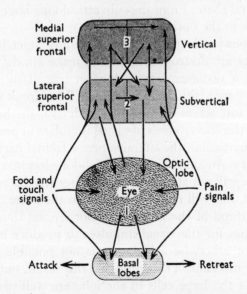

FIG. 68. Diagram to show the connexions of the optic lobes (1) with the pathways indicating 'results' (food and pain), with the motor centres (basal lobes) and with the two tiers of balancing circuits (2 and 3). (Young, 1964b.)

No investigation has been made to show whether the tendency to seize nearby objects can be increased or decreased in animals deprived of all the higher centres. Fibres reach to the optic lobes from the chemotactile centres and presumably rewards can exert effects, but not enough to raise the 'attack potential' to a level that will move the whole animal.

4. *The second tier. Lateral superior frontal and subvertical lobes*

For an attack to occur the second circuit is needed. Other fibres from the optic lobes pass to the lateral superior frontal (Figs. 67 and 68). Here they meet fibres from the inferior frontal, and perhaps other chemotactile sources and a large component from the vertical and subvertical lobes. These and the optic fibres make a dense plexus through which run the axo-dendritic trunks of the cells of the lateral superior frontal lobe itself. These trunks are relatively large and carry many long receptor branches as they pass through the neuropil. Their axons then proceed medially to the subvertical lobe and end there. From the subvertical lobe large cells send axons back to the optic lobe.

An octopus in which this second circuit is intact, but the still higher ones are destroyed, is able to make attacks at objects moving at a distance, but it does so irregularly and often slowly compared with a normal animal. The circuit as a whole, therefore, can act as an amplifying device, in the sense of increasing the effectiveness of visual impulses in producing an attack. In particular, the lateral superior frontal itself seems to be necessary. An animal in which that lobe has been damaged on one side will not attack objects moving at a distance in that visual field, but will do so if they are in the other one.

The neuropil of the lateral superior frontal thus provides opportunities for the visual impulses to produce effects that they cannot otherwise achieve. It is not possible to specify exactly the mechanism that produces this result, but the many branches of the large cells of the lobe are well placed to be stimulated by visual and chemotactile fibres. These latter probably include 'taste' fibres from the arms and lips, which have

the function of signalling when food is taken. Many of these
fibres come through the inferior frontal-subfrontal, posterior
buccal system (p. 246). The interactions in the lateral superior
frontal neuropil must be complicated. In an intact animal
fibres from the vertical and subvertical lobes also end here
providing a positive feed-back (p. 230). These influences
together thus constitute what we may call an amplifying
system, ensuring that impulses in a relatively small number of
optic tract axons are spread into sufficient pathways to produce
an attack.

Part of the output of the lateral superior frontal that produces
this effect may return directly to the optic lobe, but the evidence for this pathway is doubtful. It is certain that a large part
of the output of the lobe proceeds through the subvertical lobe
and thence to the optic lobe. This subvertical relay may pro-
visionally be considered to provide a part of the suppressor
system, allowing pain signals to have their effect in reducing
the tendency to attack. The subvertical lobe is exceptionally
difficult to study experimentally and at present we can only
argue from its connexions. Large tracts of fibres from the arms
and other skin areas reach it and either end or pass on to the
vertical lobes. These are presumed to be fibres carrying pain
signals. There is no direct evidence for this and the interpretation of a suppressor function for the subvertical lobe may
be wrong. But pain signals must reach the system somehow
and there is strong experimental evidence that the vertical
lobe, which projects to the subvertical, can have the effect of
suppressing attacks (p. 212).

The lateral superior frontal and subvertical, lobes will thus
be considered as a pair; the former spreads and multiplies the
visual and tactile signals that tend to produce attack and passes
them back to the optic lobe largely through the subvertical.
This latter allows the impulses to pass unless impulses in pain
fibres intervene. The evidence that these two lobes form a pair
with opposite effects on the tendency to attack is admittedly
incomplete. Lesions in the subvertical lobe inevitably interrupt
much of the output of the lateral superior frontal, median

superior frontal, and vertical lobes. It is therefore hardly to be expected that the results of injuries to the subvertical will tell us very much about the particular contribution that is made to the attack system by the cells and neuropil of the lobe itself. Indeed its 'function' seems to be to assemble the information, from various sources, by means of which Maldonado's 'empirical parameter' (EP) is determined. This is the value that is influenced by experience both from recent and remote past (p. 74).

The large cells of the subvertical lobe seem well suited for this function. After removal of the lobe, or injury to it, animals attack seldom and slowly, as would be expected if the EP is reduced. This assembling of signals is probably the main function of the lobe but as explained the fibres that we presume to carry pain signals run through the lobe and many end there. It will therefore be assumed that the lobe serves also to allow any pain signals to have their effect in reducing the tendency of impulses from the lateral superior frontal to produce attack. It is a good working hypothesis that the lateral superior frontal and subvertical form a pair of centres, one having its output through the other and thus working together but in opposite directions on the production of the command to 'attack'. The median superior frontal and vertical lobes, which lie above them work similarly together and they fortunately are more easy to investigate.

13

EFFECTS OF
REMOVING THE VERTICAL LOBE

1. *The third tier. The vertical lobe circuit*

THE lateral superior frontal and subvertical lobes mentioned in the previous chapter have been described first and separately, but only for convenience. In normal life they work under and with the loop provided by the much larger median superior frontal and vertical lobes (Figs. 66 and 67). These lie superficially and are easy to operate on; we therefore have much experimental information about them.

The median superior frontal receives its input mainly (? wholly) by fibres that have passed through the lateral superior frontal lobes. Many of the fibres of the optic to superior frontal tracts do not end in the lateral lobe but pass through its neuropil to the median lobe. Here they break up into numerous bundles, which interweave with other bundles that come from the inferior frontal lobe and other chemotactile pathways. The bundles divide and recombine repeatedly, producing a neuropil with a characteristic appearance, similar to that of the inferior frontal lobe (Fig. 69). The neuropil constitutes by far the greater part of the volume of the whole lobe. This interweaving of bundles gives us a clue to the method of functioning. The system allows fibres that were previously together to separate and to have opportunity to interact with other fibres, with which they were not previously associated. The 2 million cells of the median superior frontal lobe itself are of moderate size, up to 5μ nuclear diameter, and are all alike in appearance. Their trunks run irregular courses through the neuropil to the hilum at the back of the lobe and thence through an interweaving plexus into the vertical lobe (Fig. 70). Although the cells are small they are none of them of the character of minute amacrines, without axons, which are so characteristic of the vertical lobe (p. 207). The median superior frontal fibres carry collateral dendritic

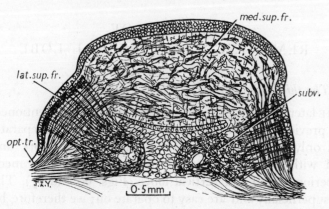

FIG. 69. Transverse section of superior frontal and subvertical lobes of *Octopus*. lat.sup.fr., lateral superior frontal; med.sup.fr., median superior frontal; opt.tr., optic tract; subv., subvertical.

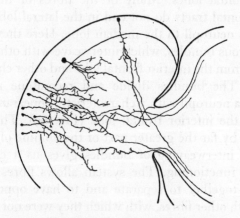

FIG. 70. Drawing of sagittal section of median superior frontal lobe. Golgi stain. (Young, 1964b.)

twigs as they pass through the neuropil and are thus able to be stimulated by the combinations of impulses presented by the incoming bundles.

The vertical lobe has an entirely different structure (Figs. 71 and 72). It consists of five cylindrical lobules, each with a very thick cortex composed mainly of masses of minute cells. On the other hand, the proportion of neuropil is relatively less than in the median superior frontal. There are some 30 million cells in the vertical lobe, the vast majority being

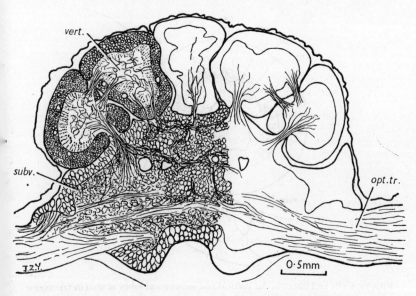

FIG. 71. Transverse section of vertical and subvertical lobes. opt.tr., optic tract; subv., subvertical; vert., vertical.

amacrines, each having a single trunk that breaks up in the neuropil into a bush of equal branches, no one being distinguishable as an axon (Fig. 72). The output of the lobe is produced by a small number of larger cells. Their trunks turn and twist about in the neuropil, carrying numerous dendritic side branches. Finally, these fibres leave the lobe, passing downwards in bundles to end in two destinations (1) the subvertical, and (2) lateral superior frontal lobes.

The fibres of the superior frontal to vertical tract are so mixed in the plexus at entry that fibres originating together in the superior frontal may be in different lobules of the vertical (Fig. 70). In addition there are further crossings of bundles of fibres between the vertical lobules. Clearly here again there is great opportunity for mixing of fibres; any original topographical display of excitation must be lost in the redistribution. The fibres of the tract run in bundles close

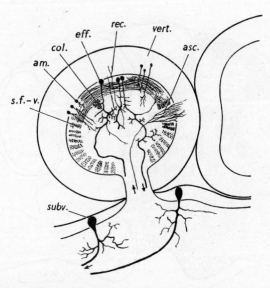

FIG. 72. Cells and fibres of the vertical and subvertical lobes as seen in transverse sections stained with Golgi's method.

am., amacrine cells; asc., ascending fibres from the subvertical lobe, perhaps carrying nocifensor (pain) signals; col., collaterals of large cells; eff., large cells carrying impulses away from the lobe; rec., recurrent branches of the large cells; s.f.-v., bundles of fibres of the superior frontal to vertical tract; subv., subvertical lobe; vert., vertical lobe. (Young, 1964b.)

to the edge of the neuropil, crossing the trunks of the amacrines and other cells of the lobes. They break up and end here, but the details of their connexions with the amacrine cells and with the output cells of the lobe are not known. Nor is it clear how they are related to the second set of fibres that ends in the vertical lobe. These run up in the bundles connecting the vertical and subvertical lobes (Fig. 72). They can be seen undegenerated after complete removal of the vertical lobe.

They are presumed to be nocifensor (pain) fibres, coming either direct from the periphery or after synapse in the subvertical lobe (p. 203).

Large tracts reach the subvertical lobes from the arms and other regions (the cerebro-brachial tracts of Fig. 73). The

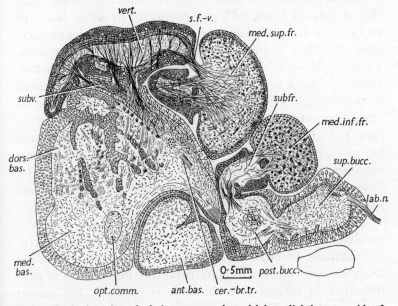

FIG. 73. Sagittal section of whole supraoesophageal lobes, slightly to one side of the mid-line, of *Octopus*.

ant.bas., anterior basal; cer.-br.tr., cerebro-brachial tract; dors.bas., dorsal basal; lab.n., labial nerves; med.bas., median basal; med.inf.fr., median inferior frontal; med.sup.fr., median superior frontal; opt.comm., optic commissure; post.bucc., posterior buccal; s.f.-v., superior frontal to vertical tract; subfr., subfrontal; subv., subvertical; sup.bucc., superior buccal; vert., vertical. (Young, 1963c.)

nature of the fibres in these tracts is not known for certain but it is a reasonable hypothesis that they contain nocifensor (pain) fibres, with perhaps others as well. In preparations with the Golgi method sprays of fibres of these ascending pathways can be seen reaching up through the neuropil of the vertical lobes. They thus run across the incoming fibres of the superior frontal to vertical tract.

This pair of centres thus provides two further circuits.

Firstly, it extends the loop provided by the second tier, so that impulses can run from the optic lobes to lateral superior frontal to median superior frontal to vertical, to subvertical and back to optic. Secondly, it provides an additional short loop running from lateral superior frontal to median superior frontal to vertical and back to lateral superior frontal. This plan of pairs of lobes, each pair connected in series, but with another pair in parallel above it, must have some significance, especially since it appears also in the inferior frontal system. The complex of lobes certainly intervenes in many activities. Many functions have been shown to be impaired by damage to these lobes. Without them animals are slow to learn to attack an unfamiliar figure but conversely are also slow to learn not to attack crabs, which had previously yielded food but now provide a shock. They are slow to learn to discriminate between two objects shown successively, whether by vision or touch. They are unable to transfer learning from one visual field to the other.

The list of activities in which the vertical lobe system is involved suggests that it is likely to be difficult to summarize its functions. In order to try to find a means of formulating them we may consider in more detail the impairment of performance of various tasks by animals in which the system has been damaged.

2. *Irregularity of attack after vertical lobe removal*

An octopus that has lived in one situation for some time and is familiar with one type of food object, or cue for food, comes out very regularly to attack whenever the object appears. Maldonado has investigated this subject by making the octopus use as home a box attached to a balance arm. When the animal left the home a contact was made, and another contact recorded the moment of seizing the prey. By these means Maldonado showed that a 'well-adapted' octopus regularly attacks crabs with a short delay. As he puts it, 'the animal system has rapidly learnt to build up a command to attack this particular visual figure'.

After removal of the vertical lobes the attacks become much slower and the times are more variable (Fig. 79). Later the animals can partially re-learn to attack either crabs or, say, a white rectangle, but the times remain slower and more variable than in normals. The vertical lobe system is therefore concerned with producing a strong and stable level of attack. We could say that it is concerned with motivation to eat, but this does not add much to our picture of how it functions. The vertical lobe system is presumably in some way influenced by the hunger mechanism but certainly does not need to be intact for the animal to become hungry again after satiation.

The best formulation on the evidence that we have considered so far is that the vertical lobe system is concerned in building up the command to attack. Later we shall try to define the part it plays more clearly. Here we may notice that because it contains re-exciting circuits it could provide an increase in the 'command to attack' by what amounts to a positive feed-back. The circuit lateral superior frontal to median superior frontal to vertical to lateral superior frontal seems especially well suited for this.

It is an interesting question whether the vertical lobe system is equally concerned in the building up of commands to retreat. There is no doubt that learning not to attack a given figure is seriously impaired after removal of the vertical lobe (p. 226). There has been no investigation of the question whether the actual retreat, in response to a given painful stimulus, is altered by this operation. It is postulated that signals for pain reach the vertical lobe from below. It might therefore be expected that after its removal the animals would retreat more slowly from a shock.

3. *Failures of the memory system after vertical lobe removal*

From the earliest experiments that Boycott and I made it became clear that the vertical lobes are concerned in some way with the working of the memory store, but the true nature of their functions is only now beginning to be clear. It is relatively easy to remove the lobes from an anaesthetized octopus, but about 5–10 per cent must be left at the front end if damage to the median superior frontal or subvertical is to be avoided. Animals without vertical lobes do not appear to superficial observation to differ in any way from normal ones. They remain at home among the rocks, come out to attack and eat, and walk and swim normally. The lobes are evidently not necessary for any simple motor function. This agrees with the fact that electrical stimulation, which causes movements when applied to many parts of the brain (e.g. anterior basal lobe, centre of optic lobe) produces no obvious effects when applied to the superior frontal or vertical lobes.

The deficiencies that follow vertical lobe removal become apparent in some situations in which the animal has to learn, or to perform an action learned before operation. Thus Boycott and I found that by giving shocks we could train octopuses not to come out to attack when a crab was shown with a white square, while continuing to attack a crab shown alone. If we then removed the vertical lobes the animals began at once to come out in both situations. In spite of receiving many shocks they continued to attack. Only if the square and crab were shown at very short intervals (two minutes) would the animals cease to attack after some shocks. They would show signs of retaining this representation preventing attack only if the situation was presented very frequently. If the crab and square were shown after an interval of, say, five minutes they were again attacked.

These early experiments reveal many of the fundamental features of vertical lobe functioning, although we did not properly understand them at the time. We thought at first that the representations must be stored in the vertical lobe, because when it was removed they seemed to be no longer present. And yet, although no long-lasting representations could be built after operation there were clear signs that they could be established, at least for a short time in some remaining part of the nervous system.

The representations that we were studying at that time were peculiar in that both situations contained crabs, which the octopus had already learned to attack while in the sea. To learn not to come out when the crab is accompanied by a white square is a difficult task. However, the situation has the advantage that it reveals two essential features, first, that the vertical lobes are especially concerned with preventing attack,

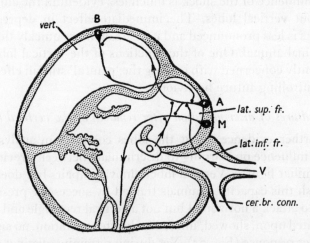

FIG. 74. Vertical lobe system of the cuttlefish (*Sepia*), showing the circuits by which a memory record may be maintained. The optic nerve fibres o cannot by themselves fire either the superior frontal vertical system (A–B) or the motor system (M). If they fire together with visceral food reward fibres (v) they start up the chain ABA whose collaterals facilitate M so that O can now fire it. (Young, 1938.)

and, secondly, that they help in some way to preserve a record based on the events of the immediate past.

We have since learned more about the first of these functions, but the second may prove to be the more interesting. This may be the means by which a record is kept in being for long enough to be printed in the permanent memory. The circuit may be part of what may be called the mechanism for reading in to the memory. It was suggested long ago that the self-re-exciting chains of the vertical lobe circuit might be the basis for memory storage (Young, 1938; see Fig. 74). It is not probable that long-lasting representations are stored in this way, but the immediate effects may be so held (p. 276). One way of investigating this has been to study the time for which signs of a previous shock can be detected. One or more shocks are given when attacks are made at crabs; then at intervals of, say, 2, 4, 8 minutes, &c., the crab is shown again. By testing several octopuses in this way we can use the number of attacks as a measure of the effect of the shock (Fig. 14). The influence of the shock is much less evident in the animals without vertical lobes. The immediate effect in depressing attacks is less pronounced and it wears off more quickly than in a normal animal. One of the functions of the vertical lobes is evidently concerned with making the 'painful' stimuli effective in controlling future behaviour.

4. *Failures of discrimination after removal of the vertical lobes*

Further evidence about the lobes comes from analysis of their influence on learning to discriminate between previously unfamiliar figures. Vertical lobe removal impairs but does not abolish this capacity. Animals trained by successive presentation to attack a horizontal but not a vertical rectangle and then operated upon, showed, immediately after operation, no sign of correct response (Fig. 75). Yet during retraining distinct signs of discrimination appeared. These signs were only really clear in the animals that were trained by trials given in two sessions daily at short intervals, five 'positive' and five 'negative' trials at each session. In a sense the appearance of correct response is misleading because the animals learned during each session but often performed incorrectly at the beginning of the next (Fig. 76). However, there was some slow overall improvement. Once again we see evidence that the representations are not actually within the vertical lobes.

In the experiment shown in Fig. 56 the animals without vertical lobes at first showed quite accurate discriminations in a relatively easy task. However, when the rewards were reversed they completely failed to learn in the new direction. Such reversal is quite possible for normal animals (though signs of the original representations persist, p. 177). This difficulty in reverse learning is an important clue because it again shows that the vertical lobe is concerned with attaching enough of the right reward to the appropriate elements in the memory.

Yet there is no doubt that correct coding of at least some elements can proceed after operation. In the experiment of Fig. 77 the animal seemed at first to have learned nothing. It

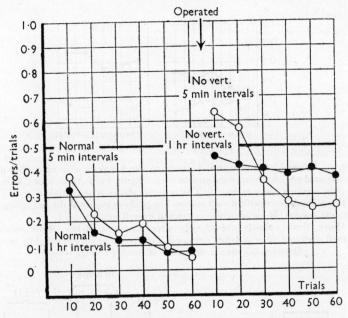

FIG. 75. Effect of removal of the vertical lobes on a previously learned discrimination. The first part of the graphs show the results of training to attack a horizontal rectangle but avoid a vertical one (O trials at 5-minute intervals, ● trials at 1-hour intervals). The vertical lobes were then removed and training continued. (Young, 1961.)

attacked both rectangles on every occasion that they were shown during training. Yet when tested by showing the figures without reward it often showed perfectly 'correct' responses, coming out to the rectangle with which it had been fed but not to the other. The defect of the animal was, therefore, that when during training it received food it thereafter attacked when any moving object appeared. One function of the vertical lobe circuit thus seems to be to ensure a proper balance of

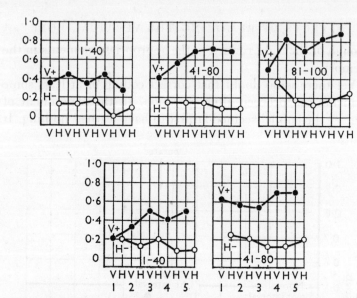

FIG. 76. Vertical lobes removed. Training to attack a vertical rectangle but not a horizontal one. Analysis of the attacks at each figure within the sessions, groups of eight sessions being averaged. The ordinate shows attacks/trials.

The animals learn within each session but perform poorly at the beginning of the next session. However, there is gradual overall improvement.

Above, three animals trained only after operation. Below, three animals trained, operated upon and then retrained. The second group show slightly better performance, but the difference is small. (Young, 1960c.)

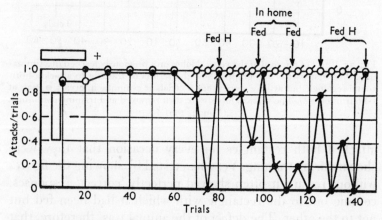

FIG. 77. An octopus without vertical lobes (85 per cent removed) was trained for sixty trials but showed no capacity to discriminate between vertical (closed circles) and horizontal (open circles) rectangles when response to the horizontal rectangle was rewarded with fish. In a series of tests without reward ($\emptyset$ horizontal and ϕ vertical), however, performance was correct, but again deteriorated when food was given at the points shown with arrows, whether the food was given in the home or with the horizontal rectangle. (Young, 1961.)

tendencies to attack and retreat, so that the immediate effect of reward by food is not excessive. We shall see later that it also does the same for the effects of shock. Only if the tendencies of an animal are properly balanced in this way will the behaviour be controlled by the representations set up in the past, rather than by the effects of immediately preceding

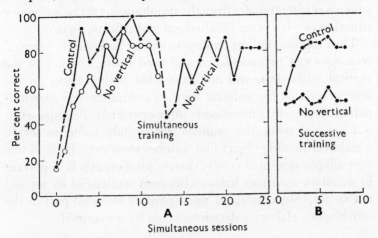

FIG. 78. Percentage correct responses by control and no-vertical animals when trained to attack a black but not a white square by first simultaneous (A) and then successive (B) presentation. (Muntz, Sutherland, and Young, 1962.)

food or painful stimuli. We can thus say that the vertical lobe system is necessary for 'reading-out' of the memory as well as for 'reading-in'.

5. Discrimination of figures shown simultaneously after vertical lobe removal

The best way of proving that representations are present after vertical lobe removal is to eliminate the effects of food or shock by making the animals choose between figures shown simultaneously. Fig. 78 shows that animals without vertical lobes can learn to do this moderately well, though always with less accuracy than normals. When the vertical lobes were removed from animals previously trained, their performance with simultaneous discriminations at first deteriorated, though not to chance level. With further training it reached the same asymptote as that of the animals not trained before operation. (Muntz, Sutherland, and Young, 1962). When these animals that had been trained to discriminate between figures simultaneously were shown them successively they failed to react correctly and could not be taught to do so (Fig. 78). Normal animals readily transfer from the simultaneous to the successive situation or vice versa (Sutherland and Muntz, 1959).

Thus representations tending to ensure biologically 'correct' responses can be established and used in the absence of the vertical lobes. It is still not clear what is the reason for the inaccuracy that the animals show in a simultaneous discrimination, especially immediately after operation. Perhaps without vertical lobes the animals are unduly liable to attack whichever moving object first 'catches their eye'. Even in this very simple system to ensure correct prediction it is important to maintain a correct balance between tendencies to act and not to act. Such balances must play an essential part in the much more elaborate decisions taken by a mammal.

14

PAIRED CENTRES FOR ADDRESSING
THE SIGNALS OF RESULTS

1. *Consecutive operations on vertical and median superior frontal lobes*

As we have seen interruption of the vertical lobe circuit produces an incapacity to discriminate between figures shown successively to an octopus. Careful investigation of the effects of removal of various parts of the circuit has shown, however, that the different lobes are not by any means equivalent, indeed there are indications that they act in opposite directions (Young, 1962e). This can be seen clearly in an experiment in which the lobes were removed separately at consecutive operations (Fig. 79). After the vertical lobes had been removed the octopuses came out to attack more often than before operation. After the median superior frontal had been subsequently removed they then came out much less. When the operations were done in the reverse order the octopuses attacked first less and then more.

This experiment shows that the lobes act in opposite directions and especially that the vertical lobe exercises under these conditions a suppressing influence on the tendency to attack. Since the level of attack fell even after dummy operations (presumably due to the effect of anaesthesia) the experiment does not prove that removal of the median superior frontal specifically reduces the level of attack, but only that removal of the vertical lobe raises it.

2. *Reversal of previous tendencies after operation*

A large series of animals was therefore prepared in which tests were made at much longer periods after operation. Besides dummy operations and removal of either vertical or

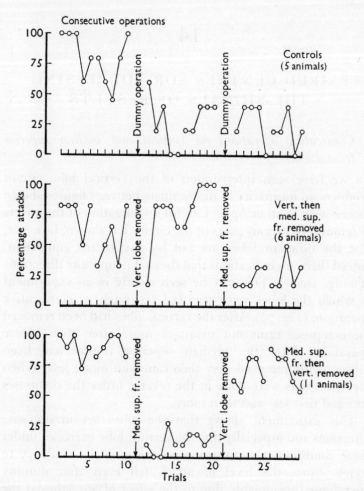

Fig. 79. Consecutive operations to show the different effects of removing the median superior frontal and vertical lobes. The octopuses were tested by showing crabs and recording the attacks, but not allowing them to capture the crabs. No food was given throughout.

After the initial ten tests (one day) the animals were operated as shown. Next day they were further tested. Those without superior frontals attacked less, those without vertical lobes more. All were then operated again and the other lobe removed.

As controls the animals were anaesthetized and the brain exposed.

median superior frontal lobes, in other animals *both* lobes were removed, and in still others the tracts between them cut. Since octopuses vary greatly in their tendency to attack all were tested before operation by showing them crabs, which they were not allowed to eat. The octopuses were then distributed

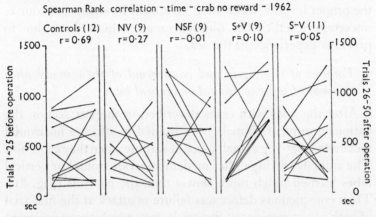

Spearman Rank correlation - time - crab no reward - 1962

FIG. 80. Changes in 'motivation' to attack after operations on the vertical lobe system. The ends of each line show the total time to attack taken by one animal in 25 trials before and after operation. In the controls dummy operation produced relatively little change in tendency to attack. There is a correlation of 0·69 between the rank order before and after operation. After all the other operations the changes were much greater. Most of the operations reversed the 'character' of the animal. Those that attacked much before did so less after and vice versa.

NV., no vertical; NSF, no median superior frontal; s+v, both lobes removed; s−v, superior frontal to vertical tract cut.

to ensure as far as possible, equal initial tendencies in the groups. After the operations they were tested again. In the control animals the operation did not greatly alter the tendency to attack (Fig. 80). The differences between them remained mostly unchanged and the rank correlation before and after operation was 0·69. The animals from which either the vertical or median superior frontal lobes had been removed showed much greater changes in response. In general those that before operation attacked often did so less often after operation. The rank correlations were only 0·27 and −0·01 respectively. The effect of either operation thus depends to some extent on the previous tendency of the animal. Clearly these individual differences are of great importance and seem to be stable characteristics of the animal, depending at least in part upon the median superior frontal and vertical lobe system. We might thus say that a function of these lobes is to maintain the proper level of 'motivation' to attack. It remains, of course, uncertain whether the differences are inherited or due to previous experience in the sea.

3. *Failures of reading-in and reading-out of the memory after removal of superior frontal or vertical lobes*

After the tests with crabs described in the last section the various groups of animals were trained to attack a horizontal rectangle by giving a small piece of sardine when they came out. The animals lacking either median superior frontal or vertical lobes learned much more slowly than the controls (Fig. 81). Their conspicuous defect was failure to attack at the first trial of each of the sessions of five trials, into which the experiment was divided. At the first trial of each session, if the octopus did not attack, it was given a piece of food, which *increased* the subsequent probability of attack (p. 8). The operated animals proved able to make this response of increased attacks but *did not properly attach this reward effect to whatever system represented the horizontal rectangle*. Evidently a further function of this system is to ensure such attachment. It is necessary for correct 'reading-in' to the memory store. In the absence of either lobe no 'conditioning' occurs and many of the animals do not attack the rectangle at the first trial of the next session. In the animals with either median superior frontal or vertical lobes removed, however, there was a slow improvement in this respect, showing as we have seen before that some learning is possible in the absence of either one of the lobes alone.

When both lobes had been removed the animals could still respond with increased attacks as a result of feeding, but showed no sustained increase between sessions (Fig. 81). In this respect there is a sharp contrast with the animals from

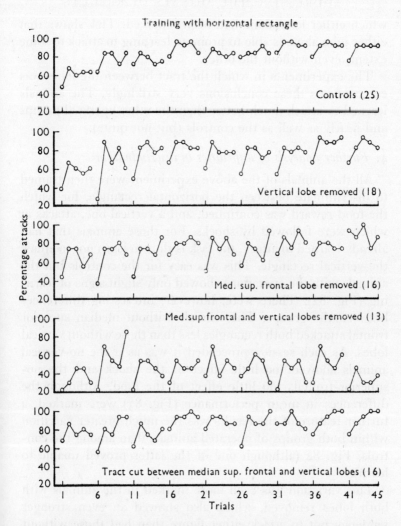

FIG. 81. Training to attack a horizontal rectangle. Trials were given in sets of five, twice daily. At the first trial of each set every animal was fed with a small piece of fish, whether or not it had attacked the rectangle. All groups responded by more frequent attacks at subsequent trials of the sets. Learning to attack was impaired by all the lesions, especially by removal of both lobes. The number of animals in each group is indicated within parentheses.

which either lobe alone had been removed. This shows that either lobe alone is able to promote learning to attack to some extent, even without the other.

The experiments in which the tract between the lobes was cut confirms these conclusions very strikingly. The animals learned to attack much better than the other operated groups and nearly as well as the controls (but not quite).

4. *Further analysis of difficulties in discrimination*

All the animals of the above experiment were then trained to discriminate between the horizontal rectangle, for which the food reward was continued, and a vertical one, attacks at which were followed by shocks. For those animals that had already learned to attack, the task is thus to learn not to attack the vertical rectangle. This was easy for the controls but the animals with the operations showed only slight signs of learning (Fig. 82). There were, however, interesting differences between the groups. The animals without median superior frontal attacked both rectangles less than those without vertical lobes. As each session proceeded it was as if the no-vertical animals showed too little effect of the shock and the no-superior-frontals too little effect of the food. Although the differences in mean performance (Fig. 83) were marked, a further feature of the results was the much greater variation within both groups of operated animals than among the controls, Fig. 82 (although one of the latter proved unable to learn).

This variation was even more marked in the animals with both lobes removed, which also showed an even stronger tendency not to attack either figure than had those without median superior frontal lobes. Conversely, the animals with the tract between the lobes cut came the closest to the normals both in variability and in tendency to attack. However, even at the end of the experiment they showed only slightly less than 50 per cent of errors.

The discrimination experiment thus confirms that the presence of both lobes and the connexion between them is necessary to produce what we have called the proper addressing of signals of results in the memory. But beyond this it also suggests that the two lobes play distinct parts, the median

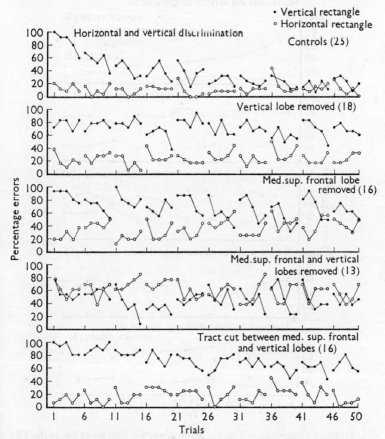

FIG. 82. Learning not to attack a vertical rectangle while continuing to attack a horizontal one. Each series consisting of five trials with each figure shown alternately. The horizontal rectangle was shown first and food given to every animal whether or not it attacked. Subsequently food was given only after attacks at the horizontal rectangle. Shocks (10 V a.c.) were given for attacks at the vertical rectangle. Performance was impaired after all lesions.

superior frontal being the more important for attaching signals indicating food reward, the vertical lobe those indicating pain. However, it must be emphasized that the two lobes normally work in series and injury to either of them influences the functions of both.

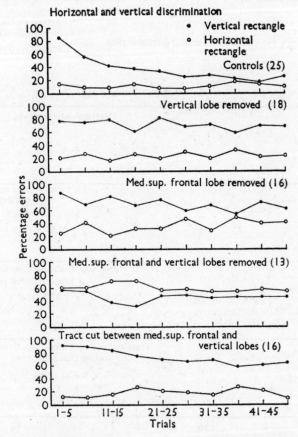

FIG. 83. Same experiment as Fig. 84. Mean errors for each set of five trials. The animals without vertical lobes make mistakes mainly by attacking the 'negative' figure (vertical rectangle) too much. Those without median superior frontal attack the positive figure (horizontal rectangle) too little.

5. *Difficulties in learning not to attack crabs*

One of the first symptoms that Boycott and I found after removal of the vertical lobes was inability to learn not to attack crabs when shocks were given for the attacks. Control animals are readily able to do this. By the fifth trial (at 10

min intervals) only 40 per cent of them attacked and by the
ninth trial 5 per cent (Fig. 84). The animals without vertical

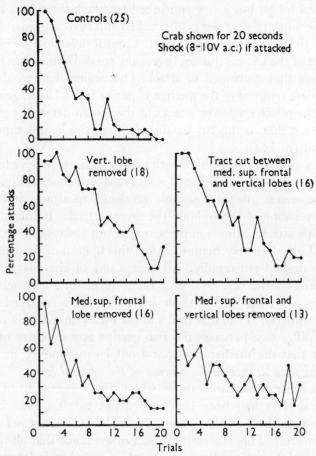

FIG. 84. Learning not to attack crabs when attacks result in shocks. A crab was
shown to each animal twenty times, at 10-minute intervals. If there was no attack
within 20 s. the crab was pulled away by a thread. No feeding throughout the
experiment.

The learning was impaired by all the operations. The animals with the vertical
lobe removed attacked more vigorously than those without median superior
frontal.

lobes continued to attack for very much longer; at the ninth
trial 65 per cent still came out and some continued to do so
until the last of the twenty trials of the experiment.

The animals without the median superior frontal lobe mostly ceased attacking much sooner than those without vertical lobes, but a few continued to attack for a long time. At the ninth trial 12 per cent attacked and two continued to do so to the end of the experiment. Careful investigation of the extent of the lesions did not reveal any special features in those animals that continued to attack. One animal had an almost complete removal of the median superior frontal lobe, proving that the relatively fewer attacks of the remainder of the group were not due to the cut passing close to the lateral superior frontal (p. 202).

The animals from which both lobes had been removed were most interesting when tested with crabs and shocks (Fig. 84). There was a low and variable tendency to attack, but this hardly changed throughout the twenty trials. Some of the animals attacked the crab persistently, but always in a characteristically leisurely manner. After this operation the animals never dashed out rapidly. All except one of the no-verticals attacked at the first trial and their mean time to reach the crab was 5·8 sec, but of those with both lobes removed only 8/13 came out at the first trial and the mean time was 11·0 sec. The difference between the two groups is a measure of the effect that the median superior frontal can produce in promoting attack, *even in the absence of the vertical lobe*.

By contrast the animals in which the superior frontal to vertical tract had been cut learned not to attack the crabs faster than the animals without vertical lobes, but not so fast as the controls. This is a further piece of evidence that although the two lobes normally work in series each has independent input and output pathways through which it can influence behaviour independently of the other.

6. *Functions of the vertical lobe system for control of attack and addressing of rewards*

These experiments with removal of different parts of the complex thus allow us to proceed considerably further with the analysis of the significance of these lobes. They show that by the distribution of signals indicating the results of action the lobes ensure that the octopus learns to attack or to retreat when particular figures occur. The changes that occur in the rank order of the frequency of attack after operation show that both the median superior frontal and the vertical lobe influence the tendency to attack.

After removal of either lobe the characteristic frequency of attack often changes; they may either increase or decrease according to the previous level. Animals that were attacking strongly before operation usually attacked less after removal of the median superior frontal. Conversely, removal of the vertical lobe was often followed by an increase in attacks by animals that previously attacked seldom.

These facts do not necessarily mean that long-term changes in the level of attack are produced by changes within these lobes, though this cannot be excluded as a possibility. The hypothesis may be advanced that each lobe has a constant effect. The median superior frontal lobe acts to increase the probability that any movement in the visual field will produce an attack. The vertical lobe further increases this probability, unless there has been trauma, in which case the vertical lobe increases the probability of *retreat* from that figure. The long-term differences that are produced by experience thus lie elsewhere, probably in the optic lobes. If an octopus has acquired a high level of attack at a given figure this means that there are cells (or systems of cells) in its optic lobes that are able to produce the attacks, provided that the median superior frontal lobe is there to multiply the signals. After its removal there is, therefore, a fall in attacks. This will also follow after vertical lobe removal. An animal that was seldom attacking had presumably suffered much trauma so that some visual attributes of any situation will cause the optic lobes to signal 'retreat'. Since such signals are multiplied by the vertical lobe it follows that removal of the latter will produce increase in attack.

There is not sufficient evidence to be certain that this is how the system operates but the evidence that the vertical lobe increases the effect of signals of pain is strong (p. 214). It is reasonable, therefore, to adopt the hypothesis that the two lobes exert their effects in opposite directions but that the effects do not themselves change with learning. The evidence suggests that the actions of these two lobes also do not change with satiation or food deprival (p. 222). They cannot, therefore, quite be called centres for 'motivation' or 'drive'. It is probably best for the present to say simply that they are centres for the spreading, multiplication, and balancing of the signals of the results of action.

Since the two lobes are linked in a circuit it is not surprising that the effects of removal are not simple. Thus the time taken for an attack is reduced after removing either of them, since this breaks the positive feed-back system. One interpretation is that the output from the median superior frontal lobe will tend to increase the probability of attack unless the vertical lobe intervenes, as it were, with a suppressor action, produced by the operation of nocifensor (pain) fibres. The tract from the vertical lobe to the lateral superior frontal may be the pathway that provides further excitation by positive feed-back. The vertical lobe probably has in itself largely inhibitory or suppressor effects, and yet animals from which it has been removed attack more slowly and learn more slowly to attack than do normals (Maldonado, 1962). This apparent paradox, that the lobe appears to be both excitatory and inhibitory, is explained by the fact that the excitatory effect of the median superior frontal is exercised largely through the vertical lobe, where the pain signals can intervene. We do not know whether, in the absence of pain signals, the vertical lobe has any further amplifying effect on the signals from the median superior frontal lobe tending to produce attack. It certainly allows spreading and distribution of the fibres of the superior frontal to vertical tract and may have the effect of amplifying both pain and food signals.

7. *Function of the vertical lobe circuit in transfer of representations*

One of the most baffling problems presented by this system is to decide whether it plays a part both in the establishing of representations elsewhere in the brain and in their use. Animals with these circuits damaged perform less well than normals even with a simultaneous discrimination (Fig. 78). But this does not necessarily mean that the 'printing' of representations has been impaired. The poor performance might well be a result of the irregularity of behaviour that has been produced by upsetting the balance of the system.

It seems probable that both functions are present, indeed perhaps it is artificial to try to think of them separately. One piece of evidence is that animals without vertical lobes can reach the same asymptote of performance in a tactile discrimination, but more trials are required for them to do so (Wells, 1959a). The tactile learning system has its own lobes for addressing signals of results (p. 250). The vertical lobe system may be simply ancillary to these.

A characteristic feature of the organization of the superior frontal and vertical lobes is that they allow the mixing of influences from different parts of the receptor fields, and indeed of different receptors themselves (eyes, touch, and chemoreceptors). It seems likely that this enables them to play a part in the process of generalization; that is to say, transfer of representations from one part of the nervous system to another. This is a very important feature of the building of a model with which effective forecasts are made. No transfer between modalities has been demonstrated in *Octopus* and indeed discriminations that have been learned by sight cannot then be made by touch (Wells, 1961b).

Within each modality transfer is well marked, however. Objects that have been presented to one arm only are correctly identified by the others. Visual discriminations learned by presentation in one part of the visual field of one eye only are correctly performed when the object is presented in another part of the same field or in the field of the opposite eye (Muntz, 1961). The representation is actually transferred to the optic lobe of the side that has not been trained. This was proved by removing the lobe on the trained side and showing that the discrimination was still performed by the opposite eye. The transfer across the mid-line no longer takes place if the vertical lobe has been removed or divided by a cut down the mid-line. This dependence on the vertical lobe system is all the more remarkable because there is, in addition, a very large optic commissure joining the two optic lobes, but this alone does not allow transfer of learning. We can, however, explain this in terms of the above hypothesis. It seems unlikely that the information as to which cells in the optic lobes have been stimulated is passed through the vertical lobe circuit. The function of this circuit is rather to maintain a lowered threshold in the cells that have been stimulated from the retina and then to deliver the signals of results back to them. For transfer to the opposite side, therefore, it is necessary to find the addresses of the appropriate cells there. For this we must assume that the ventral optic commissure contains fibres connecting similar types of cells in the two lobes. This is a large assumption, but it is difficult to see how the information can be transferred without some such specific links. The vertical lobe circuit would then be necessary to maintain the addresses in the opposite optic lobe after they had been found through the commissure, and then later to deliver the conditioning signals to that side.

8. *The functions of tiers of circuits in the balancing and addressing of signals indicating results*

The various influences that the signals indicating food or pain exercise upon behaviour are thus produced by several sets of circuits arranged in tiers, as it were in parallel, one above the other (Fig. 68). The same circuits also serve to maintain the cells that were stimulated by the exteroceptor in a suitably receptive state to receive the signals that indicate results. Each circuit contains paired elements, one increasing and the other decreasing the probability of a given action. These two elements are arranged in series at each level but the output of each element also influences the opposite element at a lower level. It is evident that with such a system of connexions it will not be easy to work out exactly how a given set of signals will influence behaviour. The result may well be to provide a spreading and multiplication of food and pain signals so that their effects in changing the probability of action are properly evaluated and balanced. The details of how this is achieved by the quantitative features of the networks remain to be discovered and should be of great interest.

The optic lobes of an octopus presumably contain pathways by which food or pain signals tend to initiate attack or retreat. The lateral superior frontal certainly increases the attack tendency and the subvertical probably reduces it. The median superior frontal increases attack and the vertical may inhibit it. The vertical lobe increases the tendency to retreat when pain signals occur. We have, therefore, evidence for the existence of paired centres for spreading and multiplication of the signals that indicate the results of action (food or trauma). The centres ensure the arrival of these signals at the cells that are involved in encoding the visual impulses. Thus the latter become appropriately 'addressed', that is to say, connected with either the pathway that ensures attack or that for retreat. This function of signalling the results of action is obviously of fundamental importance for any organism and we may hope to find further details of its operation by study in *Octopus*. In particular it would be very important to clear up some of the problems deriving from the fact that the median superior frontal produces much or all of its effect through the vertical lobe. Do the two parts then truly work in opposite directions or should both be considered as parts of a single system for spreading and multiplying signals both for feeding and avoidance?

9. *Tiers of circuits in vertebrates*

It is tempting to speculate that similar tiers of circuits exist in the vertebrate brain. Certainly there are signs that the three functions of signals of results discussed on p. 197 can be recognized in different regions. Thus the effect of food reward in producing consummatory actions is mediated by the reflex centres of the medulla. The second effect of raising or lowering the tendencies to take certain actions appears in the functions of the basal forebrain centres, and these operate by circuits. Thus the well-known 'Papez circuit' influencing 'emotional' behaviour includes the hippocampus, mammillary body, anterior nucleus of the thalamus, and cingulate cortex. These areas are certainly concerned with 'reward', as is shown by the fact that with stimulating electrodes implanted in them animals can be made either to seek self-stimulation from one centre or to avoid it if the electrode is in another one near by (Olds, 1960; Lilly, 1960). No doubt centres for many different actions are involved and it is a major problem to envisage how they may be integrated. Perhaps the variety of basic action patterns is much less than might be supposed.

The maximum complexity in the regulation of behaviour undoubtedly comes at the highest level, where signals of results are used to register that certain particular external events or actions are likely to be favourable or unfavourable for survival. This 'addressing' is the third function that we have listed for these signals and it is interesting that it is effected in mammals by the thalamo-neocortical circuits, superimposed on top of those of the forebrain base. Although it is notoriously dangerous to try to speak of the locality of 'engrams' in a mammal, there can be little doubt that they reside largely in the neocortex. And yet for both their establishment and use the underlying circuits are needed. Human beings from whom both hippocampal lobes have been removed for the cure of epilepsy show gross defects of memory for recent events (Scoville and Milner, 1957). Yet in such people the basic model that enables them to maintain their personal identity and behaviour remains intact. Conversely, during electrical stimulation of the temporal region under local anaesthesia, a patient may discover to his surprise that he is unable to remember a number he was told shortly before (Penfield and Roberts, 1958).

It is difficult to see in detail at present how these basal circuits are linked to the neocortical ones. The thalamo-neocortical systems correspond to the optic lobes of the octopus system, as the distance receptor input pathways. They must somehow come under the influence of the signals indicating results (pain and pleasure, &c.). If the centres of the limbic system are concerned with the proper balancing and addressing of such signals, how are these then conveyed to the neocortex? The pathways that we know, such as those of the Papez circuit seem complete in themselves. Since, however, they are certainly concerned with recording in the memory, we may search with some confidence for the pathways through which they teach the neocortex.

Knowledge of these regions has grown remarkably in recent years but their actions are of quite baffling complexity. This is hardly surprising if they include many paired centres, each tending to produce or to inhibit some action. No doubt to think only of a large set of pairs is too crude an approach. Indeed, a classificatory system of this sort that was able to perform all the actions of a human would seem to demand even more neurons than we possess (see Uttley, 1961). Almost certainly the brain uses some system of compromise. By means of suitable analogues it avoids a full binary classification. It may be that the secret of how this is achieved lies in the arrangement of tiers of circuits. Each lower level establishes a general tendency to act or not to act in some whole range of situations. The tiers above are concerned with finer and finer detail. And so it may be even within the neocortex, with the primary, secondary, and tertiary representations of the receptor and motor fields.

It is idle to pretend that we yet understand the system, much as we should like to do so. But it is interesting to find strong evidence that spreading and amplification of signals indicating the results of action and optimizing their effects are produced by paired centres and tiers of circuits in such different animals. The assessment of probabilities is a similar problem for octopuses and men.

15

LEARNING OF CHEMO-TACTILE
RESPONSES AND DISCRIMINATION

1. *The chemo-tactile investigatory system*

IN the eight arms and their suckers an octopus has a tactile
system probably better developed than that of any other
invertebrate, and indeed than of most vertebrates. Moreover,
elaborate exploratory movements are made, and the arms can
be extended to surprising lengths, so that a small octopus,
weighing, say, 500 g, has tactile information about a territory
some 120 cm in diameter. There is therefore an appreciable
delay between the moment when an arm seizes an object and
draws it towards the mouth and the arrival of taste signals
from the latter. The arms of an octopus are in a sense used as
distance receptors. It is therefore most interesting to find in
the part of the brain concerned with touch that there are two
pairs of centres organized into long and short loops, exactly
as in the visual system (Figs. 93 and 94).

The receptors are mainly in the rims of the suckers and they
send fibres into chains of ganglia in the arms, one ganglion to
each sucker (Fig. 18). In these ganglia connexion is made with
motor cells that operate the muscles of the suckers. There are
connexions between neighbouring ganglia, and fibres also pass
centrally in the brachial nerves, through the anterior suboesophageal mass, to the inferior frontal/subfrontal lobes. The
more elaborate tactile discriminations depend upon the integrity of the inferior frontal system (p. 255) but the ganglia
of the arms, acting alone, are capable of much independent
control. If a piece of food is touched the suckers make movements that transfer it towards the mouth. These movements
will take place in an orderly manner in an arm that has been

completely isolated from the body, during the few minutes before it dies from ischaemia.

The movement of taking food to the mouth is the basic action of the arms. The process of discrimination learning involves continuing to do this for one type of object but not for another. Wells and Wells (1956) have studied various forms of this learning. They have used mainly octopuses that had been blinded by severing the optic nerves, having previously shown that neither this operation nor removal of the optic lobes has any effect on tactile learning.

When an octopus encounters an unfamiliar object with an arm it draws the object in and 'examines' it for times varying from a few seconds to 30 minutes. If the object is edible it is held with the beak and broken up by the radula, if inedible it is ultimately rejected by a movement of the suckers and muscles of the arms that is the reverse of the previous acceptance. The time taken to examine inedible things falls rapidly with repeated presentations, until the objects are rejected within a few seconds, or indeed are examined cursorily with an arm tip but not picked up at all. This change in behaviour presumably has the nature of habituation (extinction), that is to say, the failure to continue with an inborn response that does not yield a reward. It is specific for the object learned; if another object is given it will be drawn to the mouth.

After removal of the vertical lobes octopuses show an interesting change in that they examine inedible objects for about six times longer than normal animals, before rejecting them (Wells and Wells, 1957a). This suggests that the superior-frontal/vertical system is somehow concerned with the classification of tactile inputs. The hypothesis we shall put forward is that, as for visual learning, the vertical lobes have, as one of their functions, the maintenance of the 'address' of the tactile cells that have been stimulated and the delivery to them of the signals that indicate the results of the action.

The animals without vertical lobes show a further difference from normals in that they retain the effects of tactile habituation less well. If tested shortly after they have stopped accepting an object they will again draw it in. Wells and Wells showed that this habituation, learning not to draw in objects, occurs within the tissues of the inferior frontal/subfrontal complex of lobes (Fig. 85). It continues in animals that have

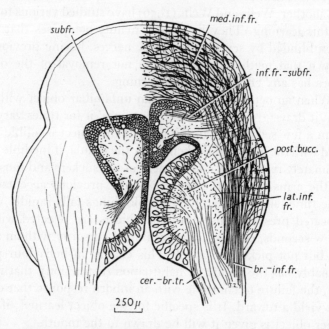

FIG. 85. Transverse section of the chemotactile centres. br.-inf.fr., brachio-inferior frontal tract; cer.-br.tr., cerebro-brachial tract; inf.fr.-subfr., inferior frontal to subfrontal tract; lat.inf.fr., lateral inferior frontal; med.inf.fr., median inferior frontal; post.bucc., posterior buccal; subfr., subfrontal.

been deprived of any or all of the other parts of the supra-oesophageal lobes, though it is impaired after removal of the vertical lobes. After the median inferior frontal and subfrontal lobes have been removed an octopus continues to draw objects to the mouth as often as they are presented even if they are inedible. This is important evidence that the ganglia of the arms, acting alone, are unable to mediate even simple learning processes and in this they resemble the vertebrate spinal cord.

2. *Chemo-tactile discriminations*

The receptors of the arms have been shown to be capable of sending to the brain signals about the degree of 'roughness' of objects touched and about their chemical nature (Wells, 1962a and 1963). The chemical sense was investigated by rewarding octopuses with fish for drawing in objects soaked in one solution but giving shocks when they drew in another one. Remarkably high sensitivity was found. Hydrochloric acid, sucrose, and quinine were detected in sea-water at concentrations 100 times less than the human tongue can detect them in distilled water. It is not certain how this chemical sense in the arms is related to that of the lips around the mouth. The latter contain abundant receptors and it is assumed that these signal the presence of 'food', but there is no evidence of this.

3. *Mechano-tactile discrimination*

In their early discrimination experiments Mr. and Mrs. Wells trained octopuses with the shells of lamellibranchs and found that the animals readily learned not to draw in specimens that were filled with wax, while continuing to take live ones (Fig. 86a). This discrimination was probably based on chemical receptors. Even isolated arms make writhing movements when meat extracts are placed near them.

More extensive experiments were made with the more strictly tactile receptors. Octopuses were shown to be able to discriminate, after training, between the shells of different species of lamellibranchs, even when filled with wax, *provided that the pattern of ribs was different*. Species that differ in shape but not in roughness could not be distinguished (Fig. 86b).

Further investigation showed that octopuses cannot easily discriminate shapes by touch and this has been confirmed by presenting to them objects cut out of plastic and grooved in various ways (Fig. 87a). The octopuses can recognize as distinct those that differ in degree of roughness, but not when the grooves differ only in direction or 'pattern'. Moreover, the accuracy with which the animals distinguish between objects is proportional to the extent of the difference in roughness (Fig. 87*b*).

It is not quite true that no discrimination between shapes is possible. Octopuses trained to pull a sphere but not a cube towards the mouth, made far more mistakes than with the ribbed

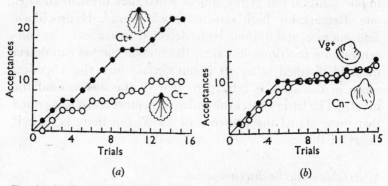

FIG. 86. (*a*) Training of a blind octopus to distinguish by chemical clues. The animal was presented with live *Cardium tuberculatum* and allowed to eat them (Ct+). When wax-filled shells of the same species were taken the animal was given a shock (Ct−). There were eight trials daily and the curves show the cumulative acceptances. (*b*) Failure to discriminate between wax-filled shells of *Venus gallina* (Vg+) and *Cardium norvegicum*, which differ in shape but not texture. Fish was given for acceptance of the positive object, shocks for the negative. (After Wells and Wells, 1956.)

and smooth cylinders. However, after an intensive course of training at forty trials a day something like 75 per cent accuracy with the sphere and cube was achieved. Further tests showed that the cue used was the sharp edges of the object. When tested with a cube with rounded edges the octopuses were still able to distinguish it from a sphere, but made even more mistakes than before. Moreover, when presented with a smooth cylinder of narrow diameter and rounded ends they confused this with the cube rather than with the sphere (Wells, 1962*a*).

This all suggests that such information as can be gathered about the shape of objects depends upon measuring the

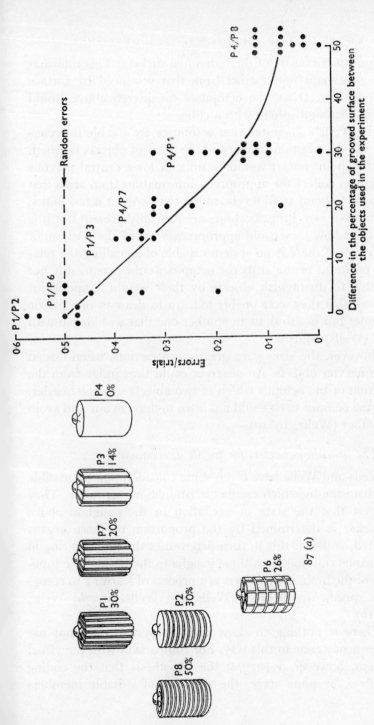

FIG. 87: (a) Perspex cylinders used for tactile discrimination. The percentages show the proportion of grooved surface. Octopuses find P_1, P_2, and P_6 difficult to discriminate, but can distinguish between those in the top row, and also P_8 and P_4. (Wells and Wells, 1957b.) (b) Difficulty of tactile discrimination as a function of the similarity of surface sculpturing of two objects. The ratio of errors to trials is plotted against percentage difference between the objects. Each point represents the errors by a single animal. (Wells and Wells, 1957b.)

amount of curvature of the individual suckers. This information is perhaps not distinct from that produced by surface
irregularities. If so, the octopuses considered above would
confuse a rough sphere with a cube.

The Wells's suggested that octopuses are unable to recognize the distribution in space of the areas of objects touched.
As they point out, it would be difficult for a central nervous
system to collect the appropriate information from arms that
are able to bend at all levels, rather than only at a few joints,
as our own can. Proprioceptors are probably present but it is
not clear how they could appropriately signal the position of
the arms. If there is no system capable of signalling the relative positions of the arms the octopus would presumably not
be able to distinguish objects by their weight. Experiment
showed that they were unable to learn to draw in one plastic
cylinder but not to draw in another one that was loaded with
lead (Wells, 1961a).

However, the arms gave greater contractions when loaded
with heavier objects. An observer could thus judge from the
reaction of the octopus which of two objects was the heavier.
But the octopus itself could not learn to draw in one and avoid
the other (Wells, 1961a).

4. *The neural mechanism for tactile discrimination*

Wells and Wells have given some consideration to possible
mechanisms by which tactile discriminations are made. They
suggest that the state of excitation in the ganglion above
a sucker is determined by the proportion of sense organs
excited, and that this in turn determines the rate of firing in
the axons running from these ganglia to the brain. The function of the brain is then seen as a process of learning to recognize specific frequencies (Wells and Wells, 1957b; Wells,
1961b).

There is nothing to show that the system does not use
a frequency code in this way. For comparison with the visual
system, however, I suggest the hypothesis that the coding
involves, at some stage, the selection of suitable members

among a set of cells, arranged to respond to different degrees of 'roughness'. This would be achieved by a set of cells with a range of spread of dendrites. The cells with the larger spreads or more densely distributed synapses might signal the presence of much irregularity and vice versa. If each cell has alternative pathways we should have an arrangement like that in the visual system (p. 155). We shall discuss later the question of where such cells may be located.

It has been shown by Graziadei (1962) that the margins of the smaller suckers at the tips of the arms are especially richly supplied with receptors of various types. These cells have collaterals that make a plexus within the epithelium. This arrangement recalls the collaterals in the retina and may well serve to increase contrast at edges, if an active cell tends to inhibit its neighbours.

The axons of these cells may run direct to the main nerve cord but some of them end in connexion with large encapsulated nerve-cells lying beneath the epithelium. These latter cells have numerous short dendrites and each presumably serves to produce an integrated output in response to deformation of a part of the sucker rim. The details of the functioning of the arrangement shown by Graziadei clearly provide possibilities for collecting tactile information as suggested by Wells.

5. *The tactile learning centres*

Considerable progress has been made in identifying the parts that the various supraoesophageal lobes play in these mechano-tactile learning processes. A convenient technique is to teach octopuses not to draw a particular grooved plastic object to the mouth. This can readily be done by giving electric shocks when the object is taken. After a few (2–4) shocks the animals steadily reject the object but will draw in others.

If the object had been presented only to one arm during training, and was then presented to an arm on the opposite side of the body, it was at first accepted. Wells (1959b) established the curious and perhaps very important fact that this is true only if the training trials have been placed close together, at intervals of a few minutes. If the trials are spread out at intervals of half an hour, then the learning has time to 'spread' to the parts of the centres connected with all the other arms and the object will be rejected by any of them.

The organization of the tactile centres of the inferior frontal region has interesting similarities with that of the superior frontal-vertical system. Indeed, it is now possible to suggest that both sets of centres are connected with the buccal lobe system, which is primarily concerned with the mechanism for obtaining food.

The superior buccal lobe of *Octopus* is a median structure receiving numerous nerves from the receptors around the mouth and lips (Fig. 88). Through the circum-buccal connectives and inferior buccal ganglia it controls the movements of the beak and file-like radula. An octopus deprived of all the supraoesophageal ganglia, including the superior buccal lobe, cannot eat. If only the superior buccal lobe is present the octopus can eat sardines, but often has difficulty with crabs, which are taken and passed to the mouth but may remain alive there for hours. Or it may kill the crabs and devour them only partly and untidily, whereas the normal animal opens them neatly and removes all the meat.

Evidently the superior buccal is one of the motor centres for the basic operations of feeding. The whole of the inferior frontal-subfrontal and superior frontal-vertical systems can be considered as special extensions of the buccal centres, providing a learning system that decides whether a given object touched or seen shall be eaten.

The arrangement of the centres behind the superior buccal and below the inferior frontal lobes has only recently been fully described, but is of great interest because of its similarity to the superior frontal-vertical lobe system (Young, 1963c).

The superior buccal lobe divides posteriorly and continues backwards as paired lobes, which we shall call the posterior buccal lobes (following a suggestion of Thore, 1939, for *Sepia*) (Figs. 73, 85, and 88). These posterior buccal lobes are

continuous behind with the subvertical lobe and each receives
large tracts of fibres from the arms, and, through the superior
buccal, from the lips. Its walls consist of both large and small

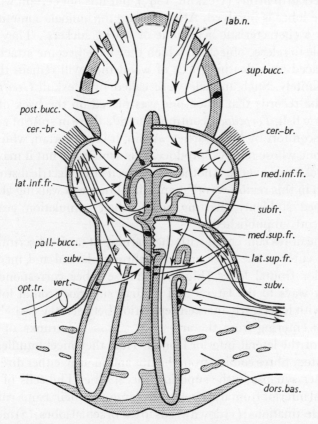

FIG. 88. Diagrammatic horizontal section of supraoesophageal lobes of *Octopus*
to show the learning centres for tactile discriminations.
   cer.-br., cerebro-brachial tract; dors.bas., dorsal basal; lab.n., labial nerve;
lat.inf.fr., lateral inferior frontal; lat.sup.fr., lateral superior frontal; med.inf.fr.,
median inferior frontal; med.sup.fr., median superior frontal; opt.tr., optic tract;
pall.-bucc., palliobuccal tract (? pain); post.bucc., posterior buccal; subfr.,
   subfrontal; subv., subvertical; sup.bucc., superior buccal; vert., vertical.

cells and it probably constitutes the main output pathway for
the tactile learning system. In this it corresponds in part to the
subvertical lobe, with which it is continuous.

The evidence about the function of the posterior buccal lobes is incomplete. Electrical stimulation in this region is said to initiate feeding movements of the beak and to make the suckers grip firmly (Uexküll, 1895), but it is not certain which of the lobes is involved. After injuries the animals sometimes show a characteristic syndrome of 'sticky suckers'. They are unable to release objects to which they have become attached. If placed on a floating piece of wood they will remain there indefinitely. Such animals were called by Uexküll *Greiftiere* and he records that when one was placed on the back of an electric fish, *Torpedo*, it continued to ride there in spite of signs of discomfort by both parties. Again, it is not certain which is the lobe whose removal produces this syndrome, but it may be the posterior buccal. Another effect seen after electrical stimulation in this region was that an animal that was walking about stopped suddenly, starting again when stimulation ceased (Boycott, unpublished).

The fibres concerned with the learning of tactile discriminations enter at the sides and pass through lateral and median inferior frontal lobes (Fig. 85). These lobes correspond in many ways to the lateral and median superior frontal lobes, but with less clearly marked separation between the two.[1] The fibres entering from the arms run across the trunks of the cells of the lateral inferior frontal. Here they meet bundles of gustatory fibres coming from the lips and mouth, either directly or after synapse in the superior buccal lobe. The cells of the lateral inferior frontal are relatively large and their axons run to four destinations: (1) downwards to the brachial lobes; (2) medially to the posterior buccal lobes; (3) posteriorly to the lateral superior frontal lobes; and (4) laterally to the optic lobes.

The lateral inferior frontal thus serves to allow interaction of signals from the arms and lips and to deliver the resulting output either back to the arms or lips, or to the vertical lobe or optic system. Moreover, the interweaving bundles of

[1] In previous publications Wells has used the term lateral inferior frontal (on my advice) to include with the lobe of that name as here defined also what we are now calling the posterior buccal. He had earlier urged on me the adoption of Thore's suggestion and I regret not having seen its aptness until recently.

brachial fibres and buccal fibres continue upwards into the median inferior frontal.

The cells of the median inferior frontal lobe are smaller than those of the lateral inferior frontal. They are all alike in size and form and have a remarkable similarity to the cells of the

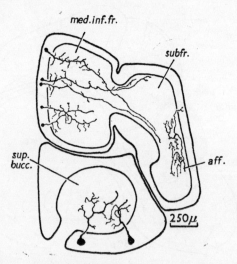

FIG. 89. Part of a thick sagittal section of buccal and inferior frontal lobes of *Octopus* stained with Golgi's method.

aff., afferent fibre, probably carrying nocifensor signals to subfrontal lobe from below; med.inf.fr., median inferior frontal; subfr., subfrontal; sup.bucc., superior buccal.

median superior frontal. Their trunks run across the interweaving bundles of incoming fibres, among which they give off collateral dendritic branches (Figs. 89 and 90). The axons of these median inferior frontal cells then proceed to the subfrontal lobe, which is composed mainly of minute cells. This relationship is thus exactly similar to that between the median superior frontal and the vertical lobes. The fibres from the median inferior frontal enter the subfrontal through a plexus and then proceed to run tangentially at the outer border of the neuropil (Figs. 90 and 91). This is a position comparable to that occupied by the fibres of the superior frontal to vertical lobe tract.

The subfrontal contains about 5 million minute cells, mainly amacrines. There are larger cells placed at intervals, just as in the vertical lobe, and it is presumed that they provide the output of the subfrontal, though it has not yet been possible

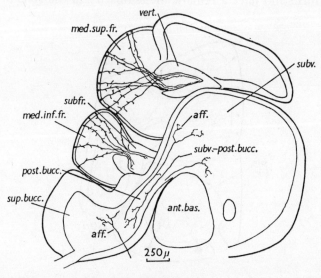

FIG. 90. Drawing of thick section stained with Golgi's method. Cells of the inferior and superior frontals have been stained and their courses show the similarity between the inferior frontal/subfrontal and superior frontal/vertical systems.

aff., afferent fibres to subvertical (? nocifensors) and to the superior buccal; ant.bas., anterior basal; med.inf.fr., median inferior frontal; med.sup.fr., median superior frontal; post.bucc., posterior buccal; subfr., subfrontal; subv., subvertical; sup.bucc., superior buccal; subv.-post.bucc., fibre running from subvertical to posterior buccal; vert., vertical.

to stain them fully with the Golgi method. At the lower (hinder) end of the lobe bundles leave it below and enter the posterior buccal, exactly as bundles pass from the vertical lobe to the subvertical. Degeneration has been seen in these bundles after injury to the subfrontal, but conversely they still contain intact fibres 10 days after removal of the subfrontal. Fibres therefore run in both directions in them, as they do between the vertical and subvertical. Fibres can be seen branching and terminating in the outer regions of the subfrontal lobes in a manner suggesting that they are similar to the afferents presumed to signal 'pain' that reach the vertical lobes from below (Fig. 89). Degenerating fibres are seen entering the lobe from below after more anterior lesions that interrupt the pathways from the arms.

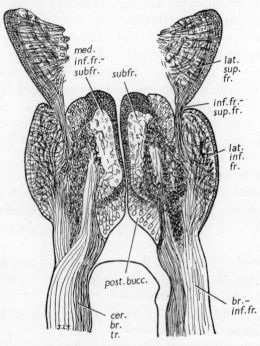

FIG. 91. Oblique transverse section to show how the small cells of the subfrontal lobe are continuous with the inner layers of the posterior buccal lobe.

br.-inf.fr., brachio-inferior frontal tract; cer.-br.tr., cerebro-brachial tract; inf.fr.-sup.fr., inferior frontal to superior frontal tract; lat.inf.fr., lateral inferior frontal; lat.sup.-fr., lateral superior frontal; med. inf. fr.–subfr., median inferior frontal–subfrontal tract (seen in transverse section); post.bucc., posterior buccal; subfr., subfrontal.

There is thus a close similarity between the arrangement of the touch centre and visual centres. The experiments of Mr. and Mrs. Wells on tactile discrimination also suggest significant similarity in functioning. The median inferior frontal seems to serve to spread the tactile information between the eight arms and presumably to mix it with signals indicating food reward from the lips and mouth. This system probably reinforces the tendency to draw in whatever object an arm touches, *unless* impulses signalling trauma arrive by the median part of the cerebro-brachial tract. These impulses, spread and amplified in the subfrontal, would then produce the suppressor action that produces the learning *not* to draw in objects, which is characteristic of the system.

The median inferior frontal lobe is not necessary for learning not to draw in objects. There is evidence that it serves to allow interchange of information between the arms, but not for actually recording it. If one arm of an animal lacking the median inferior frontal lobe is trained to reject an object, then the other arms continue to accept it and show no changes in behaviour as a result of the training of the first arm (Wells, 1959*b*).

The presence of the subfrontal lobe is, however, necessary if the animal is to learn to reject objects by touch. This certainly suggests that the subfrontal, like the similar vertical lobe system, serves in some way to suppress the tendency to 'attack'.

The similarity between the two sets of pairs of lobes is so striking that they must surely have similar functions. It is therefore suggested that the inferior frontal/subfrontal system serves to maintain the 'address' of the cells of the tactile system that have been activated and in due course to deliver to them the signals generated by the result of the action (food or pain). In the touch learning system *both* inferior frontal/subfrontal *and* superior frontal/vertical systems have this function.

Some capacity to reject objects associated with a shock was found in all animals in which even a small part of the subfrontal lobes was left intact after operation. Wells believes that even as few as 13,000 of these cells make it possible for the octopus to learn to reject objects.

In experiments with tactile discrimination learning, however, it was found that greater quantities of subfrontal tissue were needed for any appreciable accuracy of performance. Thus animals estimated to have about a million subfrontal cells remaining after operation learned an easy discrimination well. With 300,000 there was some sign of learning, but not with less, although such animals readily learned to reject an object.

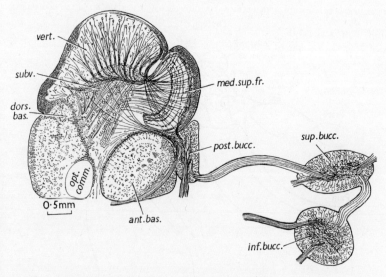

FIG. 92. Drawing of sagittal section of the brain of *Sepia*.
    ant.bas., anterior basal lobe; dors.bas., dorsal basal lobe; inf.bucc., inferior buccal lobe; med. sup.fr., median superior frontal lobe; opt.comm., optic commissure; post.bucc., posterior buccal lobe; subv., subvertical lobe; sup.bucc., superior buccal lobe; vert., vertical lobe (Young, 1963c).

6. *Differences between the tactile systems of decapods and octopods*

The proof that the power of learning is given by a tissue containing these small cells is strong evidence of their importance in the memory. Moreover, in decapod cephalopods, which make less use of the sense of touch, there is no differentiated inferior frontal or subfrontal lobe. In these animals the superior buccal lies far forward (Fig. 92). The lobe that occupies the front of the supraoesophageal mass is sometimes called inferior frontal, but is better named posterior buccal (Thore, 1939). It is interesting that it receives a bundle of fibres from the pedal and pallioviscteral regions exactly as does the posterior buccal of *Octopus*. These may well be 'pain' fibres from the funnel and mantle.

In *Sepia*, when the arms have seized the prey (usually a prawn) it is very quickly drawn in and bitten. The arms are

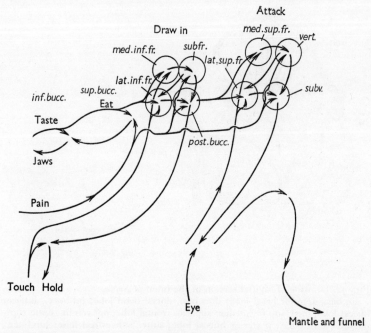

FIG. 93. Diagram of the organization of the two sets of pairs of centres, that are involved in tactile and visual learning in *Octopus*.

inf.bucc., inferior buccal; lat.inf.fr., lateral inferior frontal; lat.sup.fr., lateral superior frontal; med.inf.fr., median inferior frontal; med.sup.fr., median superior frontal; post.bucc., posterior buccal; subfr., subfrontal; subv., subvertical; sup.bucc., superior buccal; vert., vertical.

therefore used as part of the eating mechanism, rather than as a distance receptor. Correspondingly there is no special development of a small-celled system to deal with information from them.

The visual system of *Sepia* is, however, served by a fully developed superior frontal/vertical lobe system (Fig. 92). This is organized essentially, as in *Octopus*, with long and short loops (Fig. 93). There is, however, no separation into lateral and median superior frontal. The whole superior frontal corresponds to the lateral part in *Octopus* and receives a conspicuous pathway from the vertical lobe which also has a very different structure from that of *Octopus* (Figs. 73 and 92).

The significances of these similarities and differences are not yet fully clear. The well-developed vertical-superior frontal tract suggests that an important function of the system is the positive feed-back, keeping up the attack potential. Experiment confirms this; after vertical lobe removal a cuttlefish does not continue to hunt a prawn that has disappeared out of sight (Sanders and Young, 1940). The capacity to do this must be important in normal life in the sea. Perhaps learning what to attack and what to avoid is little developed in *Sepia* (see, however, Wells, 1962*b*). If so, the special features of the median superior frontal and vertical in *Octopus* may be connected with such learning. But further experiments are badly needed with *Sepia* and other cephalopods.

Comparative studies of this sort can provide most valuable evidence about the functions of the parts. We have still further evidence from the pelagic octopods such as *Tremoctopus* and *Argonauta*, which have presumably lost the use of the arms as distance receptors. In these the inferior frontal system is secondarily reduced (Fig. 16). A most interesting development is the appearance in these animals of many small cells in the inferior buccal lobes.

7. *Function of the vertical lobes in tactile learning*

We have already seen that octopuses without vertical lobes examine objects with the arms for longer than do normal octopuses. These lobes also play a part in learning tactile discrimination. Animals from which they have been removed take longer than before to reach a given standard in an easy discrimination and may fail altogether with a difficult one (Wells, 1961*b*). If the lobes are removed after learning an easy tactile discrimination the animals at first take the negative object, which they had previously learned to avoid, as well as the positive. However, if they are then re-trained they learn more slowly than normal animals but faster than animals that had not been trained before vertical lobe removal. Some trace

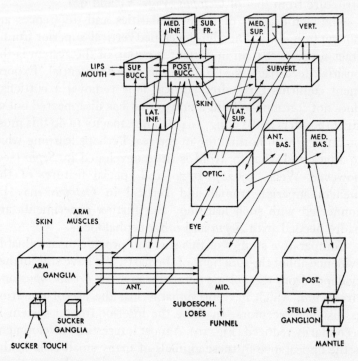

Fig. 94. More detailed diagram of the main centres involved in visual and tactile learning in *Octopus*.

ANT., anterior suboesophageal; ANT.BAS., anterior basal; LAT.INF., lateral inferior frontal; LAT.SUP., lateral superior frontal; MED.BAS., median basal; MED.INF., median inferior frontal; MED.SUP., median superior frontal; MID., middle suboesophageal; POST., posterior suboesophageal; POST.BUCC., posterior buccal; SUB.FR., subfrontal; SUBVERT., subvertical; SUP.BUCC., superior buccal; VERT., vertical.

of the original representation thus survives the operation. Wells considers that the action of the lobes depends upon 'amplifying the effect of each trial'. Such amplification is evidently one of the functions that we must assign to it in both tactile and visual learning. He believes that the vertical lobe is not itself essential to the process of tactile learning, although part of the 'store' may be in it. Learning to recognize objects by touch proceeds (though more slowly) without it, in some other part of the brain. This is strikingly similar to the situation for visual learning. The vertical lobe plays a part in the normal 'reading-in' and 'reading out' of the tactile memory. The effect of this lobe is, however, somewhat less marked with tactile than with visual learning.

8. *The tactile memory centre*

There is therefore evidence that the tactile memory system includes tiers of paired centres similar to those of the visual system (Figs. 67 and 68). From the similarities of structure it is a reasonable hypothesis that one member of each pair promotes and the other suppresses the tendency to draw in objects to the mouth. We cannot say at present where the cells that actually carry the representations for tactile discrimination are located. Wells found that the animals cannot learn without the subfrontal system. He suggests that what I am calling the representations may lie at least partly in the subfrontal lobes. It is difficult at present to be sure about this but it is interesting to consider the hypothesis that the cells that are 'switched' or 'conditioned' during tactile learning lie in the posterior buccal lobes. These lobes contain large and small cells. They receive fibres from the arms and from the lips, also from the lateral inferior frontal, subfrontal, and subvertical lobes (Fig. 90). It is tempting to consider that the posterior buccal and the lateral inferior frontal constitute a lower pair of centres, their relations to the tactile fibres being similar to those of the lateral superior frontal and subvertical in the visual pathway. The posterior buccal cells would thus play a critical part in the whole arrangement. It may be that it is here that the actual learned representations of tactile situations are carried. We can well suppose that these cells have initially alternative pathways that either increase the tendency to draw in an object touched, or decrease the tendency to produce a rejection. However, the tactile memory store mainly contains information about what should *not* be pulled in and the posterior buccal lobe is probably mainly a centre concerned with rejection.

The cells that represent the tactile qualities of objects that have been associated with pain would thus become switched to produce rejection. The median inferior frontal and subfrontal in this scheme form an upper pair of centres serving to maintain the address of the tactile cells stimulated and then to feed to them the signals indicating the results, perhaps mainly if those signals indicate 'trauma' or inedibility. This ensures the conditioning of cells in the posterior buccal. There is probably also a positive feed-back loop serving to amplify the tendency to draw in food. However, as we have seen, the tactile system is heavily biased in its lower part to draw in objects *unless* they have proved to be inedible. Learning to draw in is therefore a less marked feature than for the corresponding visual behaviour.

A further function of the inferior frontal/subfrontal system is probably to stabilize the level of investigation, for instance the time for which an object is examined for edibility before rejection. The vertical lobes also play a part in this. Presumably by the numbers of its pathways and their connexions the inferior frontal system also ensures that changes in response characteristics occur at suitable rates. The exploratory activity needs to be maintained at a suitable level. The more perfect is the classification and learning system the higher can the exploratory potential be maintained. Failure to explore is only a second line of defence when classification has proved to be incorrect and may be so again.

It cannot be said that this hypothesis, even if mainly correct, gives us a complete view of the origin and functioning of the system. Much remains to be explained. The posterior buccal and subvertical lobes undoubtedly form one continuous system anatomically, and in a sense they are the centres of the tactile and visual learning systems. But whereas the tactile memory store may be in the posterior buccal (or near it), for the visual system it is in the optic lobes. This difficulty is perhaps met by regarding the optic lobes as an outgrowth of the centre of the

supraoesophageal ganglion—as it were a specialized part of the
subvertical lobe. This agrees with its position at the side of
the supraoesophageal lobe in *Nautilus* (Fig. 95). The anterior
suboesophageal mass forms an unknown feature of the whole
system. There are many small cells here, especially in the front
part ('prebrachial lobe'). It is possible that the cells storing

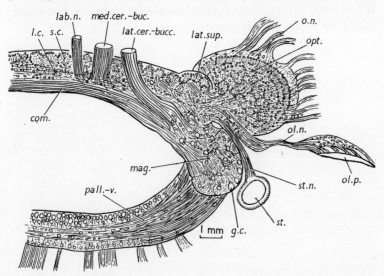

Fig. 95. T.S. central part of the nervous system of *Nautilus*. Reconstructed by
tracing from photographs. The sizes of the various nerve-cells are shown in
correct proportions, but all are much larger than in reality.

com., commissural region of supraoesophageal cord; g.c., giant cell; lat.cer.
buc., lateral cerebro-buccal connective; lat.sup., lateral supraoesophageal lobe;
l.c., large-celled region of supraoesophageal lobe; lab.n., labial nerve; mag.,
magno-cellular lobe; med.cer-buc., medial cerebro-buccal connective; opt.,
optic lobe; ol.n., olfactory nerve; ol.p., olfactory pit; o.n., optic nerves; pall-v.,
pallio-visceral cord; s.c., small-celled region; st., statocyst; st.n., static nerve.

the tactile representations lie here. The prebrachial lobe would
then correspond functionally to the optic lobe. This is by no
means unlikely. There is other evidence that the anterior suboesophageal mass is the much modified anterior part of the
original cerebral commissure (Young, 1964*a*).

A further intriguing problem is the relation between visual
and tactile learning. The significance of the tract running from
the lateral inferior frontal to the lateral superior frontal is

obscure. Experiments show that the median inferior frontal plays little part in visual discriminations, which can readily be learned without it. However, there is certainly an effect of the vertical lobe on touch discrimination (p. 253). Since the two systems overlap in the vertical lobe it may well be that there is some sort of co-ordination between them. However, it has been shown that objects learned by sight are not recognized by touch (Wells, 1961b).

16

DISTANCE RECEPTORS AND
THE ORIGIN OF PAIRED CENTRES

1. *The macrosmatic system of* Nautilus

THE special paired centres for promoting and preventing
attack have certainly been evolved from much simpler
arrangements. In *Nautilus* there is little sign of the separate
lobes that are found in higher cephalopods. It is interesting to
relate this greater simplicity of the nervous system to the fact
that *Nautilus* is less well equipped with distance receptors
than are the higher cephalopods. Its eyes are dioptrically poor
(Fig. 25), though it has large olfactory organs. Our hypothesis
is that the systems of paired centres are necessitated by the
fact that when distance receptors are used there is a delay
before the reward arrives. It is therefore interesting to see if
there is any sign of them in *Nautilus*. The cells are certainly
not all of the same size or uniformly arranged around the
cords that form the nervous system of *Nautilus*. The two
suboesophageal cords, anterior ('pedal') and posterior (palliovisceral) contain almost entirely large cells ($> 10 \mu$ diameter)
arranged at the periphery of the cords. In the supraoesophageal cord there are also mainly large cells around the anterior
surface, and it is from this part that the nerves to the buccal
mass arise (Figs. 95 and 96). The dorsal and posterior parts of
the cord are composed of islands of smaller cells ($< 5 \mu$ diameter), recalling the islands at the centre and back of the supraoesophageal lobes of an octopus. The organization of part of
this small-celled region is quite complicated, involving an
outer plexiform layer surrounding what may be called a
laminated zone (Fig. 96). In the plexiform zone fibres passing
back from the buccal region interweave with others coming in
from the sides, that is, from the tentacles, optic lobes, and

olfactory organs. These plexuses vaguely recall those of the median inferior and superior frontals. The similarity is especially marked at the sides, where fibres from the arm nerves run directly into a lateral cerebral lobe, which is a special part of the plexiform layer. This is essentially the plan of the inferior frontal lobes of higher forms. There is certainly some

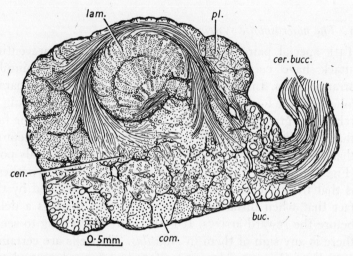

FIG. 96. Drawing of sagittal section of supraoesophageal cord of *Nautilus*. The cells are all shown rather larger than they really are.

buc., buccal zone at front, with large cells; cen., central zone with medium-sized cells; cer.bucc., cerebro-buccal connective; com., commissural zone; lam., laminated zone; pl., plexiform zone.

similarity and both systems allow the signals from the various receptors to interact.

The means by which this system assists in the control of behaviour are uncertain. The centre of the supraoesophageal cord is occupied by a region of moderately large cells, which may well, with the more ventral cells, provide the efferent pathways. The optic lobes are lateral expansions of the cerebral cord and the plexiform layers of the two are continuous (Fig. 95). The optic lobes are large but presumably with its pin-hole eyes *Nautilus* is less efficiently equipped to deal with distant visual events than are the forms that are provided with lenses. In compensation it has a much larger olfactory organ. This is connected with a large olfactory lobe, which, like the optic lobe, is a lateral extension of the cerebral cord. Perhaps in cephalopods, as in vertebrates, the earlier flesh-eaters were macrosmatic and mainly scavengers. The higher developments of their brains came with the introduction of hunting by means of distance receptors. Such concepts were already implied in the discussion of the evolution of the vertebrate forebrain by Sherrington in 1906.

Presumably the cerebral cord of *Nautilus* and its lateral extensions are concerned with making the decisions as to eating behaviour that are indicated by information arriving from the arms, eyes, olfactory, and static organs. The whole system of centres for the signals of results as we see them in *Octopus* and other higher cephalopods must have been evolved by modification of this small-celled region of the supraoesophageal cord.

2. *Differences in organization of command centres with different time scales*

When distance receptors are involved learning probably requires that there shall be some system to bridge the time gap between receipt of a stimulus, causing the initiation of action, and the advent of signals indicating the nature of the reward. In an octopus we can see how the various lobes that mediate this function have come to be developed out of the simple 'reflex' centres that control eating (Fig. 97). The superior and inferior buccal lobes operate with the signals from the taste receptors in the lips and mouth, and then issue the command to eat. Here the delay involved is minimal, but decisions not to eat must be made if the object is noxious.

When an octopus touches an object and draws it in there is a delay of a second or two before the appropriate taste signals are given by the lips. The posterior buccal lobe, the centre of the system that bridges this time gap, is directly continuous with the back of the superior buccal lobe. The subfrontal, with its numerous small cells, is a special development of the inner layers of small cells that are found in the superior and posterior buccal lobes (Fig. 73).

When a distant object moving in the visual field precipitates an attack there is a still longer delay before the signals indicating results arrive. This interval is bridged by the system

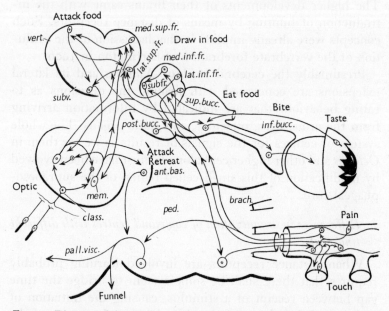

FIG. 97. Diagram of the tactile and visual learning systems of *Octopus* to show that they are developments of the eating system, serving to bridge the delays introduced by the use of distance receptors. (Young, 1963c.)

ant.bas., anterior basal; brach., brachial; class., classification neuron; inf.bucc., inferior buccal; lat.inf.fr., lateral inferior frontal; lat.sup.fr., lateral superior frontal; med.inf.fr., median inferior frontal; med.sup.fr., median superior frontlat; mem., memory system; pall.visc., palliovisceral; ped., pedal; post.bucc., posterior buccal; subfr., subfrontal; subv., subvertical; sup.bucc., superior buccal; vert., vertical.

that is centred on the subvertical lobe, a further backward continuation of the buccal system. On top of this is the circuit of the superior frontal/vertical system, involving even more numerous minute cells.

The simple set of buccal motor neurons at the front of the brain of *Nautilus* has thus been replaced by a whole series of centres allowing for more and more sophisticated and delayed commands. The superior buccal command is 'Bite', the posterior buccal one 'Draw in with the arms', the subvertical one 'Attack at a distance'. The series involves an increasing delay before the reward arrives, and probably an increasing efficiency of the exploratory, coding and memory systems if the potentialities of the distance receptors are to be fully exploited. We can recognize a corresponding increase in complexity of the centres that operate these actions. In particular there is an increasing development of the system of tiers of circuits involving pairs of lobes, one of each pair containing minute cells. Moreover, we can see a parallel in at least some of this with the development of tiers of circuits, one above the other in the vertebrate brain.

3. *Significance of centres with many small cells*

The development of the higher centres is presumably concerned with increasing the capacity to make decisions between alternative lines of conduct, this being made possible by the presence of suitable encoding and learning systems. The operation of these mechanisms is somehow connected with the presence of small cells. In *Octopus* these are almost or quite absent from the most simple 'reflex' centres, such as the pedal lobes. Some are found mixed with larger cells in the brachial lobes, which control the arms, and in the superior buccal lobe for the beak. In the posterior buccal lobes there is an even higher proportion of small cells. It may be that small cells are characteristic of the organization of regions of the nervous system from which alternative actions are controlled. When large and small cells are found together the small ones are mostly in the inner cell layers, around the axo-dendritic trunks of the larger unipolar cells, which lie peripherally. The details of the relations between the branches of the large and small cells are not known, but presumably the small ones are somehow concerned in increasing or decreasing the extent and duration of effects of incoming afferent impulses. The larger cells produce effector actions (either directly or through further synapses) and the 'correct' response is determined by a balance in the neuropil between impulses that promote action (food reward) and those signalling trauma (pain).

The small-celled lobes of the more highly developed paired centres for the signals of results can be regarded as a special development of the small-celled regions of less highly specialized lobes. Indeed, the lateral and median inferior frontal and the subfrontal can be seen to be directly continuous with the inner part of the cell layers of the posterior buccal lobe (Fig. 73). We can regard the subfrontal and vertical lobes as regions where the axo-dendritic trunks of the median inferior frontal and superior frontal cells are submitted to a particularly intense barrage of the small-cell influence and the suggestion is that this influence is inhibitory.

4. *The origin of memory systems*

Presumably nervous tissue that is able to store records has arisen out of tissue of a more strictly reflex nature. It is therefore interesting that during embryonic development of an octopus the whole set of inferior frontal lobes differentiates from a single simple lobe. The medial basal wall of this lobe becomes the posterior buccal and the medial lateral wall becomes the lateral inferior frontal. The median inferior frontal first appears as a commissural region, joining the two lateral lobes. The subfrontals remain for a long time as shallow evaginations of the medio-dorsal walls.

We may suppose that this part of the supraoesophageal lobe first became differentiated for control of the arms acting at a distance in detecting food and drawing it in. The basal parts of the lobe, the lateral inferior frontal and posterior buccal, were concerned with ensuring that objects touched were drawn in. However, inhibition of this 'reflex' action was allowed for when noxious objects were touched, and this involved small cells. The median inferior frontal and subfrontal have differentiated by proliferation of these small cells in the upper part of the lobe, as a means for keeping a record indicating those configurations of tactile stimuli that have proved to be advantageous or the reverse.

Although we cannot see exactly how this record is made there are some most useful hints. The cells concerned with memory storage have purely local effects within the system. Whereas the posterior buccal sends its axons to activate motor centres and the lateral inferior frontal sends them to other supraoesophageal regions the median inferior frontal sends its axons *only* to the subfrontal and the axons of the latter mostly end *within the lobe itself*. These facts indicate strongly that we should look to the development of these lobes with small cells as the special feature that makes the establishment of an enduring record possible.

We cannot yet see entirely clearly what advantages are gained by the segregation of such special pairs of lobes from the simpler arrangements with large and small cells mixed. There can be little doubt that the arrangement has substantial advantages, presumably in ensuring rapid learning and reliability of performance in attack or retreat.

Some clues that are available for interpretation of such paired centres are:

1. That they allow mingling of the effects of impulses from various parts of each receptor field (tactile or visual) with each other and with fibres indicating food reward or trauma.

2. That the lower pair of centres makes a long loop leading from and to the receptor analysing centre. In the visual system this loop is necessary for an attack to be made at a distant moving object. In this sense it amplifies the effects of impulses from the optic lobes. In the tactile system this loop is less prominent, perhaps because the system is already heavily biased to draw in objects with the arms.

3. The short upper loops are superimposed in parallel on the lower ones. They receive their inputs from them and send outputs back through them.

4. Interruption of these upper loops produces animals that attack slowly and inconsistently. They learn only slowly to attack a figure that yields food. There is thus a failure to 'read-in' to the memory. They are unable to perform adequately in situations involving discrimination of objects

shown successively. This is apparently not because of the absence of tissue capable of storage but to the undue influence of rewards recently received. The animal acts under the influence of these rather than of what is stored in its memory. There is inaccurate 'reading-out' from the store.

5. The effects of removal of median superior frontal and vertical lobes suggest that the former multiplies signals tending to produce attack and passes its output mainly to the vertical lobe. Here they are further increased *unless* signals indicating trauma arrive from below.

6. The median superior frontal contains cells with many receptive dendrites in the extensive neuropil. These are well suited to be activated by the fibres entering through interweaving bundles.

7. The vertical lobe has a very different structure, and includes numerous minute cells without long axons. The fibres of these cells contain numerous synaptic vesicles and they make 'serial synapses'. This suggests that they inhibit the passage of impulses from the superior frontal to the sub-vertical lobe.

8. The median inferior frontal and subfrontal lobes have relations identical to those between median superior frontal and vertical. There is good experimental evidence that they also are concerned with learning, although less detail is known of the functions of the separate lobes.

The similarities between the inferior frontal-subfrontal and superior frontal-vertical systems are so striking that it should surely be possible to extract from them an understanding of the principles that are at work.

17

THE NATURE OF THE
CHANGES INVOLVED IN LEARNING

1. *How is the code of the nervous system established?*

WHATEVER may be the devices by which signals indicating results are multiplied and dispersed there must be some points at which, when these signals are applied, changes take place in the transmission characteristics of some elements of the nervous system. In spite of much speculation there is still no definite knowledge of what this change is. In this sense we have so far failed almost completely to identify the memory of the nervous system. Nevertheless, there is much that can be said about the problem that was not possible a few years ago. At least we begin to see in outline what sort of change it may be and how we can try to devise a strategy that may find it. This is indeed an essential preliminary operation, which has usually been omitted by those who go on to discuss whether the memory change is, say, chemical, or electrical, or a growth process.

It is first of all worth recalling that the nervous memory is likely to be very different from the memory store of a digital computer (Chapter 3). Whatever may be its physical principle the memory of such man-made machines has the characteristic that it contains a large number of elements, each simple in itself, registering a presence or absence, and significant because it is precisely addressed and can be rapidly and frequently consulted. In such a system there is a sharp distinction between the memory and the calculating engine that consults it. In brains there is no such sharp distinction and in this sense it might be said to be misleading to compare the 'memory' in the two cases. The neural memory is probably more like an analogue calculator, made by selecting parts from a code set.

Moreover, we cannot assume that the effects of past experiences are stored in the brain in the same individual and particulate manner in which this is done in a computer. In animals operations are performed actually in the memory and by the actions of the code elements themselves. The memory is a characteristic of the network itself and in this sense the memory and the representation it contains are the same thing.

The problem thus becomes to discover how these characteristics are established. Obviously they must in some way be made to correspond to features of the environment, the function of the memory being to recognize certain events when they recur in the world around. There seem to be two ways in which this can be achieved. The nervous system might have properties that allow it to be moulded so that in a sense it resembles those features of the input that are to be recognized. Thus if the visual world contains a preponderance of vertical and horizontal contours these directions may be, as it were, printed on the nervous system during its growth (see Hebb, 1949). In the auditory system again the fact of the occurrence of certain frequencies might tune certain neurons (Hydén, 1960; Hydén and Egházi, 1962). Wells and Wells have suggested that in the tactile learning of an octopus the frequency of occurrence of irregularities of the surface are recorded.

Building representations in this way may perhaps be compared with modelling by moulding, as in sculpture. It is not easy to see how it can provide representations of the detail and subtlety that must be available at least to higher animals. Detailed information can only be conveyed if a code has been established and the transmitter selects from the code certain items to represent the message to be sent. It seems likely that the memory of the nervous system operates by selecting from a code in this way. We have seen above some evidence that in an octopus this is so and that the 'language' of the visual code is provided by the shapes of the dendritic trees of certain cells. We know that the dendrites and cell bodies provide the region in which 'decision' is taken as to whether nerve impulses shall be fired down the axon (see Bullock, 1958). These are, as it were, the computing regions of the cell. There is therefore every reason to look to them for the varied features that provide our code. It does not necessarily follow, of course, that the actual shape of each field is the significant characteristic. There are, however, good reasons for thinking that the field shape is important. First, perhaps, the fact that the dendrites are spread out and, in octopuses, cats, and monkeys at least, some fields have 'shapes' and are polarized in directions that are known to be significant for the coding system. A striking feature of these networks is that fibres run more or less straight in one direction for quite long distances (p. 148). They certainly do not interlace in a random fashion as they may do in lower centres. Further, we know that the summation of electrical changes distributed over the surface of the dendrites is one means at least by which the discharge is regulated (see Bishop, 1956; Purpura and Grundfest, 1956, for discussion of dendritic functioning).

If the pattern of dendrites provides the basic responders, and hence the code, how is that pattern or set established? It would be entirely reasonable that it should be determined by heredity. The requirement is that the memory shall contain an alphabet suitable to set up representations of those situations that the animal is likely to meet in its lifetime. We have seen how experiments have shown that the frog's retina reports to the frog's brain only certain features of the visual world, features that are likely to be of 'interest' to a frog. Presumably a frog's brain contains a simple alphabet that will allow storage of information about a few such simple changes. Heredity may well be able to provide the necessary simple set.

There is some evidence that the dendritic patterns are established in their main outlines rather early even in a mammal. The number of major branches of the dendrites of stellate cells of the cerebral cortex of the guinea-pig is little less at birth than in the adult (Peters and Bademan, 1963). In the mouse there is considerable change after birth, but the adult condition is essentially reached at 17 days (Haddara, 1956). In the cat the number of dendritic branches does not increase during postnatal development, but the dendrites increase in length and acquire spines during the second postnatal week. However, the basilar dendrites of the pyramidal cells develop only after birth. It is interesting that these postnatal changes occur even in a piece of cortex that is neurally isolated on the day after birth (Purpura and Housepian, 1961).

On the other hand, if the orientation of some of the dendritic fields follows main axes such as horizontal and vertical it is tempting to think that these forms may be imposed during postnatal life. For an octopus, as for many animals, the world contains a preponderance of lines running in these directions and of objects that move horizontally. There is every reason to think that some changes occur in the forms of the cells during the later stages of development. Thus the characteristic distribution of stellate and pyramidal cells in the visual cortex develops only after birth in the rabbit (Mitra, 1955).

There are too few facts available at present to allow us to settle this great problem of how much of the capacity to learn is laid down by heredity. It may be that even in ourselves the models in our brains are built out of units provided by the hereditary memory system. It is perhaps more likely that the latter provides their rough outlines, which are later moulded by experience during lifetime. There may be large differences in this respect between the brains of species that learn little and those in which elaborate models can be built up.

2. *Where are the learning changes likely to be found?*

If the memory contains an alphabet that is partly provided by heredity and partly altered by use, then the distinction drawn at the beginning of the previous section between two possible forms of coding becomes blurred. The model may be made partly by moulding, partly by selection from a code. But in any case the memory and the representations in it are constituted by the connexions of the network. This means that the changes, whatever they are, that go on during learning are likely to be widely distributed through a large mass of nervous tissue. Experiment has fully confirmed that this is so. Removal of portions of the brain usually does not lead to the loss of

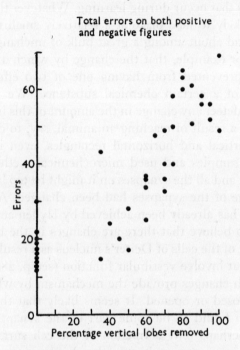

FIG. 98. Relation between extent of lesions to the vertical lobes and accuracy of visual discrimination. Each point shows the total of errors by an octopus in sixty paired trials, plotted against the percentage of vertical lobe removed.

single particular representations, but to a general lowering of the accuracy of discrimination (Lashley, 1950, &c.). This has been shown to be so also for an octopus. Removal of an increasing proportion of the vertical lobe leads to decreasing accuracy (Fig. 98). However, we must be cautious in the interpretation of this if the vertical lobe is not the seat of the memory, but is responsible for maintaining the balance that is necessary for its use. More relevant is the fact that removing one optic lobe and part of the other one, or making cuts in the optic lobe, do not lead to particular memory losses.

This fact of the dispersion of the memory store has important and rather disconcerting implications in the search for the changes that occur during learning. Whatever their nature these are likely to take place at a relatively small number of points spread about among a great bulk of unchanged tissue. Suppose, for example, that the change by which a particular neuron is prevented from having one of two effects is the deposition of a certain chemical substance. We should be unlikely to detect any change in the amount of this in a sample of tissue as a result of teaching an animal, say, to distinguish between vertical and horizontal rectangles, even if we took very small samples and used microchemical methods. Even a single cell and all the synapses on it might be too large a unit if only some of the synapses had been changed. Analysis of single cells has already been achieved by Hydén and Egyházi (1962), who believe that there are changes in the base ratios of the RNA of the cells of Deiter's nucleus as a result of learning tasks that involve vestibular function (see p. 280). It may be that such changes provide the mechanism by which pathways are closed or opened. It seems likely that the relevant unit will be found to be some part of the synaptic system, involving perhaps only a fraction of the cell surface. Small chemical changes may so alter the threshold as to make the cell inexcitable, closing one of two pathways. This path may, perhaps, then eventually atrophy. However, it is difficult to see how to plan an experiment that is likely to reveal the initial chemical changes. Presumably the only situation in which differences could be detected, except at the scale of the electron microscope, would be where there was a large difference in the total amount of information stored by two animals over the whole previous period of their lives. This shows the necessity for hard thinking to work out a strategy to find learning changes. An experiment where the total amount of learning during the life of an animal is varied can be imagined, though it might be hard to conduct effectively.

3. *What are the prospects of recognizing synaptic changes produced by learning?*

The electron microscope seems to provide the only tool with the necessary spatial resolution to be able to show the individual changes that go on during learning. But here we meet other difficulties in deciding where to look! Electron microscopy has confirmed in numerous situations the belief established by Cajal and other light microscopists that there is a discontinuity where one neuron makes synapse with another. The membranes of the two cells remain intact at such points and the two surfaces are usually separated by a gap as wide or wider than that separating cells elsewhere (Figs. 5 and 6). The trouble is that in any given piece of tissue there are so many contacts present that it is impossible to say exactly where the transmission is taking place, if indeed it is meaningful to think of it as sharply localized at all. The pre-synaptic terminal branches of the axons are often crowded with small spherical 'vesicles'. Similar vesicles are present at the nerve endings at a motor end-plate and the suggestion is that they may be released to liberate the acetyl choline or other chemical molecule that serves to ensure transmission. At motor end-plates the transmitter is released in quantal packets (Fatt and Katz, 1952), though it has never been proved that these are related to a release of vesicles.

At some synapses parts of the membranes are differentiated, with thickenings on both sides, perhaps indicating closer union here than at other parts of the surfaces (Fig. 5) (Gray, 1959). The vesicles are often crowded at these points. It might perhaps be that these differentiated areas represent regions of especially active excitation (or inhibition), which can increase or decrease with use. But it is still not certain whether they are the significant areas. By centrifugation a fraction containing much choline acetylase can be isolated, and electron microscopy shows that this fraction also contains an adhering fragment of the post-synaptic membrane, with the pre-synaptic regions attached (Gray and Whittaker, 1962). But there are disconcerting hints that the relevant excitable regions may be dispersed in ways that we have not yet considered. Thus, in the bird's retina there have been seen profiles that seem by the distribution of vesicles to be both pre- and post-synaptic (Kidd, 1962). These might, of course, as Kidd suggests, be the seat of pre-synaptic inhibitory fibres and are possibly connected with the abundance in the bird's retina of amacrine cells, with no axons (see p. 145).

The point for the present discussion is that it is by no means always clear exactly what structure we refer to when we speak of 'a synapse'. The concept is still essentially physiological, though we have some information about its morphology in some simple situations. How then can we expect to see changes with learning in 'objects' that we cannot recognize properly anyhow? Such changes are certain to be widely distributed and therefore we meet the difficulty already mentioned of finding an experimental situation in which we might expect to recognize them. Even a very small piece of nervous tissue contains hundreds of possible synapses. In any animal that can learn, and has done so, some of these have presumably changed, but how can we tell which?

To emphasize these difficulties is not to say that they cannot be met. The point is that we must devise a strategy that has a chance of revealing what we wish to know.

4. *Some physiological evidence of changes in the nervous system*

There is some evidence that the amount of transmitter produced at a synapse varies with the previous history. For example, Brown and Pascoe (1954) were able to render synapses in a sympathetic ganglion inactive for 7 days. When first tested thereafter the synapses then produced little transmitter, but after subjection to volleys of impulses the amount increased in proportion to the activity.

Indeed, when any synaptic region is subjected to repeated stimulation its capacity for response is altered. Thus after tetanic stimulation of the optic nerve for 15 sec, there is post-tetanic depression of transmission through the lateral geniculate nucleus, lasting five hours or more. (Bishop, Burke, & Hayhow, 1959). This certainly constitutes a memory change in the sense that for a short period it makes more or less probable the passage of impulses along pathways recently used. What part, if any, it plays in the establishment of more enduring changes remains uncertain (see Eccles, 1953, 1964). Portions of the central nervous system that have been isolated so that they are not used for a while, lose their power of post-tetanic potentiation, but regain it after a period of reactivation. Thus Eccles and McIntyre (1953) rested dorsal root ganglia by severing them from the periphery. Tested after the period of rest these fibres gave small evidence of post-tetanic potentiation, but this greatly increased after several thousand impulses had been passed through the system (Eccles and Krnjević, 1959).

Unfortunately, it is in the nature of such experiments that the duration of the changes can be followed only for the few hours during which an animal can be kept alive in an acute experiment. After true learning the result of some situations may contribute to the production of a change that lasts a lifetime.

5. *Bridging the time gap between excitation and consummation*

There are many indications that the operation of the memory system involves some special short-lasting process by which the more permanent record is 'printed'. Indeed, as we have seen, learning the appropriate response to signals from a distance receptor necessarily involves some mechanism that keeps the cells that were initially stimulated appropriately 'addressed' while the action takes place, until the signals indicating its results arrive. The mapping of the time course of this initial process is of great interest. This, or a similar process, can be followed in octopuses by presenting an unfamiliar figure and giving a food reward (Fig. 13). Tests made immediately thereafter show an increased tendency to attack, but this soon disappears. A second presentation with food, however, gives a greater increase in attacks, showing that something had survived. A similar experiment can be made by giving shocks to animals when they attack a figure that had previously been associated with food (Fig. 14). During the subsequent hours they show less tendency to attack, but ultimately do so apparently as before.

The facts of retrograde amnesia in man for events preceding a blow on the head or electric shock can also be interpreted as measuring the time course of whatever neural systems maintain the shorter-lasting representation. Interruption of these systems prevents the formation of the longer-lasting representation in the memory (Russell, 1959). Interruption of the memory system by anaesthetics is another ingenious means of throwing light on the processes that are involved (Burns, 1958; Steinberg and Summerfield, 1957).

Of course these experiments do not prove that two distinct changes are involved. There might be only one, the remaining effects of which become so slight after a few hours that they are not detected in the behaviour. Nevertheless, it is convenient as an hypothesis to consider that short-lasting and long-lasting representations are involved, recorded by different mechanisms. One hypothesis is that the short-lasting representations are maintained by the persistence of self-re-exciting chains (Young, 1938). These, as it were, serve to maintain the relevant features of the original situation for long enough for them to leave some record that endures. Octopuses without vertical lobes that have received shocks for attacks at a crab will not attack them again for as long as the crab is left in the visual field (p. 212). Thus re-presentation from the outside may be considered to substitute for that from within.

Study of the time course of the formation of representations after single occasions should have much to provide towards understanding of the processes. Most of the experimentation on learning has directed attention to the results of repeated presentation, for example in the classical conditioned-reflex situation (Pavlov, 1927). But the final result is the sum of single occasions, whose character we need to study.

6. *Evidence of electrical changes during learning*

A very interesting set of observations has shown that changes in electrical activity can be detected during the processes of conditioning (e.g. Jasper *et al.*, 1958). Many of the characteristics recorded in this way indicate the persistence in the brain of rhythms that correspond to temporal features of situations experienced. Thus after a cat has been given shocks when a light flash occurs 7 times per sec, there are 7 features per sec in its brain waves even in the dark (Yoshii, Pruvot, and Gastaut, 1957). Single cells of the visual cortex can be shown under suitable conditions to carry a record of past visual events. Thus a cell that initially fires a single burst of nerve impulses in response to a flash of light, will, when subjected to a series of flashes at 5 per sec, together with the passage of a current through the cortex, respond to a single flash with trains of impulses at 5 per sec. This condition lasts for up to 30 minutes. It is presumably not a 'true' learning and the problem is to see how such phenomena are related to selection among certain elements to make what we have called a 'representation'. Microelectrode studies do indeed suggest that the seat of 'closure' (i.e. the actual learning change) is in the dendrites (Morrell, 1960). But they have not so far served to define what this change may be.

The passage of polarizing currents through the cerebral cortex is followed by either increased or decreased frequency of discharge of neurons and changed responses to afferent stimuli. The effects last for five hours or more. They are produced by polarizing currents of the order of those that occur naturally and even if these are localized to a small volume of tissue. Such experiments show that long lasting changes in activity can be produced by small temporary alteration of the physical environment of the nerve cells (Bindman, Lippold, & Redfearn, 1962).

7. *Possible significance of glia for learning*

It has been suggested several times that long-lasting changes are in some way a property of the neuroglia and neurons together. The glia cells outnumber the neurons by perhaps ten times and occupy the greater part of the volume of the brain. It is difficult to believe that their function is only 'trophic', or that of support or even insulation. It may well be that in their properties we shall find the explanation of changes such as those of learning that cannot be adequately understood by what has been called 'millisecond physiology' (Galambos, 1961). There is evidence that astrocyte cells can produce electrical changes (Tasaki and Chang, 1958). In the retina the glial types of cell produce slow potential changes and have been discussed as 'anti-neurons' (Galambos, 1961).

It is perhaps relevant to notice that there is a really remarkable similarity in the glia found in nervous systems as distinct as those of cephalopods and vertebrates, although these animals have evolved independently for 500 million years or more. The space between the neurons of an octopus is packed with glial protoplasmic masses strikingly like those of vertebrate astrocytes. Evidently the operations of the nervous system depend essentially on such tissue.

8. *Possible growth and metabolic changes during learning*

If two processes with different time-courses are involved it might be that the longer-lasting one has a character similar to that of growth. There is some evidence that peripheral nerve fibres are able to change their form rapidly, at least under the somewhat drastic condition of destruction of their neighbours. Hoffmann (1950) discovered that when some of the nerve fibres to a muscle are removed the nerve fibres of the remaining areas sprout. This process takes place rapidly enough for the new fibres to reach several hundred microns in a few days (Fig. 99) (Morris, 1953). Further, there is evidence that the growth of fibres may itself be influenced by the connexions that they make, those that do not reach suitable endings fail to increase in diameter, or even undergo atrophy (Aitken, Sharman, and Young, 1947). Embryologists investigating the development of the nervous system after removal of a receptor or muscle have shown in many situations that neurons that are unconnected may begin their development but then fail to grow and may disappear. The whole complex of facts about the effects on the growth of neurons of stimulation from above and connexion below suggests that they are subject to a delicate system of 'double dependence', according to the functions they perform (Young, 1948; Szentágothai and Rajkovits, 1955).

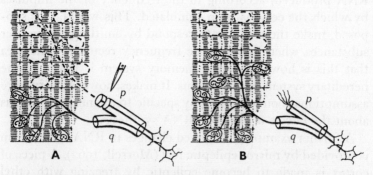

FIG. 99. Diagram of effects of partial denervation of a muscle.

A, the branch p is severed but q is left intact. B, some days later fibres from the end-plates innervated by q have grown into the empty end-plates previously innervated from p. (After Morris.)

Although much knowledge is available in this field, it has not yet been possible to correlate it with events in the nervous system during learning. The gap may seem wide between such relatively large growth changes and the results that we might consider likely to follow from a single appearance of a figure to an octopus and the eating of a piece of fish. Yet, of course, every metabolic change that uses materials in the cell may be regarded as influencing growth if it stimulates the enzymes that procure replacement of metabolites, especially perhaps if these involve alterations in the proteins or other molecules that constitute the more permanent 'fabric' of the cell.

There is much evidence that activity on the part of nerve-cells has the effect of increasing the metabolism of RNA, proteins and lipids in them. This may lead to a decrease in these substances, as in motor nerve cells after excessive running activity, or to their increase, as in vestibular ganglion cells after moderate rotatory stimulation (see Hydén, 1960). The metabolic rate of these substances is very high in the nerve-cell, which has indeed been called 'an enormous gland-like cell, fulfilling its function under steady and rapidly changing production of proteins and lipoproteins'. Hydén suggests that there may be a specification of the detailed structure of the RNA produced, according to the frequency of the impulses by which the cell has been stimulated. This would, it is supposed, make the cell able to respond by emitting transmitter substances when this impulse frequency recurred. The idea that this is how the neural memory system is linked to the hereditary system has attractions. It makes, however, very large assumptions about encoding by specific frequencies, as well as about the effects of these on RNA synthesis.

A further example of induced changes in RNA metabolism is provided by mirror epileptic foci (Morrell, 1962). A piece of cortex is made to become epileptic by freezing with ethyl chloride. The corresponding cells of the opposite hemisphere become epileptic, after some days or weeks, and continue so even if isolated from the inducing foci by section of the corpus callosum. The feature that interests us here is that these cells show by their staining reactions that there has been an enduring change in their RNA. As Morrell says this situation may provide a useful model for the study of the changes that occur in learning.

The increased production of material when it is in 'demand' is the basic adaptational process that occurs in most or all tissues, e.g. in bacteria. It is a type of response that the enzyme systems must have acquired very early in their evolution and it is reasonable to think that it is still at the basis of the most complex of all adaptational changes, namely those that go on in the memory of the nervous system. It is a form of change that automatically establishes a correspondence with the environment, which we have seen to be an essential feature of the memory of a homeostat. What is lacking in the environment is made by the organism. Unfortunately in our ignorance of the biochemistry of neurons we cannot yet say whether changes of this sort are involved in learning, though it is a reasonable hypothesis upon which to work.

One sign of the longer-lasting changes that occurs following nervous activity is an increase in volume (Hill, 1950; Tobias, 1952). Hill found an increase of diameter of 0·22 μ in a giant axon of 200 μ after passage of 10,000 impulses. It has been calculated that a comparable change in a pre-synaptic terminal knob of diameter 0·3 μ would double its volume (Eccles, 1953). This would certainly be likely to change its synaptic efficacy. Unfortunately in our ignorance of the interrelations of the pre- and post-synaptic regions and glia we cannot say how the surface relations would be changed (p. 278). But the volume changes show that rather large alterations in metabolism must occur and these may stimulate the enzymes to still further change.

9. *Are there special memory cells?*

Growth in size may, of course, be a misleading analogy. The fact is that we have really no clear ideas about the nature of the changes involved. In this situation we can perhaps advance a little farther by considering firstly what are the time courses of the processes involved, and secondly where to look for these processes. Some methods for studying the time courses have been considered already. One clue to follow as to their location is the possibility that there are cells, or parts of them, that are specialized for undergoing the learning change. It may be that this is a function of the very numerous small cells that are so characteristic of the higher nervous centres. Cells in lower parts of the nervous system, such as the spinal cord or cephalopod suboesophageal ganglia, may show changes of excitability lasting for many minutes, but in spite of much search no one has found in these lower centres changes that endure. They do not learn in the ordinary sense.[1] The neurons of such

---

[1] A possible case of learning in a 'lower centre' has been shown in headless insects. The preparations were held suspended so that whenever a foot fell to a certain level a shock was given. The leg was raised for longer and longer intervals, so that fewer shocks were received (Horridge, 1962). This is evidence

centres are large and they have long axons. There are few or none of the very small amacrine cells. These small cells are, however, characteristic of the centres that can store representations, the cerebral cortex, or the octopus optic lobes, or the 'pedunculated bodies' of the brains of arthropods.

This can hardly be an accident. The common request of physiologists that psychologists shall find them a 'simple learning system' is perhaps based on a misunderstanding. It may be that there are no simple learning systems. An octopus can, perhaps, only learn when to attack and when not to do so, but in order to do this it is required that there be sufficient relatively large cells with motor pathways connected with these two alternatives, and gated, as it were, by numerous small cells (p. 155). These somehow ensure the switching or conditioning by which after one or a few stimulations of the larger cells, associated with a given reward, one channel only is left open.

10. *Learning what not to do*

Whatever process operates in learning it seems likely that it involves the choice between two or more possibilities. It is usually assumed that this choice is made by some form of facilitation in the pathway that has been excited (see e.g., Eccles, 1953). But if the actions are initially equally probable and balanced against each other then the probability that one of them will occur can be increased by reducing the effectiveness of the other. Perhaps at least a part of training, even in apparently simple conditioning, consists of learning what *not* to do.

This could be achieved by inhibitory collateral pathways such as those suggested in Fig. 47. The small amacrine cells may be the agents responsible for the change. They occur, accompanying the larger cells, in all the types of nervous tissue that are known to be involved in learning. Their action may be to reduce the probability of use on a subsequent

of some change in the neurons concerned, just as post-tetanic potentiation is evidence of changes in an isolated sympathetic ganglion or spinal cord. It is not yet clear whether such changes are related to those ordinarily considered as constituting learning.

occasion of the alternative pathways that were not used on the learning occasions. The fact that the vertical lobe, which produces a suppressor action on the tendency to attack, contains an exceptionally large number of these small cells suggests that it is a region specialized to produce such inhibition.

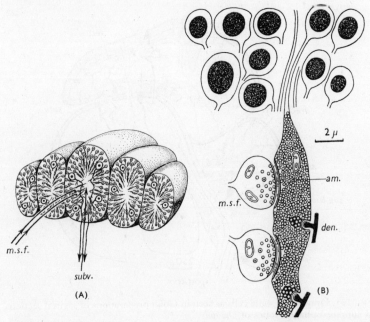

FIG. 100. (A) Diagram of the vertical lobe of *Octopus* to show the two inputs (from median superior frontal, m.s.f., and subvertical, subv.) and output to the subvertical lobe. (B) Small cells of the vertical lobe as seen by electron-microscopy. m.s.f., endings of the median superior frontal fibres, making synapse with the trunks of the small amacrine cells (am.) These are themselves filled with synaptic vesicles and they make contact with dendritic spines (den.) which are probably attached to the trunks of the large (output) cells. (Gray & Young, 1964.)

Study of the fine structure of its cells has already provided some hints about the mechanisms that may be operating. The trunks of the amacrine cells are packed with dense masses of synaptic vesicles (Fig. 100). In contact with these trunks there are at least two other types of structure, one *also filled with vesicles*, the other post-synaptic. The former are almost certainly the fine endings of the fibres coming from the superior frontal lobe. The latter are probably dendritic branches of the large cells that provide the output from the lobe (Fig. 101). Unfortunately it has not yet been possible to identify the endings of the fibres that enter the vertical lobe from below and are believed to be inhibitory.

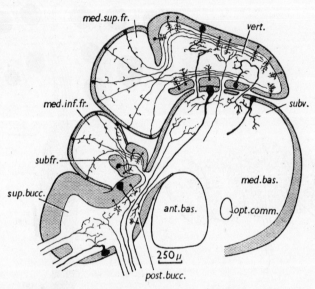

FIG. 101. Drawing of some cells as seen in Golgi preparations of sagittal sections of supraoesophageal lobes of *Octopus*.

ant.bas., anterior basal; med.bas., median basal; med.inf.fr., median inferior frontal; med.sup.fr., median superior frontal; opt.comm., optic commissure; post.bucc., posterior buccal; subfr., subfrontal; subv., subvertical; sup.bucc., superior buccal; vert., vertical. (Young, 1963c.)

For our present purpose all that we can say is that the minute amacrine cells, packed with vesicles, seem to intervene to reduce the influence of the pathway in promoting attack. An alternative possibility is that in the untrained condition both pathways are held inhibited, again perhaps by the action of small cells. Learning would then consist in removal of the inhibition from one path. Such a mechanism recalls the suggestion that enzymes exist in an inhibited form and that demand brings them into action by disinhibition (p. 52). At present we can do little more than discuss these possibilities as a means to orientate our thoughts and direct our experiments.

It is not difficult to see how suppression of one pathway might occur over a short period. If the connexions in the optic lobe are appropriate the collaterals could inhibit the alternative pathway, perhaps by pre-synaptic inhibition (Fig. 47). How this might produce a more per-manent reduction in the probability of this pathway is a matter of specu-lation. It might be by the production of agents that promote a de-growth of the terminals of the classifying cells. A very simple possibility is that the collaterals, or amacrine processes stimulated by them, might them-selves grow and squeeze out the other terminals. The electron microscope shows a web of processes of various types, among which interaction could well be understood to occur in vari-ous ways.

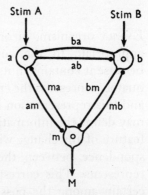

FIG. 102. Diagram of three in-terconnected neurons to show the type of modification that is usually assumed to occur dur-ing learning. Impulses in the channel A are supposed initially to fire M, whereas those in channel B fail to do so. Simulta-neous firing of A B is then said to alter the channel bm, so that later B is able to fire M. (From Burns, 1958.)

A great advantage of a theory of this type is that it avoids a difficulty, pointed out by Burns, in most theories that imagine learning by facilitation. In such theories activity of synapses on one part of the cell is supposed to produce facilitation of synapses elsewhere on the same cell (Fig. 102). No physiological basis for this remote effect has ever been suggested.

That learning occurs by elimination of the unused path-ways is a hypothesis that has many attractions. It becomes clear that learning is of the nature of a reduction of the initial redundancy of connexions, comparable to that by which the contour of individual features is emphasized by a receptor. The outlines of a general theory of the encoding and storing process can thus be seen.

18

THE CONTROL OF
THE COLLECTION OF INFORMATION

EVERY organism, in order to survive, takes actions that are
appropriate to the surrounding conditions. It does this
because it contains in its nuclei a controlling system that adequately represents the environment. The surroundings change
and this representation is continually brought up to date. We
may define the information that flows into the organism as the
feature of any change within that serves to increase the correspondence between the organism and the environment it
represents. This correspondence is achieved by selection of
certain among the possible states of the system, states that
have been set by its previous history.

How such homeostatic systems first arose is, of course, a
fascinating question, especially if asking it should help to
allow us to arrange for them to synthesize themselves again,
that is, to 'create life'. The capacity of an organism to make
such 'choices' and hence to build up its own 'instructions'
need not be so mysterious as it might seem. Granted the
presence of suitably complicated molecules, natural selection
provides that the combinations that adequately represent the
surroundings shall survive (see Bernal, 1962).

Of interest for the present discussion are certain features of
the timing of the methods of collection of information and
revision of instructions. Every organism, as its molecules turn
over and change, continually adapts to the conditions of the
recent past. If some raw material is in short supply, more
enzymes for its synthesis are produced. If the conditions
require more movement, then muscles hypertrophy, and so on
through all the range of 'adaptations'. Each such change is
produced by selection between two or more alternatives, the

selection being made by means of the 'information' flowing from the environment. As we saw in the previous chapter, learning in the nervous system can be considered as a special case of such adaptational changes.

But in every sort of organism there occur at intervals the more complete changes of instructions that we classify as 'reproduction'. It seems to be a fundamental instruction of every species that from time to time it shall discard nearly the entire organism, then shuffle together the instructions of two individuals and start over again. We need not be concerned here with the various types of shuffling that have been discovered, especially in 'lower' organisms. Some nuclear reorganization seems to occur in all of them. The position of the viruses is ambiguous, but they are the exception that proves the rule; they are not autonomous homeostats dependent on acquiring their own instructions.

To find the significance of this universal property of nuclear change we may consider the mechanism by which the adaptational changes and repair processes are made possible. Each system responsible for change or repair of adult structure must itself be liable to error and hence requires a further system to control it. This regress seems to dictate the impossibility of devising an indefinitely self-maintaining system. On the analogy of a homeostatic factory, there must be instructions that provide for repair shops to repair the repair shops that repair the repair shops that repair the repair shops, &c.

Living systems seem to have escaped this regress, at least within the limits of the 2,000 million years or more during which they have continued. The secret seems to lie in the fundamental instruction that ensures the occurrence of reproduction at intervals. The effect of reproduction is to reduce the homeostat to a state that includes almost nothing except its 'instructions'. In bisexual species the male contributes little but a nucleus, while the egg contains, in addition, the minimum complement of 'working equipment' to allow the new instructions to begin to operate. Yolk provides the fuel for this period, and mitochondria the enzymes.

At the same time as the homeostat is reduced to its instructions these are shuffled. The elaborate genetical mechanisms of meiosis, crossing over, and fertilization ensure that the various 'words' of the DNA code are recombined to provide new combinations in each individual. Some are thus able to represent the environment adequately. Mutation provides a further method of changing the representation, apparently by random alteration of the symbols of the code.

Such methods of adaptation by random small changes and shuffling demand selection among large numbers and over long periods. It is difficult to realize that such methods are capable of producing the extraordinarily precise representations by which organisms are fitted to their environments. Many people of a 'practical' turn of mind, whether engineers or medical men, find it difficult to believe in the efficiency of such a mechanism. It is convenient to remember that the best means of producing 'perfectly' flat or spherical surfaces, say for mirrors, is to allow suitable 'random' movements of two opposed members (see Platt, 1958). Indeed, the spherical form of the eyeball, which is so important for vision, is produced by the numerous small movements of an initial roughly spherical rudiment. It has been said that 'all really precise methods are simple and random'.

By means of such random rearrangement of the instructions at regular intervals, followed by rigorous selection among the numerous new sets that result, the species is able to transcend the apparent limitation set by the above regress. It succeeds in remaining alive by repeatedly changing into something else. This seems to be the significance of the fact that all organisms must reproduce, and equally that they grow old and die. Our purpose is to investigate the variables that are significant in the operation of such a system that continually renews its own instructions.

First we may compare the genetic method of obtaining an adequate representation of the environment with the method provided by 'adaptational' changes and learning in the nervous system. Both systems operate by selection from a code.

Indeed, it is basically the same DNA code in the two cases. However, in neural learning, as we have seen, the symbols among which selection is made may be more complex products of the genetic code, such as the dendritic trees of the neurons. The important difference between the two methods of acquiring information seems to be that a random selective element enters into one, but the nervous system functions with rapid and precise feed-backs. These are themselves designed by the hereditary instructions to provide precise information about the results of each action, whether it is good or bad for the organism, whether it yields pleasure or pain.

This presumably means that the nervous system can make representations of the environment much faster than can the genetic system. Yet the nervous system has the limitations that we have considered, it needs repair and cannot proceed indefinitely alone. We have, therefore, to discover how the homeostat is adjusted to ensure that both methods are used, with an effective timing.

It is clear enough that the two methods must stand in some reciprocal relationship. The better the means of repair, adaptation, and learning, the less often will it be necessary to undertake a basic revision of the instructions of the homeostat. And indeed, it seems to be a rough general rule that types of organism that learn better live longer. However, we need to be very cautious about generalizations in this field of study, the rules that regulate the methods for the acquisition of information by each species are complicated and any simple generalizations will have exceptions. For example, men almost certainly learn faster and learn more than tortoises, but tortoises can live longer.

It would be a great mistake to abandon the study of this problem, as many people do, because of such difficulties. The mechanisms for the control of these long-term features of homeostasis are just as much open to investigation as are the more obvious adjustments, say of respiratory rate, which we ordinarily classify as part of physiology. The systems for acquiring information by reproduction and evolution might be classified as 'long-term physiological control'. We may expect to find 'mechanisms' for this, as much as for the minute-to-minute regulation of the heart beat.

The differences in the length of life of individuals are very great. A bacterium lives for the order of ten minutes. A protozoon lives for some days, say, 10^3–10^4 minutes. Many animals live for about a year, 5×10^5 minutes. The larger animals live for ten or more years, say, up to 10^7 minutes, and a very few may approach or pass 10^8 minutes. It must surely be of biological significance that the intervals between nuclear reorganizations vary by more than a million times. Presumably in each type of organism this time interval is set at the appropriate level for exploiting a particular habitat. Thus bacteria often live in environments that have little permanence. They are organisms that vary much and adapt well, for example by changing their enzymes. They can thus 'choose' their environment within a certain range, but it is rather small. Corresponding to this limitation of 'choice' the 'lower' organisms have much less DNA per cell. This is calculated to be only of the order of $10^{-5 \text{ to } -6}$ picogrammes (1 picogramme $= 10^{-12}$ g) for a single small virus particle (rabbit papilloma virus). In a bacterium there is much more, 2×10^{-2} picogrammes. In a human cell the value is 350 times more, 7 picogrammes. The 'instructions' for making even such a simple homeostat as a bacterium are thus immensely more detailed than is necessary for the 'parasitic' virus. Surprisingly little further elaboration is necessary to make a man! However, the detailed significance of such figures is doubtful. A frog contains 15 picogrammes of DNA per cell.

It is interesting to consider how many nucleotide base pairs are involved—that is, how many proteins could be made. The papilloma virus probably has about 6,600 base pairs, enough to code for one protein, bacteria 20×10^6, and man 7×10^9. This last figure gives the possibility of a fantastic number of different DNA molecules and hence of protein types (see Kit, 1963).

In fact the bacteria not only have much shorter lives than Metazoa, they are also measurably smaller and simpler in their organization. This means that they are homeostats organized for self-maintenance only under a limited range of circumstances. In a man there are 'devices' for keeping alive in spite of environmental changes that would destroy a bacterium. This is one of the senses in which the Metazoa are the 'higher' organisms; they have invaded more 'difficult' habitats (see Young, 1938, 1962*b*).

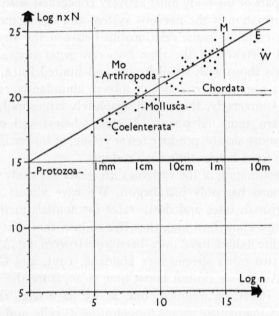

FIG. 103. Plot of the number of cells in each organism (*n*) against the total number of cells of that species *Nn,* where *N* is the number of individuals. E, elephant; M, man; Mo, mosquito; W, whale. (From v. Foerster, 1962.)

The 'higher' organisms thus take a longer time to unfold their more elaborate homeostatic systems. These systems also occupy a greater bulk; accompanying the differences in length of life there are even greater differences in weight. A bacterium weighs 10^{-5} g, a fruit-fly 10^{-3}, a rat 10^2, and a whale 10^8 g. Again, we do not find exact correlations. A rat's life is perhaps 50 times longer than a fruit-fly's, not 100,000 times longer, and an old whale is not 10,000 times older than an old rat.

The significance of the more complex organization of the 'higher' organisms is presumably that they provide homeostatic mechanisms that ensure survival under conditions that are 'difficult' for life (see Young, 1962b). The larger organizations also allow for the support of *more* life than do the simpler. v. Foerster suggests that there are more cells in a man than in all the Protozoa in the world put together (Fig. 103).

The part of the body most actively concerned with acquiring information is the nervous system and among metazoans there is certainly some relationship between the size of the nervous system and the time between generations. Among mammals those with small brains and limited learning (e.g. rodents) also mature quickly, breed abundantly, and die young. Conversely, those with absolutely large brains probably learn more (elephants, horses, whales) and certainly mature more slowly, produce fewer young, at longer intervals, and live for a longer time than rodents.

The estimation of the variables necessary for study of these correlations has only just begun. We have almost no data about growth rates and death rates for animals in the wild. We do not know how long they live or how they die; indeed, proper life tables have only been constructed for Man and one or two other species (see Haldane, 1953, and Comfort, 1959). Again, we do not know how to measure the nervous system. It can be weighed, but, as we have seen, there are only very inadequate means for counting its cells, and only the crudest beginnings of a model that may tell us what are the parameters of its functioning.

These defects in biology are bad enough, but it is worse still when we come to try to measure the 'learning capacity' of an animal or its 'capacity to adapt to environment' in any other way. It is indeed hard to imagine how these can be estimated under natural conditions. Yet nothing less is necessary if we are to be able to make a proper study of homeostasis.

In spite of all these difficulties it is already possible to see the first signs of the emergence of some systematic knowledge about how organisms regulate their means for acquiring information. Ultimately, the mechanisms that ensure this are regulated, like everything else, by the nucleic acid code. We know that this code contains instructions that control the relative rates of development of each part of the body, including the genital system. Moreover, in many higher organisms the regulation of the time interval between generations is by an endocrine mechanism and this, in turn, is controlled by the brain. Indeed, the highest part of the brain is directly concerned with this regulation, although nearly all other functions are controlled only indirectly, through higher motor centres.

Control of reproduction by a system of nerve centres and glands has long been known in vertebrates and arthropods, and it is now clear that a similar system operates in cephalopods. This was discovered when it was noticed that after removal of the vertical lobes some young female octopuses rapidly become mature and may lay eggs (Boycott and Young, 1956). The phenomenon is due to removal with the vertical lobe of a small centre that lies close beneath it and from which a nerve proceeds to a gland on the optic stalk (Fig. 104a). After interruption of the nerves the glands rapidly become enlarged and of deep orange colour, their cells enlarge and fill with secretion (Fig. 104b). Wells (1960b), who investigated this phenomenon in detail, showed that female *Octopus vulgaris* do not normally mature until they are quite large (2 kg). After denervation of the optic gland, however, the ovary even of a small (200 g) octopus immediately begins to grow. After two to three weeks ripe eggs are produced and may be laid and brooded, the female then dying as she normally does after reproduction at a much larger size. Denervation of the optic gland of the male produces enlargement of the testis, but males normally mature much earlier than females (at about 200 g).

This system of nerves and glands thus regulates the time of breeding of the females. Unfortunately we do not know what stimulus normally initiates the ripening. It may be connected with light, since Wells and Wells also found enlargement of

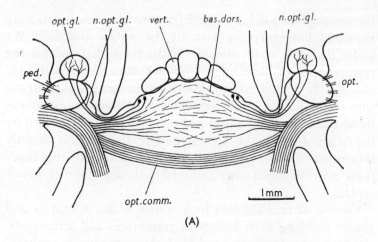

(A)

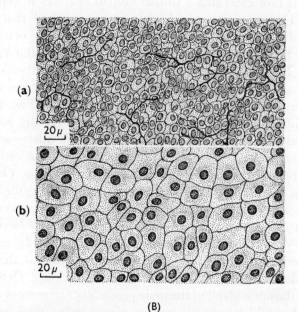

(B)

FIG. 104. (A) Diagram of T.S. hind part of brain of *Octopus* to show the innervation of the optic gland. bas.dors., basal dorsal lobe; n.opt.gl., nerve of optic gland; opt.comm., optic commissure; opt.gl., optic gland; opt., optic lobe; ped., peduncle lobe; vert., vertical lobe. (B) Sections of the optic gland of an octopus. (a) normal with nerve fibres among the cells. (b) after 25 days of denervation. The cells have enlarged.

the optic glands after cutting the optic nerves. For our present interest the important point is that the gland is controlled from a centre lying very near to the vertical lobe circuit, that is, close to the lobes that are involved in maintaining an appropriately balanced system of investigation by the adult animal. This proximity can hardly be an accident and suggests that there is a mechanism for suitable correlation of the two basic means by which information is gathered—through the nervous system and through hereditary rearrangement.

As a correlate of the development of better powers of learning there is likely to be some means of ensuring that the individuals live long enough to learn. Having learned at some risk to follow certain lines of conduct that adequately meet the conditions of a given environment, it is presumably then effective for the individual to make use of its knowledge to grow large and produce many offspring. It will pay the species to allow each well-trained brain to direct a large mass of living matter and to pass on its capacity, if not its actual wisdom, to many others.

It is not equally obvious why the system controlling reproduction should be operated directly by the higher nervous centres. Since maturation of the gonads is a relatively slow process it is not surprising to find that the immediate stimulus for it comes from endocrine organs, such as the pituitary in vertebrates, corpora allata in insects, eye-stalk glands of crustacea, or optic glands in cephalopods. That all these organs should be directly controlled by centres close to those able to learn must surely indicate some important principle of operation. The method of innervation of these glands is especially remarkable because they are almost the *only* structures directly innervated from these highest centres. No muscles or other glands are directly controlled by the diencephalon, only the pituitary. The supraoesophageal ganglia of insects send no motor nerves except to the corpora allata. In octopuses also there is no undoubted efferent nerve leaving the supraoesophageal ganglia except the nerve to the optic gland. There is, however, a mysterious 'subpedunculate nerve' leaving from a centre close to that for the optic gland nerve. It innervates some tissues in the orbit and carries efferent as well as afferent fibres. Its function is not known but may be concerned with control of intra-ocular pressure and hence perhaps of the growth of the eye (Boycott and Young, 1956). It would be interesting to investigate whether this subpedunculate nerve also has any relationship to the reproductive system.

There must be some common principle involved to produce these similar neuroglandular arrangements in completely independent phyla (Wells and Wells, 1959). Perhaps it is not fanciful to regard the efferent fibres leaving these higher nerve centres as similar in functional value in the system to the efferent fibres that are known to control many afferent pathways. In the octopus itself there are such fibres proceeding from the optic lobe to the retina (p. 146). A similar efferent pathway has been investigated in insects (see p. 164). In some vertebrates there are efferent fibres in the optic nerve (Maturana, 1958). There is an efferent bundle of fibres ending in the cochlea (Rasmussen, 1960, and Iurato, 1962). In fact the regulation of the means of obtaining information is a commonplace, and includes such phenomena as control of the pupil, or of the conditions of the tympanum and ear ossicles by the muscles of the middle ear. Similarly, we may regard the pituitary innervation, the optic gland nerves, and other such systems as pathways that regulate the conditions of collection of information by the hereditary mechanism. It should prove interesting to discuss the characteristics of these circuits that control the whole tempo of the life of the species.

Changes in these circuits, altering the relative rates of development of the gonads and the rest of the body, have been one of the most potent influences in producing new types during evolutionary history (de Beer, 1958). One of the characteristic features of a shift in the direction of a longer period of growth and learning is the development of parental care. If individuals are to learn a lot it will pay the species to care for them and to guard them, either through parental action, or in some other way, against the results of the mistakes they make while overcoming the risks that they are learning to meet. Thus, among the birds, those whose brains are ultimately the most highly developed hatch in a very immature state and remain for a long time in the nest ('nidicolous'). In the more 'primitive' orders of birds the young can look after themselves from an early date ('nidifugous'), but they never become very 'clever'.

This question is of special importance to Man because our own evolution seems to have consisted largely in delaying the onset of maturity, even to the point at which we remain permanent juveniles. Understanding of the mechanism by which this adjustment has been produced might well be of great value to us. Many of our most serious dangers arise from the difficulties of adjustment that are experienced by individuals who mature so slowly. We suffer on the one hand from the frustrations of delayed and incomplete adulthood and on the other from the violence that is produced by the adult reactions that we still achieve. Do we need to be more grown-up or less? One way of finding the answer is surely to investigate the fundamental principles that regulate maturation.

The circuits have become so adjusted in man that the mechanism for acquiring information by the individual is greatly hypertrophied and the hereditary mechanism is relatively less effective (though still, of course, fundamental). The recent acceleration of the rate of change of man's condition has been the result of the elaboration of codes by which information can be passed directly from one individual to another. By speech and writing we acquire information not just from two parents, as in ordinary heredity, but from many. Such 'multiparental inheritance' provides immense possibilities for evolution. By allowing for the rapid development of new combinations of the code it enables evolutionary experiments to proceed at a rate that would not be possible by the slower recombinations of two by two. Indeed, the characteristic of man is that by means of language and tools he constructs models of the world outside his own brain and outside his own genetic system. By proper use of these models he should be able to overcome all the risks that the environment offers. But there are evidently risks within the language systems and social-economic systems themselves. The proper use of these means of communication depends upon a degree of co-operation that is not always readily elicited, especially between larger groups of people. Perhaps inquiry into the fundamental nature of the information-gathering circuits and the types of models that they produce may help towards ensuring the stability of human life.

19

A MODEL OF
THE MODEL IN THE BRAIN

ONE purpose of a model is to summarize, and this chapter is a summary of the summary. Moreover, it is a deep-seated characteristic of human activity to make working models, which not only demonstrate the principles of some subject under examination but frequently also prove to be useful tools for promoting human welfare. I shall therefore finish by describing the apparatus that Dr. Wilfred Taylor has constructed, partly on the principles that have been discussed here.

1. *Homeostasis and choice between alternatives*

A brain is part of the control system of a homeostat. All homeostatic systems known to us operate by making choices between alternatives. This indeed is probably the 'secret of life', invented by some fortunate coming together of various molecular species, an event that occurred on this planet perhaps 2,000 million years ago. It may have happened in many other parts of the universe, perhaps using other sets of molecules (though the carbon atom seems to present special opportunities for the development of alternatives).

The system of alternative choices is found everywhere throughout the living world. Genes are carried in pairs on the chromosomes. Each act of fertilization therefore consists in the making of new sets of pairs among previously given units of the code. Selection among these many sets of pairs ensures that the organisms that result adequately represent the environment. The process thus constitutes a transmission of information in the sense defined (e.g. at the beginning of the previous chapter) as that which increases the correspondence between a homeostat and the environment that it represents.

In each type of protoplasm there is present a large set of enzymes, some only in small amounts, or held in an inhibited state. The adaptational processes by which bacteria come to be able to synthesize materials that they lack may be a disinhibition (or inhibition of an 'antagonist'), allowing the enzyme to make more material like itself (Crick *et al.*, 1961). A requirement for this to take place is that there shall be some 'receptor' sensitive to the absence of the material in question. The action of this in disinhibiting the enzyme then constitutes a transmission of information in the above sense.

All the adaptational changes, such as those by which muscles hypertrophy, glands enlarge, bones become strong, or blood becomes richer in haemoglobin, must depend upon similar processes of choice between alternatives, though we know little of how they operate. These changes, too, obviously improve the organism as a representation of its environment. They make it more likely to be able to meet the conditions that will arise if the future resembles the past.

2. *The nervous system as a decision maker*

Similarly, we find that the whole nervous and muscular system operates by repeated choices between alternatives. Each organism is provided with a limited number of muscle fibres, each of which either contracts at a given moment or does not (i.e. relaxes). By the same principle these muscle fibres are nearly always arranged in paired sets of 'antagonists'. The limbs work by flexor and extensor muscles at each joint, the food moves in the intestine by alternating action of circular and longitudinal muscles, the pupil is controlled by sphincter and dilatator muscles, and so on. All behaviour is therefore produced by selecting certain patterns of action between alternatives. Perhaps the most complicated of all behaviour is human speech or writing and even this operates by continual choice among a set of preselected muscular combinations—the movements permissible within the language (see p. 66).

Whether a given muscle fibre contracts or not depends upon the presence or absence of nerve impulses that arrive along the motor nerve fibre at its motor end-plate. These nerve impulses are characteristically all-or-nothing events. Whether a nerve impulse is fired down a fibre is decided by the temporal and spatial distribution of nerve impulses converging on the synaptic system of the dendrites of its cell. Here numerous influences from different sources interact to control the 'decision'. The nerve-cell bodies and dendrites, with their associated terminal '*boutons*' have the best claim to be considered as the actual computers of the nervous system (p. 56). The computing registers of an ordinary digital computer are few and each by its very rapid and repeated actions plays a large part in determining the result of the calculation. But each motor nerve-cell can only control the actions of a small number of muscle fibres (p. 46). The elaborate patterns of action are produced by having relatively large numbers of muscle fibres (p. 47).

The more subtle features of behaviour depend upon the fact that these motor nerve-cells themselves are under the control of much larger numbers of 'higher' nerve-cells. Indeed there is a hierarchy of levels of centres, each level having more numerous and smaller cells than the one below (p. 263). The system thus operates essentially by the parallel action of numerous channels, from the muscle-fibre level upwards. It is the presence of many layers and many cross-connected channels, providing great possibilities of alternative actions, that allows for the delicate shades of choice that are characteristic especially of the 'higher' nervous systems.

Delicate and selective systems of action can only be effective if the homeostat is provided with equally sensitive detectors, able to respond to many features of environmental change. That there must be some such correlation between the two ends of the system is obvious. A motor system capable of many detailed manipulations seems to require the guidance of a highly sensitive and discriminative receptor system. The principles controlling such relationships have indeed been studied by control theorists but more is required before we understand their application to animal life. Elaboration of the receptor side is often considerable even with a simple effector apparatus. Thus a sedentary worm has little choice but to withdraw into its tube or not, a movement that is operated by one giant neuron (p. 46). Yet the ring of tentacles is provided with numerous receptors. Similarly, a parasitic round-worm in the intestine has a central nervous system of only a little over one hundred cells with which it decides chiefly whether to wriggle or not, but it has quite numerous receptors. Perhaps these animals are capable of more subtle actions than are apparent.

The question of the significance of the numbers of channels in the receptors of higher animals is still more complicated and little explored (p. 64). Since the principles of the system depend upon this multiplicity there is obviously much more that could be revealed by its study. The types of receptor present are those that will detect the changes likely to be relevant in the habitat that the species adopts (p. 32). This point is so obvious that it is often overlooked. We ourselves have such extensive powers of reacting to events in the outside world that we are apt to ignore the limitations of our receptors and to forget that animals with simpler brains may react to an even more limited range of features of the environment than we do (p. 33).

In many receptors there is a simple relationship between the intensity of stimulation and the frequency of response. The mechanisms by which certain patterns of response by groups of these primary receptors are recognized are only just beginning to be known. For each organism the input is classified into a limited number of categories, which may be called 'universals' (p. 33). We have no complete list of these for any one receptor system except the very simplest. Animals as different as octopuses and cats seem to analyse the visual input into oval fields, perhaps especially in the horizontal and vertical planes. Many other 'invariants' are also extracted, such as brightness, extent of contour, or number of angles.

The detection of oval fields probably depends upon the presence of cells with spreading dendritic trees of the appropriate shape. The patterns of the dendritic fields may thus provide the code system with which the nervous system operates for both unlearned and learned responses. There is evidence that the main outlines of dendritic patterns are determined very early, at or about the time of birth (p. 269). Thus the 'instinctive' reactions to certain 'sign stimuli' may be released by the activation of cells with particular dendritic patterns, which are connected by heredity with given motor centres.

Such predetermined couplings are of course common throughout the simpler parts of the nervous system. It is a basic feature of the homeostat that it has receptors to indicate the appropriate action for each condition that may occur. The system continues along the course provided by its instructions because each deviation from this course is measured by feed-back circuits and produces the appropriate correction.

3. *Learning homeostats and the indicators of results*

Such reflex homeostats can of course function only within rigidly prescribed environments. Learning homeostats have the added feature that they can vary their actions when any situation occurs, according to the probable outcome of that situation as determined by their individual past experience. As we have seen all living homeostats have some powers of 'adaptation' of their enzyme systems and to this extent are learning homeostats.

In the special case of learning in the nervous system the mechanisms are developed out of those by which reflex homeostatic actions are performed. The receptor systems for reflex action already allow the encoding of various combinations of signals to produce different actions. The development of a learning system depends upon elaborating the possibility of alternative responses to given code combinations. Which of the possible responses is given is then determined by special development of the feed-back signal systems that determine reflex behaviour. Thus the taste signals indicating food have the primary function of activating the motor mechanisms of eating. In a learning homeostat they have the further function of enabling the memory to establish a record indicating that after the appearance of a certain distant stimulus (say a square) food was available. In order for this function to be performed there must be some mechanism for bridging the time gap between the detection of the signal by the distance receptor and the operation of the detectors of results at the end of the action.

For learned reactions the hereditary mechanism provides only the sets of cells necessary for encoding, each able to respond to a particular configuration of stimuli at the receptor surface. Each of these cells must be able initially to produce more than one effect. Thus in the octopus any visual stimulation can produce either attack or retreat. In the classical conditioned reflex situation with a dog, ringing a bell might produce either less saliva or more. The action that the cells come to produce is determined during learning. Whatever change is involved in learning increases the probability that one of the two possible actions will occur. This may be effected by inhibiting the tendency of the cell in question to produce the opposite effect. Thus in the Pavlovian conditioning situation the dog is perhaps learning 'not not-to-salivate'. Alternatively both pathways may be initially in the main inhibited, learning consisting in the disinhibition of one of them (p. 284). The question here becomes one of terminology until further information about the physical changes involved becomes available.

By whatever mechanism the 'switching' or 'conditioning' occurs the output of each cell becomes 'addressed', we may say, to one or other of the possible motor pathways. The addressing is done by the effects of the unconditional signals when they accompany the stimulation of the various encoding cells (p. 157). These receptors that indicate results and allow the classification of other inputs are a fundamental feature of all homeostats. With the signals indicating the need of the organism such as those of hunger, they determine the whole course of its action. Examples are the chemo-receptors for food or the pain receptors that indicate trauma. Such basic members of this class of receptors must be provided by heredity. However, as learning proceeds secondary and tertiary connexions come to be made with these primary signals for the classification of results, so that the actions of various receptor systems may come to operate secondarily as rewards or punishments.

The primary result-classifying receptors remain, however, of outstanding importance in all learning systems. In the octopus at least they seem to operate in pairs. Relatively few impulses indicating, say, food or pain are discharged and to be effective these need to be 'amplified' by spreading them throughout the whole mass of tissue that is occupied by the set of cells responsible for encoding. Special centres are provided for this amplification by spreading. In the octopus the system seems to be that the signals indicating food reward are first multiplied and then fed into the encoding centre, passing through the centre that receives nocifensor signals indicating trauma. The two centres together thus indicate food, and hence attack, *unless* pain is also present (p. 230).

There is reason to think that similar pairs of classifying centres are present in the vertebrate forebrain. Moreover, such a system has functions much more intricate than merely indicating the presence of food or trauma. It serves to adjust the whole level of tendency to exploration and hence the functioning of the learning system. With success (i.e. in obtaining food) the homeostat must be made more likely to repeat its actions, with failure, to do something different. For any given type of organism there are limits within which it is likely to be satisfactory to change performance as a result of given amounts of success or failure. The amplification factors provided by the paired centres perhaps serve to optimize changes in this way.

The experiments with the octopus show that such centres are responsible for maintaining a stable level of performance. After interference with them the animals are individually less consistent and more variable from each other. The stability of the normal animal is probably the result of the presence of at least two tiers of such paired centres, arranged above each other in the manner shown in Fig. 93. It is therefore especially interesting to find that in the vertebrate brain there are also such tiers of circuits provided, by the hypothalamus, thalamus, palaeocortex, and neocortex. Moreover, the 'lower' members of these circuits are concerned both with the control of simple consummatory acts and with the stability of motivation and drive. But these centres have yet a further and perhaps even more important function to perform, besides tending to make the organism more or less likely to repeat its actions. They must also serve to make possible the conditioning process by which the particular patterns of signals come to be associated with the subsequent arrival of food or pain. This, as we have seen, depends upon selecting one of the possible output pathways of the cells responsible for coding. In this way each becomes addressed to produce one or other of the possible motor actions.

Failure to learn associations in this way is one of the characteristic features of octopuses in which the vertical lobe circuit has been damaged. The effect is apparently connected with the fact that there are long and short loops in the system (Fig. 93). Fibres from the optic lobe pass to the lateral superior frontal/subvertical system and from there back to the optic lobe. On top of this long loop is placed the shorter one superior frontal to vertical thence either to subvertical and hence to optic or to lateral superior frontal and so round again. Together these circuits could serve to keep the appropriate memory storage cells of the optic lobes in a state of activity such that the signals of results, when they arrive, influence those particular cells. The circuits would thus serve to indicate the 'address' to which the signals of results should be sent. It is certain that the coded representation itself does not lie wholly within the vertical lobe system since after the removal of the latter the remainder of the brain can learn to discriminate, for example, between figures shown simultaneously, though it remains inaccurate (p. 214).

It is obviously to be expected that the system of centres that is concerned with unconditioned responses will also be involved in learning. This is undoubtedly so also in mammals, where the circuit involving the hippocampus seems to be essential for the establishment of records in the memory, although the actual representations probably lie largely (but not wholly) in the neocortex.

4. *The nature of the learning changes*

This brings us back to the central problem of trying to identify the changes that are involved in learning. We have to admit that we do not know what they are (p. 267). It is suggested that there are two clues that we may follow. Learning must consist in a choice between alternative possibilities and it should therefore be a good strategy to look for the cells that embody the code set, probably by their dendritic trees. We are likely to find that each has more than one possible output channel. It is here that we should expect to find the means by which one channel is opened and/or the other one closed.

Secondly, there is the clue that small cells are abundant in the regions of the nervous system that are largely concerned with learning, while there are few or none in the centres whose action is fixed by heredity. Many of these small cells are amacrines, with many short branches but no long axon. Such amacrines are numerous in the vertical lobes whose action is to suppress the tendency to attack. They are absent from the median superior frontal, which promotes attack. Multipolar amacrines are numerous in the cell islands of the optic lobes, where they accompany the large neurons that we have reason to think are those with two possible outputs, one of which comes to be used after learning. This set of facts suggests that the 'choice' is made by switching on or off by the small cells of one of the possible pathways. These cells may have an inhibitory action or it might be that their action is initially to produce some inhibition of both pathways and then by disinhibition one of them would be opened.

With at least an attempt to provide a hypothesis of the

change involved in learning our model is complete. It shows us how the homeostat operates, some of its possible actions being selected by receptor and central networks from a code that is pre-set by heredity. The principle of operation by taking one of two possible alternative actions may seem to be altogether too crude to provide a reasonable model for the subtlety and complexity of human and animal behaviour. To make the model realistic we have to try to appreciate the possibilities that are provided by the combined operations of very numerous channels with alternative actions. It is this immense range of choice, exercised at a whole series of levels, that provides the very features of unpredictability and 'free will' that we feel are so characteristic of living and especially human behaviour.

The mechanical systems with which we are familiar do not in the main provide us with much help in realizing the possibilities of multiple-channel networks. Digital computers in particular provide a poor analogy because their achievements are the result of great accuracy and speed in a few channels (p. 40). These are characteristics exactly opposite to those we wish to study, namely operation in many channels, not necessarily very fast or with great accuracy.

5. *A working model of the learning system*

The attempt to build a model that will approach a living organism in the complexity and subtlety of its classification and decisions is therefore an urgent necessity if we are to understand ourselves. It may also prove to be a valuable tool for tasks such as pattern recognition that are at present beyond the powers of digital computers. The designing of equipment that will perform such tasks as reading human handwriting involves specifying the capacities of the living system, which is an important step to understanding it. An attempt of this sort has been made by Dr. W. K. Taylor at University College, London. An outline of his discussion and plans serves both to summarize the problem and to meet the requirement that we gave in Chapter 1. If we understood the nervous system we should be able to make one. Many artefacts have been devised that imitate certain aspects of nervous behaviour (e.g. Ashby's homeostat (1960) and Grey Walter's (1953) goal-seeking artificial tortoise). Each of these machines demonstrates that we understand some aspect of the nervous system. Similarly, Taylor's machine shows that given some of the principles that have been discussed it is possible to design equipment that will learn to recognize complex patterns, perhaps to the point of being able, if it has been properly educated, to read, write, and speak, at least with a limited vocabulary.

It is not difficult to devise switching systems that recognize patterns such as letters, provided that these have been converted into a binary code form (Uttley, 1961). But this is only possible if the information that is obtained from each part of the pattern is whether it gives signals above or below a given amplitude (i.e. is black or white). Only N measurements are then needed to specify one out of 2^N patterns, provided that the measurements are made at points specified by the designer. In other words, a machine can relatively easily be constructed to read the addresses on envelopes, *if these are written in black standard letters at standard places on white envelopes.*

These limitations are the very ones that the living system transcends and is thereby able to perform its characteristically subtle tasks of classification. A human being 'can recognise an almost unlimited number of representations of the same letter, which may differ considerably in size, style or intensity and yet still contain sufficient information for the operator to make a correct selection from the alphabet' (Taylor, 1959).

In the attempt to demonstrate the principles by which such capacities may be imitated Taylor has used analogue methods throughout. This implies that a pattern is first read by transducers that record at a number of points N the amount of light (say) on a scale of levels (L). To analyse a detailed picture N must obviously be large and theoretically the L levels should be numerous. However, the human eye can only recognize about ten levels of brightness (at any given level of adaptation), so the scale may read from 1 to 10. (Incidentally a scale with only two levels is the condition imposed by binary recognition apparatus.)

The letters of the alphabet will then be represented by a very small fraction of the L^N possible patterns. Many of the signals contain little information, because they come from zones where amplitude is constant. Moreover, most patterns never occur at all, especially the complex ones. The number of classifications that can be recognized can be increased by using a learning principle, so that the machine, like the nervous system, comes to classify only those patterns that actually occur. The problem is to decide how many classes to use. In a homeostat this is basically a function of the number of actions that are likely to be needed for continued functioning by the use of predetermined principles, which must somehow be applied as 'instructions', during the process of training. A homeostat must possess such unconditioned receptors to indicate 'X has occurred, do A' (e.g. 'the finger has been burnt, withdraw the hand'). The same receptors can be used to classify the signals from other receptors (say, visual). In the machine that Taylor has devised the instructions as to the classes to be used during learning is performed by a human being or other previously instructed system. The principles by which patterns are detected and classified may, however, be similar to those used in a brain (p. 315).

First it is necessary to find some way of allowing the outputs from a number of receptor units to interact so that the 'pattern' of their activity can be recognized. Taylor does this by connecting them at random to a number of units each of which forms a signal proportional to the algebraic sum of the analogue signals derived from the transducers (Fig. 105). These may be called associative or A units and they may be considered as analogous to nerve-cells. In the first simple model made by Taylor there were nine input channels in the 'eye' and two 'unconditioned' classifying channels (1 and 2). The machine could readily be taught to recognize the image of a letter thrown on its receptors (Fig. 106). If the letter was 'seen' in various orientations it would be recognized also in these orientations.

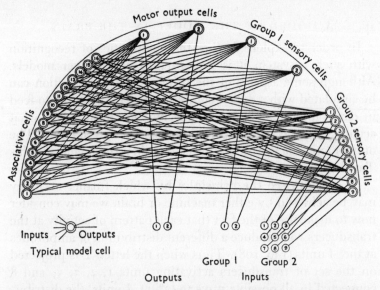

FIG. 105. Plan of Taylor's analogue learning system. Group 1 sensory cells may be compared with the stimuli for unconditional responses (e.g. pain and food reward). 'Group 2 sensory cells' are like retinal elements; in the actual model they are photocells. They are connected in a 'random' manner to the 16 'associative cells', each of which is also connected to both of the group 1 sensory pathways.

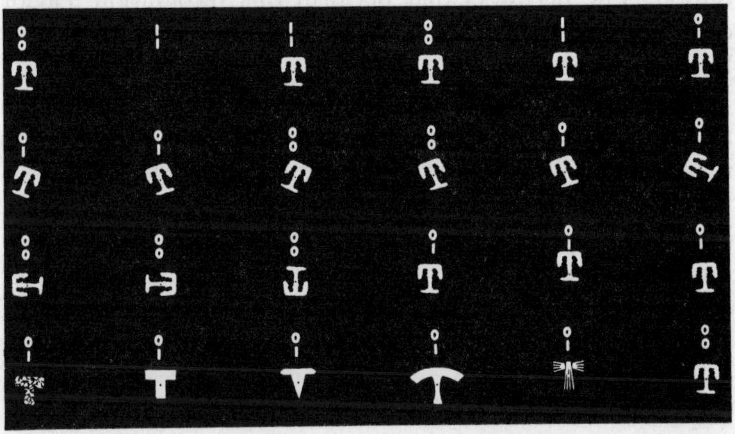

FIG. 106. When a pattern such as a T is thrown on the 'retina' it is initially equally likely to produce the output 1 or 0. The upper figure above each letter shows whether the conditioning signal 1 was pressed, the lower figure shows the output of the machine. Thus the two conditioning trials were the 3rd and 5th in the top row. The remaining figures represent tests and show that the figure is recognized as a T provided its orientation does not depart greatly from that which had been learned. The bottom right-hand test was made two hours later, when the machine had 'forgotten'.

In order to explore further the possibilities of recognition with such a system it is necessary to build larger models. Although some aspects of the principles of its operation can be simulated with a digital computer it is not possible to feed in data rapidly enough to decide by such means with what accuracy a given assembly would recognize a given figure. The only practicable way to do this is to build an analogue and this Taylor is now doing.

In order to see the principles by which further accuracy may be achieved by either machine or brain we may consider how to make use of the fact that each pattern of activity at the transducers will produce a different distribution of amplitudes at the A units (Fig. 108). Thus when the letter T is projected on the set of transducers activating units 1, 2, 3, 5, and 8 connected in all possible ways to (2^9-1) A units, the distribution of outputs was as shown, the maximum being 3·7 per cent above the five second-largest outputs. The method of recognition depends upon finding ways of identifying the maximum outputs, which will be characteristic for each pattern distribution. The networks that perform this recognition Taylor calls maximum-amplitude filters and they are themselves built of A units.

Before describing them, however, we must consider the means adopted to ensure that the difference between the maximum and the nearest outputs is as large as possible. It is the operation of these devices for amplifying differences that makes the apparatus a practicable rather than a merely theoretical possibility. There is every reason to think that similar arrangements are an essential part of the pattern-recognition systems of the brain. In general the percentage difference between the maximum and next output decreases with n_s, the number of S terminals that supply non-zero signals, according to the equation

$$d = 100/(n_s^2-1)\% \quad (n_s \geqslant 2).$$

The means adopted for increasing the value of d has been to arrange that the supply terminals of an A unit that are not

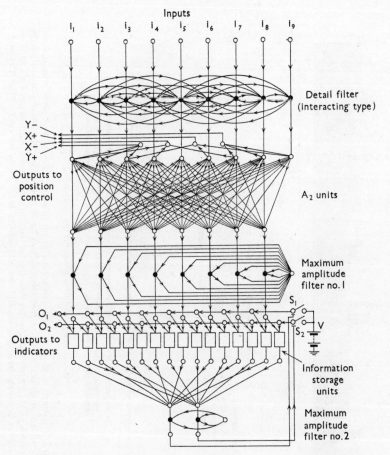

FIG. 107. Signal flow diagram of experimental automatic pattern-recognition apparatus.

The inputs to the nine detail filter terminals are supplied by photoelectric multipliers arranged in a 3×3 matrix. Patterns are centred automatically by combining outputs of the detail filter to form position controls. The filtered inputs are then connected to eight 'A_2 units', one of these will show a maximum amplitude for each pattern (Fig. 108) and this is selected by the first maximum amplitude filter. The outputs of these supply eight pulse generators and these in turn sixteen capacitor storage units.

During the teaching process the switches S_1 and S_2 are closed manually or by means of some artificial external classification system. After learning the switches are closed by electromagnets supplied by the outputs of maximum amplitude filter 2. In both cases the closed switch applied the voltage V to one of the output terminals O_1 or O_2. The same voltage is also connected to an input of the information-storage unit. (After Taylor, 1959.)

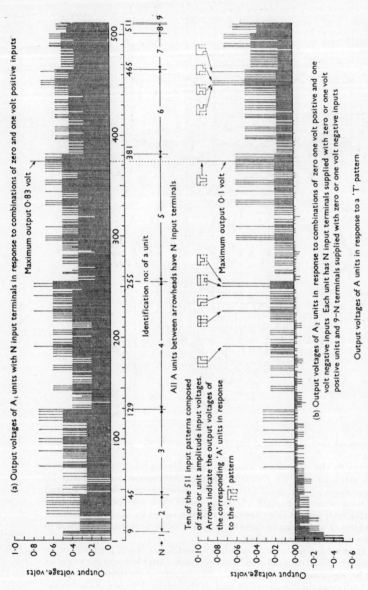

FIG. 108. (a) Output voltages to a T pattern in 2^9-1 A_1 units connected in all possible ways to nine photo-multipliers arranged in a 3×3 matrix. The pattern produces 1 volt at five terminals. The A unit giving the maximum output is connected to these five. Its voltage (0·83 V) is 3·7 per cent greater than that of the five next largest outputs (0·80 V). (b) Use of A_2 units to increase the difference between the maximum and nearest outputs. It is now 24 per cent. (After Taylor.)

occupied by positive connexions from the S supply terminals receive, through a sign-changing device, a negative (or inhibitory) input. Such units are called A_2 units by Taylor (Fig. 107) and as Fig. 108 shows their use increases the differentiation substantially.

A further advantage is obtained by making use of the fact that the detail important for recognition is in the regions where the signal amplitude changes appreciably. There are large areas within and outside a figure where it changes little. By giving special weight to the regions where the signal gradient changes rapidly the problem of differentiation is made easier. The importance of such 'detail filtering', as Taylor calls it, has been recognized by several systems that attempt to detect patterns by a binary system of edging. Even with a very fast digital computer it takes many minutes to edge a single pattern in this way. The analogue detail filter network gives a similar result in less than a microsecond. It is such advantages of perhaps hundreds of millions of times that give the living analogue systems their powers (in the brain the actual time would be more than microseconds, but the principle applies).

The method used in Taylor's machine depends upon arranging A units in rows and columns that correspond to the transducer positions. It is then ensured that each active unit inhibits its neighbours, by suitable connexions between them and the use of sign-changing units (Fig. 109a). With such an arrangement an input pattern with rectangular edges can be 'edged' as shown in Fig. 109b. Collateral inhibition of this sort has been shown to occur in the eye of the king crab (p. 115). Suitable collateral connexions exist in the eye of the octopus and, for touch, between the receptors in the arms (p. 114). No doubt they are present in the vertebrate eye and many other receptor systems. The effect of all such arrangements is to give greatest weight to the signals that contain most of the information of the detail and shape (Gerard, 1963).

The operation of identifying the unit with the maximum amplitude is made more effective in the same way by A units.

These can be connected so that if one signal is larger than the rest by more than a certain amount then all the others are reduced to zero and the first only is passed on. This 'maximum

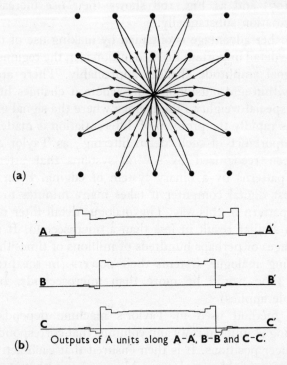

(a)

(b)   Outputs of A units along **A–A′, B–B′** and **C–C′.**

FIG. 109. (a) Signal flow diagram for one unit of a two-dimensional detail filter. The black dots are signal-summation points at each of which an input multiplied by a gain constant arrives from below the diagram and adds algebraically with the twenty signals arriving from the twenty neighbouring output nodes within a radius of $2\frac{1}{2}$ units from it. (b) Outputs of detail filter in response to a square input pattern covering numerous units each as shown in a. AA′ is taken across the diagonal. BB′ corresponds to the four edges and CC′ to both sections through the centre of the square taken at right angles to the edges. The output signals are largest at the corners of the square and smallest at the centre. The signals that contain most of the information about detail and shape are given the greatest weight. (After Taylor.)

amplitude' filter is in effect an extended form of detail filter in which the most active unit inhibits all the rest, instead of inhibiting only its neighbours.

The equipment so far described will serve to give an output

in a characteristic A unit for each pattern of intensity thrown on the transducers. This does not, however, solve the problem of classification that we have set ourselves, an essential feature of which is that many varied shapes of T are recognized as that letter by a human observer. In the system so far described each different T would give a different output. What we need is something that will as it were record the universal T. Clearly this requires additional information as to what is and what is not to be considered a T. This can only be achieved by a learning system in which the outputs for a number of input situations are recorded and in some way classified by association with other information. In Taylor's system this is done by information-storage units that record the strength, duration, and classification of the outputs of maximum-amplitude filter 1 (Fig. 107). The classification is produced by activating one of the inputs S_1 or S_2, representing pleasure or pain stimuli. The effect of each classification signal is to switch on the appropriate member of a set of information-storage units connected between the maximum-amplitude filter outputs and the output unit O_1 or O_2 that indicates the class of pattern presented. Each information storage unit acts as a gain or sensitivity control, so that the gains of the appropriate signal paths between maximum amplitude filters 1 and 2 are increased by the signals themselves. Eventually the stimulus pattern P produces a conditional response $P \rightarrow O_1$ or $P \rightarrow O_2$ that is the same as the unconditional response $S_1 \rightarrow O_1$ or $S_2 \rightarrow O_2$ elicited when the pattern was presented during training.

The general analogy between this system and the living-memory system is clear although the principles of storage may be very different. No doubt in the brain there is a hierarchy of classification signals. They begin with those that indicate the simplest good and bad for the organism, such as the signals for food reward and pain we have considered for the octopus. Such indicators of the fundamental effects upon the organism of its actions must remain important even when they are supplemented by subsidiary classifications resulting from later associations.

In a sense Taylor's model is more ambitious than our attempt to 'understand' the octopus's brain, which essentially classifies only into two categories 'to be attacked' and 'to be avoided'. Taylor's model attempts to imitate the much more subtle systems of classification involved in human pattern recognition. It is also more general than the octopus in that it does not have *any* built in encoding units such as the cells with particular dendritic spreads, which may be determined by heredity both in octopuses and cats (pp. 147 and 163).

The system has in fact all possible encoding units built in, but any number can be left out, or they can be combined. Thus encoders for vertical, horizontal, or oblique are special cases of the 511 possible combinations. The engineer is interested in the general principles of such systems and in pressing them as far as they can go. He tries to avoid selecting specific forms. It is interesting that the animal cannot afford the luxury of such a general approach. Survival depends upon appropriate recognition of certain classes of event that occur frequently and are of importance for the animal. Encoding units are provided to detect these events, and to associate them with the performance of appropriate actions.

Similarly, the problem of finding signals of results that indicate whether the decisions taken are 'right' does not arise for the engineer. The human operator can be made to teach the machine whether it has chosen correctly or not. Even so the signals must be spread to all information units, much as they are in the octopus. Each input can be made to give a 'hereditary' response, without training, such as withdrawal from pain or attack at food. The system is therefore learning to make these homeostatic responses. The rate at which learning occurs is of course also controlled by the frequency of trials, which is given by the operator, but it is possible to imagine that this too could be regulated by a system with appropriate means of adjusting its motivation.

All these special features could be incorporated into Taylor's model. Even without them the similarity between its design and the layout of actual living systems is striking (Fig. 107).

It at least helps us to think about how best to describe and name the parts of a multi-channel classifying device.

6. *The cortex as a maximum amplitude filter*

The model not only resembles the nervous system in its general layout but can be used to suggest in some detail how the mammalian cortex may perform its functions (Taylor, 1964). The connexions known to exist in the cortex could provide random connexions that allow selection with each pattern of inputs of the cell that shows the highest output. As in the model this cell would characterize the form of the '*gestalt*' that produced the input.

The essential feature of the system is that if pattern recognition depends upon the presence or absence of signals s in N channels, then the 2^N-1 patterns can be identified by a similar number of networks that form all the possible functions of the form

$$\frac{1}{n}\left(\sum_{r=1}^{n} s_r - \sum_{r=n+1}^{N} s_r \right),$$

where n is the number of active channels. The function that has the maximum value indicates the pattern that is present.

Since in man about 10^6 fibres reach the visual cortex in the optic radiation, a full classification is obviously impossible. However, the organism can produce only a limited number of motor patterns (M). Taylor poses the proposition that 'In its simplest form learning can be considered as the process of storing appropriate information in the memory so that selected members of the 2^N-1 input patterns become associated with members of the M output patterns in a way that tends to increase 'pleasure' or reduce 'pain''.

In the scheme he suggests (Figs. 110 and 111) a form of random connectivity allows impulses in the afferents arriving from a primary sensory area (s, t, u) to select as motor output the large pyramidal cell p that has received the largest amount of 'positive reward' (pleasure) in the afferents that carry what we have called signals of results (x, y). The number of things that the body can do obviously has some limit and it is suggested that there are 10^4 motor pathways (M) through the p neurons. If we assume that there are the same number of afferents (N) after encoding, then Taylor shows that the

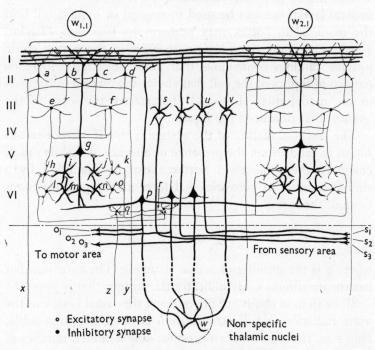

FIG. 110. Scheme to explain functioning of the cortex as a maximum amplitude filter (see text). (After Taylor, 1964.)

necessary random connexions can be made with NM neurons, which he assumes to be the small pyramids of layer 2. This is clearly a possible number, whereas the representation of all 2^N inputs would be impossible.

The s, t, and u afferents terminate on the stellate neurons of layer III. These stellates send axons to layer I at the surface and are distributed in an overlapping random way to make contact with the apical dendrites of neurons a–d. The system would require NM of these.

The cells *a*, *b*, *c*, and *d* make two types of connexion with *s*, *t*, *u*. Either they make synapse at random with any of the *N* axons (as shown by *a* and *d*), or alternatively they make the first synapse at random during development and then remain connected only with that axon (*b* and *c*). Thus if the effect on

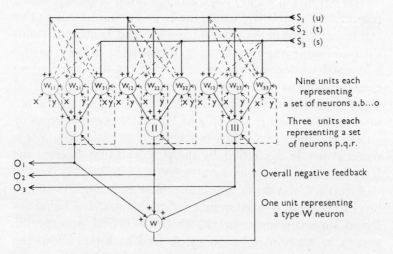

FIG. 111. Simplified computer diagram of the connexions suggested for the cerebral cortex in Fig. 110. (After Taylor, 1964.)

the output of each synapse is $1/N$ the two types will produce outputs of

$$\frac{1}{N} \sum_{r=1}^{N} s_r = \bar{s}_r \quad \text{and} \quad s_r.$$

Passing down through the cortex it is suggested that there is a system for ensuring that the largest input of these two will be passed on, and the other eliminated. This is done by what is essentially a maximum amplitude filter such as was used in the machine. *x* and *y* are the unconditional inputs corresponding to pleasure and pain signals. Their effects are inhibitory and distributed at random equally to all the cells. *e* and *f* are further stellate neurons, which take the sum of the quantities $\bar{s}_r$ and s_r for whichever of the channels is not inhibited. Crossed inhibitory connexions of e and f form the maximum-amplitude filter.

Thus if s_r is larger than the average $\bar{s}_r$ the output of f is proportional to s_r and if s_r is smaller than $\bar{s}_r$ the output of e is proportional to $\bar{s}_r$. In either case the smaller signal is eliminated.

The outputs of e and f modulate the firing of i and j, which respectively inhibit and excite the large pyramidal cell g. The transmission strength of the synapses ig and jg increases with the number of impulses arriving. Feed-backs through m and n increase or decrease the sensitivity. Thus the contribution that g makes to the efferent neuron p is raised or lowered about the initial value. There are M types of p neurons and the total input to each is a sample of all the N possible types of g neuron. The system thus functions by selecting the motor pattern that is controlled by the p neuron that receives the largest excitation.

A further maximum amplitude filter is suggested at this level to prevent a large number of motor patterns being selected simultaneously. In the thalamo-cortical non-specific system, w, there may be a negative feed-back that allows the type-p selector neuron receiving the maximum excitation to fire, but inhibits the remainder.

Thus we may suppose the system is activated by the arrival of impulses along channels such as u to c, and delivered to the apical dendrite of g. If the consequent firing of g and p brings pleasure (y) then b and d are inhibited. Since $c > a$, the excitation in $f > e$ and e is inhibited. The tendency of neuron g to fire is thus increased by the learning change in the excitatory memory synapse j–g.

This is a more general scheme comparable to that which we have considered in the case of the optic lobe of the octopus. Each input pathway (s, t, u) can either increase or decrease the probability of firing of each output pathway, p. Whether this change takes place suddenly or gradually is obviously important to discover, but in either case the principle remains the same, namely of choice between the alternative pathways that were possible.

Similarly, the principle of encoding that we have considered shows its importance. The organism cannot learn all possible combinations of all possible events. The interesting thing is to find for each species how the coding system operates. If we knew this for man we should indeed be able to discover principles that would enable us all to learn better. Taylor's model establishes the possibility that the cortex may operate by random connexion from the input to a set of neurons and then selection of those that give the maximum response. Moreover, it even suggests that the mechanism by which the maximum is selected makes use of reciprocal inhibition such as the engineer has incorporated into his device.

7. *The usefulness of models*

The biologist is endlessly curious about the details of living activity and structure. His interest in animals and plants is held because he finds these details satisfying. His value to the biological technologies is again in his knowledge of these facts. Why then be concerned with all this talk about models? Has the introduction of the theme throughout this book done any more than obscure the facts and irritate those who wish to know what the author has found out? I will confess that I often have doubts, being myself fascinated, indeed obsessed, by the beauty and interest of the structure and function of the nervous system.

Yet this beauty is far enhanced when attention to it seems to lead to something that we have called 'understanding' of how the nervous system works. This experience in turn has led to exciting problems of what is meant by 'understanding' and by 'function'. Equally exciting is the discovery that one can play a part in the process of model-building itself, producing artefacts that are both interesting and useful. Models themselves have great beauty. It is true that theirs is only a dim representation of the glories of the world around. But without them how else are we to know these beauties . . . ?

REFERENCES

AITKEN, J. T., and BRIDGER, J. E., 1961. Neuron size and neuron population density in the lumbosacral region of the cat's spinal cord. *J. Anat., Lond.* **95**, 38-53.

—— SHARMAN, M., and YOUNG, J. Z., 1947. Maturation of regenerating nerve fibres with various peripheral connexions. *J. Anat., Lond.* **81**, 1-22.

ALLISON, A. C., and WARWICK, R. T. T., 1949. Quantitative observations on the olfactory system of the rabbit. *Brain*, **72**, 186-97.

ARMSTRONG, J., RICHARDSON, K. C., and YOUNG, J. Z., 1956. Staining neural end feet and mitochondria after postchroming and carbowax embedding. *Stain Tech.* **31**, 263-70.

ASHBY, W. ROSS, 1960. *Design for a brain.* London, Chapman & Hall.

AUTRUM, H., 1958. Electrophysiological analysis of the visual systems in insects. *Exp. Cell Res.* Suppl. **5**, 426-39.

BARLOW, H. B., 1953. Summation and inhibition in the frog's retina. *J. Physiol.* **119**, 69-88.

—— 1959. Sensory mechanisms, the reduction of redundancy and intelligence, in: *Mechanisation of thought processes. National Physical Laboratory*, Symposium **10**. London, Her Majesty's Stationery Office.

BATHAM, E. J., 1957. Care of eggs by *Octopus maorum. Trans. roy. Soc. N.Z.* **84**, 629-38.

BERNAL, J. D., 1962. Biochemical evolution, in: *Horizons in biochemistry*, eds. M. Kasha and B. Pullman. New York, Academic Press.

BINDMAN, LYNN J., LIPPOLD, O. C. J., and REDFEARN, J. W. T., 1962. Long-lasting changes in the level of the electrical activity of the cerebral cortex produced by polarizing currents. *Nature, Lond.* **196**, 584-5.

BISHOP, G. H., 1956. Natural history of the nerve impulse. *Physiol. Rev.* **36**, 376-99.

BISHOP, P. O., BURKE, W., and HAYHOW, W. R., 1959. Repetitive stimulation of optic nerve and lateral geniculate synapses. *Exp. Neurol.* **1**, 534-55.

BODIAN, D., 1952. Introductory survey of neurons. *Cold Spr. Harb. Sym. Quant. Biol.* **17**, 1-12.

BOK, S. T., 1928. Das Rückenmark. *Handbuch der mikroskopischen Anatomie des Menschen* IV/1. Nervensystem I. ed. Möllendorff, W. von. Berlin, J. Springer.

BOULET, P., 1954. Experiences sur la perception visuelle du mouvement chez *Sepia officinalis* L. *C. R. Soc. Biol., Paris*, **148**, 1486-9.

BOYCOTT, B. B., 1953. The chromatophore system of cephalopods. *Proc. Linn. Soc. Lond.* **164**, 235-40.

—— 1954. Learning in *Octopus vulgaris* and other cephalopods. *Pubbl. Staz. zool. Napoli*, **25**, 67-93.

—— 1960. The functioning of the statocysts of *Octopus vulgaris. Proc. roy. Soc.* B. **152**, 78-87.

BOYCOTT, B. B., 1961. The functional organization of the brain of the cuttlefish *Sepia officinalis*. *Proc. roy. Soc.* B. **153**, 503–34.

—— 1964. [In preparation.]

—— and YOUNG, J. Z., 1955. Memories controlling attacks on food objects by *Octopus vulgaris* Lamarck. *Pubbl. Staz. zool. Napoli*, **27**, 232–49.

—— —— 1956. The subpedunculate body and nerve and other organs associated with the optic tract of cephalopods, in: *Bertil Hanström zoological papers in honour of his sixty-fifth birthday, November 20th 1956*, ed. K. G. Wingstrand. Lund, Zoological Institute.

—— —— 1957. Effects of interference with the vertical lobe on visual discriminations in *Octopus vulgaris* Lamarck. *Proc. roy. Soc.* B. **146**, 439–59.

—— —— 1965. *The brain of* Octopus vulgaris. [In preparation.]

BRAITENBERG, V., and ONESTO, N., 1962. The cerebellar cortex as a timing organ. Discussion of an hypothesis. *Atti del 1° Congresso Internazionale di Medicina Cibernetica*. Naples: Giannini.

BROWN, G. L., and PASCOE, J. E., 1954. The effect of degenerative section of ganglionic axons of transmission through the ganglion. *J. Physiol.* **123**, 565–73.

BULLOCK, T. H., 1958. Parameters of integrative action of the nervous system at the neuronal level. *Exp. Cell Res.* Suppl. **5**, 323–37.

BURNS, B. D., 1958. *The mammalian cerebral cortex*. London, Edward Arnold (Publishers) Ltd.

CAJAL, S. R., 1911. *Histologie du système nerveux* II. Paris, A. Maloine.

COLONNIER, M., 1963. Tangential pattern of dendrites and axons in the visual cortex of the cat. Ph.D. thesis, University of London.

COMFORT, A., 1959. Studies on the longevity and mortality of English thoroughbred horses, in: *Ciba Foundation Colloquia on Ageing*, **5**, The lifespan of animals. eds. G. E. W. Wolstenholme and C. M. O'Connor. London, Churchill Ltd.

CRAIK, K. J. W., 1943. *The nature of explanation*. Cambridge, University Press.

CRICK, F. H. C., BARNETT, L., BRENNER, S., and WATTS-TOBIN, R. J., 1961. General nature of the genetic code for proteins. *Nature, Lond.* **192**, 1227–32.

DE BEER, G. R., 1958. *Embryos and ancestors*. Oxford, Clarendon Press.

DEUTSCH, J. A., 1960. The plexiform zone and shape recognition in the octopus. *Nature, Lond.* **185**, 443–6.

DIJKGRAAF, S., 1961. The statocyst of *Octopus vulgaris* as a rotation receptor. *Pubbl. Staz. zool. Napoli*, **32**, 64–87.

—— 1963. Versuche über Schallwahrnehmung bei Tintenfischen. *Naturwissenschaften*, **50**, 50.

DILLY, P. N., GRAY, E. G., and YOUNG, J. Z., 1963. Electron microscopy of optic nerves and optic lobes of *Octopus* and *Eledone*. *Proc. roy. Soc.* B. **158**, 446–56.

DODWELL, P. C., 1957. Shape recognition in rats. *Brit. J. Psychol.* **48**, 221–9.

ECCLES, J. C., 1953. *The neurophysiological basis of mind*. Oxford, Clarendon Press.
—— 1961. The nature of central inhibition. The Ferrier Lecture. *Proc. roy. Soc.* B. **153**, 445–76.
—— 1964. *The Physiology of Synapses*. Berlin: Springer–Verlag.
—— and KRNJEVIĆ, K., 1959. Presynaptic changes associated with post-tetanic potentiation in the spinal cord. *J. Physiol.* **149**, 274–87.
—— and MCINTYRE, A. K., 1953. The effects of disuse and of activity on mammalian spinal reflexes. *J. Physiol.* **121**, 492–516.
—— and SHERRINGTON, C. S., 1930. Numbers and contraction values of individual motor-units examined in some muscles of the limb. *Proc. roy. Soc.* B. **106**, 326–57.
FATT, P., and KATZ, B., 1952. Some problems of neuro-muscular transmission. *Cold Spr. Harb. Sym. quant. Biol.* **17**, 275–80.
FERNÁNDEZ-MORÁN, H., 1958. Fine structure of the light receptors in the compound eyes of insects. *Exp. Cell Res.* Suppl. **5**, 586–644.
FOERSTER, H. VON, 1962. Bio-logic, in: *Biological prototypes and synthetic systems*, **1**, eds. E. E. Bernard and M. R. Kare. New York, Plenum Press.
GALAMBOS, R., 1961. A glia-neural theory of brain function. *Proc. nat. Acad. Sci., Wash.* **47**, 129–36.
GAZE, R. M., 1960. Regeneration of the optic nerve in amphibia. *Int. rev. Neurobiol.* **2**, 1–40.
GERARD, R. W., 1963. Summary and general discussion, in: *Information storage and neural control*, eds. W. S. Fields and W. Abbott. Illinois, C. C. Thomas.
GLOCKAUER, A., 1915. Zur Anatomie und Histologie des Cephalopoden-auges. *Z. wiss. Zool.* **113**, 325–60.
GRAY, E. G., 1959. Electron microscopy of synaptic contacts on dendrite spines of the cerebral cortex. *Nature, Lond.* **183**, 1592–3.
—— 1961. Ultrastructure of synapses of the cerebral cortex and of certain specialisations of neuroglial membranes. *Anatomical Society Symposium on electron microscopy*. London, Edward Arnold (Publishers) Ltd.
—— and WHITTAKER, V. P., 1962. The isolation of nerve endings from brain: an electron-microscopic study of cell fragments derived by homogenization and centrifugation. *J. Anat., Lond.* **96**, 79–87.
—— and YOUNG, J. Z., 1964. Electron microscopy of synaptic structures in *Octopus* brain. *J. cell. Biol.* **21**, 87–103.
GRAY, J. A. B., 1960. Mechanically excitable receptor units in the mantle of the octopus and their connexions. *J. Physiol.* **153**, 573–82.
GRAZIADEI, P., 1962. Receptors in the suckers of *Octopus*. *Nature, Lond.* **195**, 57–59.
GREGORY, R. L., 1961. The brain as an engineering problem, in: *Current problems in animal behaviour*, eds. W. H. Thorpe and O. L. Zangwill. Cambridge, University Press.
—— 1962. The logic of the localization of function in the central nervous system, in: *Biological prototypes and synthetic systems*, **1**, eds. E. E. Bernard and M. R. Kare. New York, Plenum Press.

HADDARA, M., 1956. A quantitative study of the post-natal changes in the packing density of the neurons in the visual cortex of the mouse. *J. Anat. Lond.* **90**, 494–501.

HAGIWARA, S., and TASAKI, I., 1958. A study on the mechanism of impulse transmission across the giant synapse of the squid. *J. Physiol.* **143**, 114–37.

HALDANE, J. B. S., 1953. Some animal life tables. *J. Inst. Actu.* **79**, 83–89.

HANSTRÖM, B., 1928. *Vergleichende Anatomie des Nervensystems der wirbellosen Tiere.* Berlin, Julius Springer.

HARLOW, H. F., 1949. The formation of learning sets. *Psychol. Rev.* **56**, 51–65.

HARTLINE, H. K., 1938. The response of single optic nerve fibres of the vertebrate eye to illumination of the retina. *Amer. J. Physiol.* **121**, 400–15.

—— RATLIFF, F., and MILLER, W. H., 1961. Inhibitory interaction in the retina and its significance in vision, in: *Nervous inhibition*, ed. E. Florey. London, Pergamon Press.

HEBB, D. O., 1949. *The organization of behaviour.* New York, John Wiley and Sons, Inc.

HICK, W. E., 1952. Why the human operator? *Trans. Soc. Instrum. Tech.* **4**, 67–73.

HILL, D. K., 1950. The volume change resulting from stimulation of a giant nerve fibre. *J. Physiol.* **111**, 304–27.

HODGKIN, A. L., and HUXLEY, A. F., 1952. A quantitative description of membrane current and its application to conduction and excitation in nerve. *J. Physiol.* **117**, 500–44.

HOFFMAN, H., 1950. Local re-innervation in partially denervated muscle: a histo-physiological study. *Aust. J. exp. Biol. med. Sci.* **28**, 383–97.

HOLMES, F. W., and DAVENPORT, H. A., 1940. Cells and fibres in spinal nerves. IV. The number of neurites in dorsal and ventral roots of the cat. *J. comp. Neurol.* **73**, 1–5.

HORRIDGE, G. A., 1962. Learning of leg position by the ventral nerve cord in headless insects. *Proc. roy. Soc. B.* **157**, 33–52.

HUBBARD, S. J., 1960. Hearing and the octopus statocyst. *J. exp. Biol.* **37**, 845–53.

HUBEL, D. H., and WIESEL, T. N., 1959. Receptive fields of single neurons in the cat's striate cortex. *J. Physiol.* **148**, 574–91.

—— —— 1962. Receptive fields, binocular interaction and functional architecture in the cat's visual cortex. *J. Physiol.* **160**, 106–54.

HYDÉN, H., 1960. The neuron, in: *The cell*, **4**, 216–308, eds. J. Brachet and A. E. Mirsky. New York and London, Academic Press.

—— and EGYHÁZI, E., 1962. Nuclear RNA changes of nerve cells during a learning experiment in rats. *Proc. nat. Acad. Sci., Wash.* **48**, 1366–73.

IURATO, S., 1962. Efferent fibers to the sensory cells of Corti's organ. *Exp. Cell Res.* **27**, 162–4.

JACOB, F., and MONOD, J., 1961. Genetic regulatory mechanisms in the synthesis of proteins. *J. mol. Biol.* **3**, 318–56.

JACOBSON, H., 1950. The informational capacity of the human ear. *Science*, **112**, 143–4.

—— 1951. The informational capacity of the human eye. *Science*, **113**, 292–3.

JASPER, H. H., RICCI, C. F., and DOANE, B., 1958. Patterns of cortical neuronal discharge during conditioned responses in monkeys, in: *Ciba Foundation Symposium. Neurological bases of behaviour*, eds. G. E. W. Wolstenholme and C. M. O'Connor. London, Churchill.

JOHN, E. R., 1963. Neural mechanisms of decision making, in: *Information storage and neural control*, eds. W. S. Fields and W. Abbott. Illinois, C. C. Thomas.

JONES, E. C., 1963. *Tremoctopus violaceus* uses *Physalia* tentacles as weapons. *Science*, **139**, 764–6.

KIDD, M., 1962. Electron microscopy of the inner plexiform layer of the retina in the cat and the pigeon. *J. Anat., Lond.* **96**, 179–87.

KIT, S., 1963. Coding by purine and pyrimidine moieties in animals, plants and bacteria, in: *Information storage and neural control*, eds. W. S. Fields and W. Abbott. Illinois, C. C. Thomas.

KONORSKI, J., 1948. *Conditioned reflexes and neuron organization*. Cambridge, University Press.

KOPSCH, Fr., 1899. Mitteilungen über das Ganglion opticum der Cephalopoden. *Int. Mschr. Anat. Physiol.* **16**, 33–54.

KUFFLER, S. W., 1958. Synaptic inhibitory mechanisms. Properties of dendrites and problems of excitation in isolated sensory nerve cells. *Exp. Cell Res.* Suppl. **5**, 493–519.

LASHLEY, K. S., 1950. In search of the engram, in: Physiological mechanisms in animal behaviour. *Symp. Soc. exp. Biol.* **4**, 454–82.

LENHOSSÉK, M. von, 1896. Histologische Untersuchungen am Sehlappen der Cephalopoden. *Arch. mikr. Anat.* **47**, 45–120.

LETTVIN, J. Y., MATURANA, H. R., McCULLOCH, W. S., and PITTS, W. H., 1959. What the frog's eye tells the frog's brain. *Proc. Inst. Radio Engrs., N.Y.* **47**, 1940–51.

LILLY, J. C., 1960. Learning motivated by subcortical stimulation. The 'start' and 'stop' patterns of behaviour, in: *Electrical studies on the unanaesthetized brain*, eds. E. R. Ramey and D. S. O'Doherty. New York, P. P. Hoeber, Inc.

LYALL, A. H., 1957. Cone arrangements in teleost retinae. *Quart. J. micr. Sci.* **98**, 189–201.

MACKINTOSH, J., and MACKINTOSH, N. J., 1964. [In press.]

MALDONADO, H., 1962. The visual attack learning system in *Octopus vulgaris*. Ph.D. thesis, University of London.

—— 1963a. The positive learning process in *Octopus vulgaris*. *Z. vergl. Physiol.* **47**, 191–214.

—— 1963b. The visual attack learning system in *Octopus vulgaris*. *J. Theoret. Biol.* **5**, 470–88.

MATURANA, H. R., 1958. Efferent fibres in the optic nerve of the toad (*Bufo bufo*). *J. Anat. Lond.* **92**, 21–27.

MATURANA, H. R., 1959. Number of fibres in the optic nerve and the number of ganglion cells in the retina of Anurans. *Nature, Lond.* **183**, 1406–7.

—— LETTVIN, J. Y., McCULLOCH, W. S., and PITTS, W. H., 1960. Anatomy and physiology of vision in the frog, *Rana pipiens. J. gen. Physiol.* **43**, Suppl. 2, 129–75.

—— and SPERLING, S., 1963. Undirectional response to angular acceleration recorded from the middle cristal nerve in the statocyst of *Octopus vulgaris. Nature, Lond.* **197**, 815–16.

MELZACK, R., and WALL, P. D., 1962. On the nature of cutaneous sensory mechanisms. *Brain,* **85**, 331–56.

MESSENGER, J. B., 1963. Behaviour of young *Octopus briareus* Robson. *Nature, Lond.* **197**, 1186–7.

MITRA, N. L., 1955. Quantitative analysis of cell types in mammalian neo-cortex. *J. Anat. Lond.* **89**, 467–83.

MITTLESTAEDT, H., 1957. Prey capture in mantids, in: *Recent advances in invertebrate physiology.* A symposium, eds. Bradley T. Scheer *et al.* Oregon, University of Oregon Publications.

MOODY, M. F., and ROBERTSON, J. D., 1960. The fine structure of some retinal photoreceptors. *J. biophys. biochem. Cytol.* **7**, 87–92.

MORRELL, F., 1960. Microelectrode and steady potential studies suggesting a dendritic locus of closure, in: *Moscow colloquium in electroencephalography of higher nervous activity,* eds. H. Jasper and G. D. Smirnov. Moscow.

—— 1962. Electrochemical mechanisms and information storage in nerve cells, in: *Macromolecular specificity and biological memory,* ed. F. O. Schmitt. Cambridge, Massachusetts Institute of Technology Press.

—— 1963. Information storage in nerve cells, in: *Information storage and neural control,* eds. W. S. Fields and W. Abbott. Illinois, C. C. Thomas.

MORRIS, D. D. B., 1953. Recovery in partly paralysed muscles. *J. Bone and Joint Surg.* **35B**, 650–60.

MUNTZ, W. R. A., 1961. Interocular transfer in *Octopus vulgaris. J. comp. physiol. Psychol.* **54**, 49–55.

—— 1962a. Microelectrode recordings from the diencephalon of the frog (*Rana pipiens*), and a blue sensitive system. *J. Neurophysiol.* **25**, 699–711.

—— 1962b. Stimulus generalisation following monocular training in *Octopus. J. comp. physiol. Psychol.* **55**, 535–40.

—— 1964. [In preparation.]

—— SUTHERLAND, N. S., and YOUNG, J. Z., 1962. Simultaneous shape discrimination in *Octopus* after removal of the vertical lobe. *J. exp. Biol.* **39**, 557–66.

NEUMANN, J. VON, 1958. *The computer and the brain.* Silliman Memorial Lectures. New Haven, Yale University Press.

OLDS, J., 1958. Self-stimulation of the brain. *Science,* **127**, 315–24.

—— 1960. Differentiation of reward systems in the brain by self-stimulation technics, in: *Electrical studies on the unanaesthetized brain,* eds. E. R. Ramey and D. S. O'Doherty. New York, Paul B. Hoeber Inc., Medical Division of Harper and Brothers.

PACKARD, A., 1961. Sucker display of *Octopus. Nature, Lond.* **190**, 736-7.

PARRISS, J. R., 1963a. Retention of shape discrimination after regeneration of the optic nerves in the toad. *Quart. J. exp. Psychol.* **15**, 22-26.

—— 1963b. Visual discrimination in the toad. *Quart. J. exp. Psychol.* **15**, 13-21.

—— 1963c. Interference in learning and lesions in the visual system of *Octopus vulgaris. Behaviour,* **21**, 233-45.

—— 1964. Interference in learning. *Behaviour.* [In press.]

—— and YOUNG, J. Z., 1962. The limits of transfer of a learned discrimination to figures of larger and smaller sizes. *Z. vergl. Physiol.* **45**, 618-35.

PAVLOV, I. P., 1927. *Conditioned reflexes: an investigation of the physiological activity of the cerebral cortex.* Oxford, University Press.

PENFIELD, W., and ROBERTS, L., 1959. *Speech and brain-mechanisms.* Princeton, Princeton University Press.

PETERS, H. G., and BADEMAN, H., 1963. The form and growth of stellate cells in the cortex of the guinea-pig. *J. Anat., Lond.* **97**, 111-17.

PLATT, J. R., 1958. Functional geometry and the determination of pattern in mosaic receptors, in: *Symposium on information theory in biology,* ed. H. P. Yockey. London, Pergamon Press.

POLYAK, S., 1957. *The vertebrate visual system.* Chicago, The University of Chicago Press.

PROSSER, C. L., and YOUNG, J. Z., 1937. Responses of muscles of the squid to repetitive stimulation of giant nerve fibres. *Biol. Bull. Wood's Hole,* **73**, 237-41.

PUMPHREY, R. J., and YOUNG, J. Z., 1938. The rates of conduction of nerve fibres of various diameters in cephalopods. *J. exp. Biol.,* **15**, 453-66.

PURPURA, D. P., and GRUNDFEST, H., 1956. Nature of dendritic potentials and synaptic mechanisms in cerebral cortex of cat. *J. Neurophysiol.,* **19**, 573-95.

—— and HOUSEPIAN, E. M., 1961. Morphological and physiological properties of chronically isolated immature neocortex. *Exp. Neurol.* **4**, 377-401.

QUASTLER, H., 1956. Studies of human channel capacity, in: *Information theory.* Third London Symposium. Ed. C. Cherry. London, Butterworth's Scientific Publications.

RASMUSSEN, G. L., 1960. Efferent fibers of the cochlear nerve and cochlear nucleus, in: *Neural mechanisms of the auditory and vestibular systems,* eds. G. L. Rasmussen and W. F. Windle. Illinois, C. C. Thomas.

ROBERTS, F., YOUNG, J. Z., and CAUSLEY, D., 1953. Flying spot microscope. *Electronics,* **26**, 137-9.

ROBERTS, M. B. V., 1962a. The rapid response of *Myxicola infundibulum* (Grübe). *J. Mar. biol. Ass. U.K.* **42**, 527-39.

—— 1962b. The giant fibre reflex of the earthworm *Lumbricus terrestris* L. I. The rapid response. *J. exp. Biol.* **39**, 219-27.

ROBSON, G. C., 1929. A monograph of the recent Cephalopoda. London, British Museum (Nat. Hist.).

RUSSELL, W. R., 1959. *Brain: memory: learning.* Oxford, Clarendon Press.

SANDERS, F. K., and YOUNG, J. Z., 1940. Learning and other functions of the higher nervous centres of *Sepia*. *J. Neurophysiol.* 3, 501–26.

SCOVILLE, W. B., and MILNER, B., 1957. Loss of recent memory after bilateral hippocampal lesions. *J. Neurol. Psychiat.* 20, 11–21.

SERENI, E., and YOUNG, J. Z., 1932. Nervous degeneration and regeneration in cephalopods. *Pubbl. Staz. zool. Napoli*, 12, 173–208.

SHERRINGTON, C. S., 1906. *The integrative action of the nervous system.* London, Archibald Constable & Co. Ltd.

SHOLL, D. A., 1956. *The organization of the cerebral cortex.* London, Methuen & Co. Ltd.

SOMMERHOFF, G., 1950. *Analytical biology.* London, Oxford University Press.

SPERRY, R. W., 1951. Regulative factors in the orderly growth of neural circuits. *Growth.* Suppl. 15, 63–87.

STEINBERG, H., and SUMMERFIELD, A., 1957. Influence of a depressant drug on acquisition in rote learning. *Quart. J. exp. Psychol.* 9, 138–45.

SUTHERLAND, N. S., 1957a. Visual discrimination of orientation and shape by the *Octopus*. *Nature, Lond.* 179, 11–13.

—— 1957b. Visual discrimination of orientation by *Octopus*. *Brit. J. Psychol.* 48, 55–71.

—— 1958. Visual discrimination of shape by *Octopus*. Squares and triangles. *Quart. J. exp. Psychol.* 10, 40–47.

—— 1959. A test of a theory of shape discrimination in *Octopus vulgaris* Lamarck. *J. comp. physiol. Psychol.* 52, 135–41.

—— 1960a. Visual discrimination of orientation by *Octopus*: mirror images. *Brit. J. Psychol.* 51, 9–18.

—— 1960b. Visual discrimination of shape by *Octopus*: open and closed forms. *J. comp. physiol. Psychol.* 53, 104–12.

—— 1961. Discrimination of horizontal and vertical extents by *Octopus*. *J. comp. physiol. Psychol.* 54, 43–48.

—— 1963a. Cat's ability to discriminate oblique rectangles. *Science*, 139, 209–10.

—— 1963b. Shape discrimination and receptive fields. *Nature, Lond.* 197, 118–22.

—— MACKINTOSH, J., and MACKINTOSH, N. J., 1963. The visual discrimination of reduplicated patterns by *Octopus*. *Anim. Behav.* 11, 106–10.

—— and MUNTZ, W. R. A., 1959. Simultaneous discrimination training and preferred directions of motion in visual discrimination of shape in *Octopus vulgaris* Lamarck. *Pubbl. Staz. zool. Napoli*, 31, 109–26.

SVAETICHIN, G., LAUFER, M., MITRARI, G., FATEHCHAND, R., VALLECALLE, E., and VILLEGAS, J., 1961. Glial control of neural networks and receptors, in: *Neurophysiologie und Psychophysik des Visuellen Systems*, eds. R. Jung and H. Kornhuber. Berlin, Springer-Verlag.

SZENTÁGOTHAI, J., 1961. Specificity and plasticity of neural structures and functions, in: *Brain and behaviour*, 1, ed. M. A. B. Brazier. Washington, Amer. Inst. Biol. Sci.

332 REFERENCES

Szentágothai, J., and Rajkovits, K., 1954. Die Rückwirkung der spezifischen Funktion auf die Struktur der Nervenelemente. *Acta morph. Acad. Sci. hung.* **5**, 253–74.

Tasaki, I., and Chang, J. J., 1958. Electric response of glia cells in cat brain. *Science*, **128**, 1209–10.

Tasaki, K., Oikawa, T., and Norton, A. C., 1963. The dual nature of the *Octopus* electroretinogram. *Vision Res.* **3**, 61–73.

Taylor, W. K., 1957. The structure and functioning of the nervous system. *Nature, Lond.* **180**, 1388–90.

—— 1959. Pattern recognition by means of automatic analogue apparatus. *Proc. Instn. elect. Engrs.* **106**, 198–209.

—— 1964. Cortico-thalamic organization and memory. *Proc. roy. Soc.* B. **159**, 466–78.

Terni, T., 1920. Sulla correlazione fra ampiezza del territorio di innervazioni e grandezza delle cellule gangliari. *Arch. ital. Anat. Embriol.* **17**, 507–43.

Thore, S., 1939. Beiträge zur Kenntnis der vergleichenden Anatomie des zentralen Nervensystems der dibranchiaten Cephalopoden. *Pubbl. Staz. zool. Napoli*, **17**, 313–506.

Tinbergen, L., 1939. Zur Fortpflanzungsethologie von *Sepia officinalis* L. *Arch. neerl. Zool.* **3**, 323–64.

Tobias, J. M., 1952. On ultrastructure and function in nerve. Nonelectrical, physical aspects of excitation and conduction, as deduced primarily from polarization experiments, in: *Modern trends in physiology and biochemistry*, ed. E. S. G. Barron. New York, Academic Press, Inc.

Uexküll, J. von, 1895. Physiologische Untersuchungen an *Eledone moschata*. IV. Zur Analyse der Functionen des Centralnervensystems. *Z. Biol.* **31**, 584–609.

Uttley, A. M., 1959. Conditional probability computing in a nervous system, in: *Mechanisation of thought processes. National Physical Laboratory*, Symposium 10. London, Her Majesty's Stationery Office.

—— 1961. The engineering approach to the problem of neural organization, in: *Progress in Biophysics and Biophysical Chemistry*, **11**, 25–52, eds. J. A. V. Butler, B. Katz, and R. E. Zirkle. London, Pergamon Press.

Vevers, H. G., 1961. Observations on the laying and hatching of *Octopus* eggs in the society's aquarium. *Proc. zool. Soc.* **137**, 311–15.

Walter, W. Grey, 1953. *The living brain*. London, Duckworth.

Weiss, P., 1950. The deplantation of fragments of nervous system in amphibians. *J. exp. Zool.* **113**, 397–461.

Wells, M. J., 1958. Factors affecting reactions to *Mysis* by newly hatched *Sepia*. *Behaviour*, **13**, 96–111.

—— 1959a. A touch-learning centre in *Octopus*. *J. exp. Biol.* **36**, 590–612.

—— 1959b. Functional evidence for neurone fields representing the individual arms within the central nervous system of *Octopus*. *J. exp. Biol.* **36**, 501–11.

—— 1960a. Proprioception and visual discrimination of orientation in *Octopus*. *J. exp. Biol.* **37**, 489–99.

WELLS, M. J., 1960b. Optic glands and the ovary of *Octopus*. *Symp. zool. Soc. Lond.* **2**, 87–107.

—— 1961a. Weight discrimination by *Octopus*. *J. exp. Biol.* **38**, 127–33.

—— 1961b. Centres for tactile and visual learning in the brain of *Octopus*. *J. exp. Biol.* **38**, 811–26.

—— 1962a. Brain and behaviour in cephalopods. London, Heinemann.

—— 1962b. Early learning in *Sepia*. *Symp. zool. Soc. Lond.* **8**, 149–69.

—— 1963. Taste by touch: some experiments with *Octopus*. *J. exp. Biol.* **40**, 187–93.

—— and WELLS, J., 1956. Tactile discrimination and the behaviour of blind *Octopus*. *Pubbl. Staz. zool. Napoli*, **28**, 94–126.

—— —— 1957a. Repeated presentation experiments and the function of the vertical lobe in *Octopus*. *J. exp. Biol.* **34**, 469–77.

—— —— 1957b. The function of the brain of *Octopus* in tactile discrimination. *J. exp. Biol.* **34**, 131–42.

—— —— 1959. Hormonal control of sexual maturity in *Octopus*. *J. exp. Biol.* **36**, 1–33.

WHITFIELD, I. C., 1957. The physiology of hearing, in: *Progress in biophysics and biophysical chemistry*, **8**, 1–47, eds. J. A. V. Butler and B. Katz. London, Pergamon Press.

WIEMER, F. K., 1955. Mittelhirnfunktion bei Urodelen nach Regeneration und Transplantation. *Arch. EntwMech. Org.* **147**, 560–633.

WIERSMA, C. A. G., 1952. Neurons of arthropods. *Cold Spr. Harb. Sym. quant. Biol.* **17**, 155–63.

WILSON, D. M., 1960. Nervous control of movement in cephalopods. *J. exp. Biol.* **37**, 57–72.

WOLF, E., 1934. Das Verhalten der Bienen gegenüber flimmernden Feldern und bewegten Objekten. *Z. vergl. Physiol.* **20**, 151–61.

WOLKEN, J. J., 1958. Retinal structure. Mollusc cephalopods: *Octopus, Sepia*. *J. biophys. biochem. Cytol.* **4**, 835–8.

WYCKOFF, R. W. G., and YOUNG, J. Z., 1956. The motorneuron surface. *Proc. roy. Soc. B.* **144**, 440–50.

WYNNE-EDWARDS, V. C., 1962. *Animal dispersion in relation to social behaviour*. London and Edinburgh, Oliver and Boyd.

YOSHII, N., PRUVOT, P., and GASTAUT, H., 1957. Electrographic activity of the mesencephalic reticular formation during conditioning in the cat. *EEG. Clin. Neurophysiol.* **9**, 595–608.

YOUNG, J. Z., 1938. The evolution of the nervous system and of the relationship of organism and environment, in: *Evolution*. Essays presented to E. S. Goodrich. Ed. G. R. de Beer. Oxford, Clarendon Press.

—— 1948. Growth and differentiation of nerve fibres. *Symp. Soc. exp. Biol.* **2**, 57–74.

—— 1956. Visual responses by *Octopus* to crabs and other figures before and after training. *J. exp. Biol.* **33**, 709–29.

—— 1958. Responses of untrained octopuses to various figures and the effect of removal of the vertical lobe. *Proc. roy. Soc. B.* **149**, 463–83.

YOUNG, J. Z., 1959. Extinction of unrewarded responses in *Octopus*. *Pubbl. Staz. zool. Napoli*, **31**, 225–47.

—— 1960a. Regularities in the retina and optic lobes of *Octopus* in relation to form discrimination. *Nature, Lond.* **186**, 836–9.

—— 1960b. The statocysts of *Octopus vulgaris*. *Proc. roy. Soc.* B. **152**, 3–29.

—— 1960c. The failures of discrimination learning following the removal of the vertical lobes in *Octopus*. *Proc. roy. Soc.* B. **153**, 18–46.

—— 1961. Learning and discrimination in the *Octopus*. *Biol. Rev.* **36**, 32–96.

—— 1962a. Courtship and mating by a coral reef octopus (*O. horridus*). *Proc. zool. Soc. Lond.* **138**, 157–62.

—— 1962b. *The life of vertebrates.* Oxford, Clarendon Press.

—— 1962c. The retina of cephalopods and its degeneration after optic nerve section. *Philos. Trans.* B. **245**, 1–18.

—— 1962d. The optic lobes of *Octopus vulgaris*. *Philos. Trans.* B. **245**, 19–58.

—— 1962e. Memory mechanisms of the brain. The thirty-sixth Maudsley lecture. *J. ment. Sci.* **108**, 119–33.

—— 1962f. Reversal of learning in *Octopus* and the effect of removal of the vertical lobe. *Quart. J. exp. Psychol.* **14**, 193–205.

—— 1962 g. Repeated reversal of training in *Octopus*. *Quart. J. exp. Psychol.* **14**, 206–222.

—— 1963a. The number and sizes of nerve cells in *Octopus*. *Proc. zool. Soc. Lond.* **140**, 229–54.

—— 1963b. Light- and dark-adaptation in the eyes of some cephalopods. *Proc. zool. Soc. Lond.* **140**, 255–72.

—— 1963c. Some essentials of neural memory systems. Paired centres that regulate and address the signals of the results of action. *Nature, Lond.* **198**, 626–30.

—— 1964a. [In preparation.]

—— 1964b. Paired centres for the control of attack by *Octopus*. *Proc. roy. Soc.* B. **159**, 565–88.

GLOSSARY

Most other words used but not defined here will be found in the *Concise Oxford Dictionary*.

acetylcholine. A substance produced at the transmitter ends of some nerve fibres, capable of initiating impulses across synaptic gaps.

action potential. The voltage difference ($\sim$ 100 mV.) produced across a nerve-fibre membrane as a nerve-impulse passes. The resulting current stimulates further regions of the membrane and so propagates the impulse.

anterior nucleus of the thalamus. A cell-station on the pathway from the mamillary body (hypothalamus) to the cingulate cortex. Part of circuit concerned with control of 'emotional' responses and with memory.

basal ganglia. Groups of nerve-cells in the mammalian brain. Functions varied and uncertain. Some concerned with the control and co-ordination of movement.

bipolar cells. Nerve-cells with two projections.

boutons terminaux ('boutons'). Swellings at the ends of axons, where they make contact with dendrites or nerve-cell bodies. They bring about stimulation or inhibition.

cell body. Main region of a cell containing the nucleus with hereditary instructions, excluding cell processes.

choline acetylase. Enzyme catalysing the formation of acetylcholine from choline and acetyl coenzyme A.

chromatophores. Special cells in the skin, changes in which modify the colour of the animal.

cingulate cortex. Most medial part of the mammalian cortex lying above the corpus callosum. Receives signals from the mamillary body, via the anterior thalamus.

Perhaps concerned with the regulation of emotional behaviour and memory.

corpora allata. Glands associated with the nervous system of insects producing a hormone for the control of moulting and development.

corpus callosum. Main transverse nerve-fibre pathway joining the two hemispheres of the mammalian brain.

crossing-over. Exchange of pieces of material between the carriers of hereditary information (chromosomes), giving a method of increasing variation.

Deiter's nucleus. Nerve-cell region receiving signals from the organ of balance via the vestibular nerve.

dendrite. The receiving apparatus of a nerve-cell, often forming a tree-like array of thin fibres.

dendritic end feet. *See* boutons terminaux.

DNA. Deoxyribose nucleic acids—the substances that comprise the 'code' of inheritance.

dorsal horn. Sensory nerve-cell region in the spinal cord.

end organ. A peripheral sensory receptor, detecting some particular environmental change.

engram. An enduring altered condition of nervous tissue that provides a record of the results of previous stimulation of receptors ($\equiv$ representation in the memory).

fibre (nerve). Thread, usually 1–10/1000 mm. diameter, capable of transmitting digital signals (nerve impulses) at about 1–100 m/s ($\equiv$ axon $\equiv$ nerve fibre).

fovea. A pit in the retina where the receptors (cones) are most closely packed producing the highest resolution.

gamma efferents. Nerve-fibres to muscle spindles. Alteration of the bias of the spindles produces afferent signals that regulate contraction of the whole muscle.

genes. Discrete carriers of genetic information, occurring in the cell nucleus (in the chromosomes).

giant fibres. Nerve-fibres of comparatively large diameter (up to 1 mm.) capable of especially rapid conduction.

hippocampus. Area of mammalian brain concerned with recent memory and emotional control.

lateral geniculate body. Layered group of nerve-cells in the mammalian brain where the optic nerve-fibres end. The axons of the cells pass to the visual cortex.

limbic system. The so-called rhinencephalon or olfactory portion of the brain. In higher mammals it is concerned with other functions, including memory, rather than with smell.

mamillary body. Group of nerve-cells in the basal (hypothalamic) part of the mammalian brain. Receives fibres from the hippocampus and sends them back to lower motor centres and forward to the anterior nucleus of the thalamus.

medullated fibre. A nerve-fibre that is enclosed within a fatty sheath (myelin) interrupted by gaps every few millimetres (nodes). The nerve-impulse jumps from node to node and is thus propagated more rapidly.

meiosis. A process of division in the sex cells where the number of carriers of genetic information (chromosomes) is halved in anticipation of fertilization.

metazoa. Those animals that are composed of many interrelating cells.

motor end plate. Synaptic structure between nerve-fibre and muscle.

muscle spindles. Receptors (proprioceptors) that record the stretch of a muscle (*see* gamma efferent).

myelin sheath. *See* medullated fibre.

nerve-cells (neurons). The cells of the nervous system that receive and send signals.

neuron. *See* nerve-cell.

noise. Factor that decreases the probability of accurate transmission of information (e.g. in the nervous system).

nucleotides. Chemical constituents of DNA.

Pearly Nautilus. A cephalopod that has survived with little change for 200-million years. It lives in the Pacific and floats with a gas-filled chambered shell.

Physalia. A floating jellyfish, with trailing tentacles that contain stinging cells ('Portuguese-man-of-war').

proprioceptors. Receptor cells recording the stretch or movement of limbs, muscles, &c. (e.g. muscle spindles).

receptor organ. Structure specialized to detect some particular change in environment and signal its occurrence in afferent nerve-fibres.

rhabdomeres. Light sensitive elements that make up the receptor cells (rhabdomes) in the eye of octopus and other animals.

rods and cones. Receptor cells of the vertebrate retina. The rods signal changes at very low illumination, the cones at higher intensities and different colours.

spermatophore. Bundle of male sex cells (sperms).

spinal fish. Fish in which a cut has been made across the main nerve trunk (spinal cord) behind the head.

statolith. Calcareous body in the statocyst: it indicates the gross spatial position of the animal's body by pulling or pressing upon the projecting hairs of the receptors.

synapse. The gap between the endings of axons (boutons) and the receiving dendrites. This is the feature of nerve pathways that allows for variation in response. Nerve impulses pass synapses usually only under certain conditions of summation in space and time and with a delay of $\sim$ 0·5 ms.

tectum. The part of the brain into which the optic nerves mainly pass in lower vertebrates (fishes and amphibia).

tetanic stimulation. The repetitive stimulation of a nerve, generally applied to a nerve-muscle system. The stimulation of the nerve to the muscle is so rapid that the muscle cannot relax between each impulse, and hence is maintained in a state of continual contraction.

thalamus. Region where nerve-fibres from the various receptor systems end. Its cells then transmit signals to the cerebral cortex.

transducer systems. Structures that change one form of energy to another (e.g. the eye, light to electrical).

ventral horn. The region of the output (effector) cells in the spinal cord.

INDEX

Nidicolous, birds, 296.
Nidifugous, birds, 297.
Nocifensors, 197, 209.
Norton, A. C., 118.
Nose, 53.
Nucleic acids, 7.
Nucleotides, 34, 290.

Octopodidae, 85.
Octopus, 9.
—, absence of hearing, 99.
—, acclimatization to tanks, 79.
— brain, 100, 102 (Fig. 22), 103 (Fig. 23), 169 (Fig. 51), 201 (Fig. 67), 209 (Fig. 73), 252 (Fig. 93), 254 (Fig. 94), 262 (Fig. 97), 284 (Fig. 101).
—, dymantic reaction, 83.
—, feeding, 70, 244.
—, habits in sea, 85.
—, larvae, 70.
—, learning to attack, 71.
—, mating, 88.
—, method of attack, 117.
—, paired centres, 219, 236, 265.
—, paired circuits, 200, 232.
—, personality, 110.
—, programme of attack, 78.
—, reactions to crabs, 71, 130.
—, receptor numbers, 53.
—, retreat, 82.
—, reversal of training, 177.
—, species of, 85; *briareus*, 70; *horridus*, 89, 90 (Fig. 17); *macropus*, 99.
—, theories of vision, 182.
Oikawa, T., 118.
Olds, J., 199, 234.
Olfactory nerves, *Octopus*, 54, 94.
— organ, *Nautilus*, 94.
— receptors, 53.
Onesto, N., 15, 78.
Optic gland, 109, 293, 294 (Fig. 104).
— lobes, *Calliphora*, 146 (Fig. 42); *Octopus*, 104, 107, 113, 121 (Fig. 31), 138, 139 (Fig. 36), 142 (Fig. 38), 143 (Figs. 39, 40), 145 (Fig. 41), 152, 154 (Fig. 46), 201 (Fig. 67), 203, 322; squid (*Loligo*), 49.
— — removal, 168.
— nerve, 11, 115, 141.
— — chiasma, 121, 123 (Fig. 32), 232.
— — numbers, 53.
— — regeneration, frog, 11.
Optimization in homeostat, 69.

Optimization in *Octopus* brain, 74, 109.
—, vertical lobe, 196.
Organized task, 26.

Pacemaker, 151, 165.
Packard, A., 89.
Pain, *see* Attack, effect of pain.
signals, *see* Signals of results.
Paired centres, functions, 209, 265.
— —, plan in *Octopus*, 252 (Fig. 93).
'Papez circuit', 234.
Parallel evolution, 42.
Parriss, J. R., 11, 33, 171, 174.
Pascoe, J. E., 274.
Pattern recognition, 309, 311 (Fig. 106).
Pavlov, I. P., 8, 15, 30, 80, 276, 304.
Peduncle lobe, 109.
Penfield, W., 234.
Peters, H. C., 269.
Physalia, 86.
Pineal eye, 124.
Pituitary, 295.
Platt, J., 194, 288.
Pleasure signals, *see* Signals of results.
Polyak, S., 160.
Pons, 15.
Posterior buccal lobe, 246.
Post-tetanic depression, 274.
Prediction, 7.
— by homeostats, 69.
Programme, 78.
Proprioceptors, 105, 242.
Prosser, C. L., 46.
Protozoa, 290.
Pruvot, P., 277.
Pumphrey, R. J., 50.
Purpura, D. P., 269, 270.
Pyriform lobe, 15.

Quastler, H., 65.

Rajkovits, K., 278.
Random methods, 288.
Rasmussen, G. L., 296.
'Reading-in' to memory, 217, 222.
'Reading-out' from memory, 181, 217, 222.
Receptors, 17, 23, 94.
—, analysers, 107.
—, crayfish, 150 (Fig. 44).
—, distance, 110.
—, efferents, 96, 296.